WISE AS A SERPENT, HARMLESS AS A DOVE

Also by Charles Strohmer:

What Your Horoscope Doesn't Tell You
Explaining the Grace of God

This book is an outstanding example of how Christians can intelligently and sensitively reach those who are involved with New Age beliefs. Charles Strohmer's inside knowledge gives him a particular advantage when dealing with this difficult area. His 'submarine' strategy provides an excellent model for apologetics and evangelism when approaching someone with any other worldview, and therefore has a much wider application than the New Age. I strongly recommend this clearly written and practical book.

—*Dr Richard Winter, Associate Professor of Practical Theology and Counselling, Covenant Seminary, St Louis, Missouri, USA. Member of the Royal College of Psychiatrists (UK).*

Wise as a Serpent, Harmless as a Dove is the first book I have seen that both explains clearly the New Age perspective and equips Christians in the art of engaging New Age people through rational and winsome persuasion. In addition to being imaginatively written, biblically informed and theologically sound, this important book records a wealth of instructive, real-life encounters with New Age people. I highly recommend it to all those who want 'to speak the truth in love' to those involved in the New Age.

—*Douglas Groothuis, Ph.D. Assistant Professor of Philosophy of Religion and Ethics, Denver Seminary.*

What is it your neighbour believes?
Do New Agers really believe in God?
How has New Age thinking become so influential?
To what degree can the gospel penetrate our culture?

Answers to these and many more questions are found in this book. If we want to reach our friends and neighbours with the gospel we must understand how they think and why. This book will definitely help us.

—*Gerald Coates*
Director, Pioneer

Charles Strohmer

WISE AS A SERPENT, HARMLESS AS A DOVE

Understanding and Communication in the New Age World

WORD PUBLISHING
Nelson Word Ltd
Milton Keynes, England
WORD AUSTRALIA
Kilsyth, Australia
WORD COMMUNICATIONS LTD
Vancouver, B.C., Canada
STRUIK CHRISTIAN BOOKS (PTY) LTD
Cape Town, South Africa
JOINT DISTRIBUTORS SINGAPORE –
ALBY COMMERCIAL ENTERPRISES PTE LTD
and
CAMPUS CRUSADE, ASIA LTD
PHILIPPINE CAMPUS CRUSADE FOR CHRIST
Quezon City, Philippines
CHRISTIAN MARKETING NEW ZEALAND LTD
Havelock North, New Zealand
JENSCO LTD
Hong Kong
SALVATION BOOK CENTRE
Malaysia

WISE AS A SERPENT, HARMLESS AS A DOVE

Published by Nelson Word Ltd., Milton Keynes, 1994.

ISBN 0-85009-583-2   (Australia ISBN 1-86258-266-1)

Unless otherwise indicated, Scripture references are from the Holy Bible, New International Version, copyright © 1973, 1978, 1984 by International Bible Society.

Other Scripture quotations are from the following sources:
    The Authorised Version (AV)
    The Revised Standard Version (RSV), copyright © 1971 by Division of Christian Education of the National Council of Churches of Christ in the United States of America.

Front cover and illustrations by Phil White

Reproduced, printed and bound in Great Britain for Nelson Word Ltd. by Cox & Wyman Ltd., Reading.

94 95 96 97 / 10 9 8 7 6 5 4 3 2 1

Contents

Preface

There is a real sense in which this book started to be written more than twenty-five years ago. It was in the late 1960s, and I was in my teens, when the inspiring idea broke in on me that 'whatever the answer to the problems of the world was, it must be Truth with a capital "T".' Within months this insight cast like iron in my soul and I resolved to make a search for Truth, whatever that was. And then when I found it, I wanted to communicate it to others who were likewise disenchanted.

A search for Truth seemed entirely sensible; not merely because of the seed that had been planted, but because it had been put into the right kind of ground. It had taken eighteen years, but I had finally become irrevocably disillusioned with the American Dream. It did not seem to matter that I had been raised in the American Midwest, in a stable family and a good school system.

RADIATION, that great bogeyman of my life during the 1950s, had haunted me into the early 1960s. Why had the adults invented this invisible menace that at any time could fry me to a crisp? Hope did dawn with the election of President Kennedy in 1960, but it was quickly snuffed out when the madness began on 22 November, 1963 in Dallas. Someone was crooking his arm and looking down the barrel of an Italian rifle, drawing a bead on President Kennedy's head, the right half of which suddenly went missing. Then, beginning in

1965, violent rioting struck the inner cities and was repeated throughout four long hot summers. The heady success of shooting missiles into outer space had left American genius too moonstruck to be concerned about the space closer to home, which had become infested with anger and burst into flames. It wasn't so much blacks fighting whites as both taking their resentment out on an unavailing social system.

The worst incident of those four summers occurred in my home city of Detroit in July 1967, a month after I left school. The squalor and death were no longer part of a television report I could turn off; it was live just down the street. During this tumultuous period the Vietnam War escalated, and when it became a personal threat from 1967 to 1968, I had had enough. The American Dream lay at my feet in pieces. Exit stage East.

America, and the West, was spiritually bankrupt; it had no answers to life's big questions. It was into this intellectual/spiritual disenchantment that the desire to find the Truth came. The first major consequence was the direction of my search. America was a Christian nation, so I concluded that there was no point in looking to Christianity for the Truth. I stopped going to church and headed East.

I already had some acquaintance with Eastern religious beliefs as a result of doing a massive school research paper on Brahmanism, years earlier. I hadn't thought much about it since, but now seemed the time to get reacquainted. A kind of ingenious spiritual synchronicity hung in the air. Suddenly it was easy to get to know the East in the West. The

Aquarian counterculture had dawned. Down the rabbit hole I plunged.

In my early twenties, astrology, meditation, visualisation, 'spirit guides', vegetarianism, asceticism and psychic healing, roughly in that order—along with a spattering of other so-called New Age beliefs and practices—dominated my search for Truth. It did not take eighteen years this time, but roughly eight, for complete disenchantment to set in. The joy within me died when the 'truth' of the Aquarian Dream was found to be lies. The hope of more and better lives through reincarnation disappeared. Trusted New Age practices like meditation no longer brought tranquillity; others lost their appeal. As a friend said, 'I was no better, I was no god.' What I now know to be the power of God had smashed my Aquarian Dream.

Not knowing then in what direction to turn for the Truth, I dropped into deep depression. If Truth wasn't in the West or the East, or in a metaphysical marriage of the two, just where was it? I hadn't a clue now.

After several weeks of bewilderment, by God's grace I met the Truth Himself and became a Christian in July 1976. What an awakening, I can tell you! And indeed I wanted to tell everyone about the Truth, Jesus Christ.

However, though I had been a spokesperson for the New Age, I quickly discovered that it was terribly difficult to communicate Christianity to the New Age world. I was bumping up against arcane intellectual/spiritual dynamics that frustrated Christian communication. Since I could not figure this out on my own, I dropped into some Christian bookstores, but I could discover no relevant material. I went to ministers and other Christian leaders, but they either answered my questions with a blank stare or pooh-poohed my zeal. I searched around on the periphery of the Church for former New Agers like myself, but the few I turned up in the late 1970s were equally at a loss about how to speak to our old friends in a way that would make sense to them.

A few years passed with only sporadic 'success'. I got established in Christian fellowship, served in the Church however I could, discovered my spiritual gifts, and went on earning a living. Yet all the while the desire to reach New Age seekers with the Truth steadily increased.

My serious hobby was writing, and in 1979 I began to transform it into a full-time occupation. I prayed earnestly and asked an increasing number of friends to pray that I would be able to write a book that spoke to New Age people. I started it in 1982; the vision came to pass with Tyndale House's publication of *What Your Horoscope Doesn't Tell You*, in February 1988, amazingly, just three months before the Nancy Reagan 'Astrology in the White House' story broke.

Two years previously, I had left my job as a parts manager to move to Scotland to marry a missionary and pursue full-time writing, editing and speaking. After the release of *Horoscope*, I began travelling to teach about the New Age 'movement'. As I travelled the grassroots of Christendom on both sides of the Atlantic, I met increasing numbers of Christians who were asking, 'How do we reach non-Christian spiritual seekers with the Truth?'

How indeed? I was meeting unexpected

numbers of believers that our Lord was raising up to reach New Age people, and there was precious little understanding about how to go about this timely and important work. The brave souls who were trying were finding themselves outwitted when in conversation with New Age enthusiasts. This constrained me to draw together the ideas that had worked for me and to develop further ones. Eventually testimonies began to trickle in. This was in the late 1980s.

As we head into the twenty-first century, New Age thinking will become increasingly influential. Already New Age motifs are steadily moving into the mainstream. Already tens of millions of secular Westerners are becoming cosmic in orientation, transformed by a non-biblical spirituality from all points East, ancient and occult. This book is prayerfully offered as part of a growing discussion by Christians everywhere as they search for ways to understand the New Age and reach its seekers with the gospel of Jesus Christ.

Acknowledgements

Producing a book is like building a house. In no way is it the labour of a lone individual. I was enormously helped by so many people, without whose generosity and candour this book would be lacking a great deal.

Thank you: John Leeper and David Booker, for turning me on to Scotty Briggs and the new parson; Dr Richard Winter, for bringing a psychiatrist's eye to the uncharted waters of Chapters 5 and 6; Joe and Melanie Adair, whose suggestions, critique and tolerance have improved Chapters 14 and 15; Jerram Barrs, whose L'Abri tapes on Christian engagement with the world scratched several of my spiritual itches; Phil White, who combined just the right mix of surrealism and humour in the artwork of the front cover and the interior illustrations; Noël Halsey, Linda Finley-Day, Beth Bissett and Win Kennedy of Nelson Word, not only for their ongoing enthusiasm about the book and for help in its preparation, but also for their patience and prayers when I was sick for a year and the project had to go on hold; the countless anonymous but not forgotten persons whom I have met during my travels, who have shared their experiences and observations and so inspired me to keep going; the affirming special individuals who 'caught the vision' and generously offered their endorsements; the ministers, leaders, principals and other risk takers who have invited me into their churches, para-church or mission organisations, schools, programmes and not a few ingenious settings, who gave me space to experiment, to make mistakes, to learn and to teach on this timely and important subject (superb hospitality too!); elders and members of Trinity Baptist Church and Trinity House Theatre and Arts Group (Livonia, Michigan), Evergreen Presbyterian Church (Sevierville, Tennessee) and Earl Soham Baptist (Woodbridge, Suffolk), for vigilance over my walk with our Lord, for intellectual stimulation, for moral challenge, for spiritual insight; the faithful and valiant souls whose prayer vigils I, my wife and my audiences rely on so deeply (your Father, who sees what you do in secret, will reward you). All of you have given more freely than I could have hoped.

Two very special people remain, to whom 'Thank you' somehow does not seem enough. One is the Revd John Peck, an esteemed Christian thinker and a dear friend. His penetrating biblical teaching on the subject of 'worldview' and his book *Wisdom in the Marketplace* have been an inspiration to me over the years. Without that, this work would be without the essential 'Inter-Mission', which is not at the heart of this book by chance. Time and time again John has helped me to clarify my thoughts and has given me confidence; but even more, his selfless Christian life has shown me how to live more consistently out of a worldview whose twin foci are a manger and a cross.

And to Linda, my loving wife, I am without reservation grateful. Her suggestions and insights as a missionary have been indispensable; her prayers, encouragement and support, unfailing; God's secret weapon from the womb of the dawn.

Introduction

On Being Wise
and Harmless

This is a book about effective communication with non-Christian spiritual seekers who are usually called New Agers. As those Christians who have been out trying it know, it is a daunting task. But perhaps it is no different in principle from other exasperating communication headaches that the Church has had to relieve. In fact, the disciples must have been really up against it back in the days of our Lord Himself, for He gave them quite a peculiar kind of guidance.

When the fullness of time had come for the gospel to hit the streets, Jesus warned His communicators that they were being sent out as sheep into the midst of wolves. This is understandable. Yet in the same breath, our Lord tells them that because of this they are to be 'wise as serpents and harmless as doves' (Matt. 10:16, AV). Now that is peculiar. Jesus' double simile seems contradictory. Yet to the Master it's not. To Him it is not an impossible juxtaposition of ideas but an ingenious method for producing effective communicators. No easy feat, considering the formidable task that lay ahead and that it was to be done by sheep!

At first, this unlikely joining of forces may

seem impossible because in the Bible 'serpent' generally represents deceptions, lies and the deceiver, while 'dove' stands for the Spirit of God and truth. And yet, however peculiar and unwise the teaming up of a serpent with a dove may seem to us, it is an apt choice of images for our Lord, and there is more to be said of both.

As a robin is the harbinger of spring, the dove is of the grace of Christ; it is a heavenly voice, a prophetic sign, of Christ's appearance to, and for, the lost. It is therefore a testifying dove, even in the face of antagonism, scepticism or counterargument. Simplicity, too, is one of its features. The dove shows a marked lack of worldliness and makes itself easily understood. The sophisticated can write volumes and still be misunderstood; the unsophisticated can communicate a lot in a few words. The dove is also one who mourns (Isa. 38:14), and is the only bird offered in sacrifice (Lev. 1:14; though a young pigeon could take its place). It is therefore a symbol of vulnerability, a word from a Latin root meaning 'to wound'. Perhaps this is why the dove represents gentleness and consolation, for it is no stranger to suffering, and it symbolises that attribute of the Holy Spirit which is easily grieved. Thus it symbolises the cautious and circumspect communicator. It will not give itself to just anyone. And as it brought an olive leaf—freshly plucked—to Noah after the flood, it is also a symbol of peace.

And you, Jesus, say this is to be an ally of the serpent? This can be understood by recognising that the image of the serpent carries with it characteristics that, in and of themselves, are not necessarily evil.

Apart from his evil intention, the serpent possesses wisdom and knowledge and is skilled at communicating it. We see from his conversation with Eve that he is quite plausible and convincing and he is not repulsive, though you might think that he would be. He is subtle and shrewd, characteristics that in themselves are not necessarily bad. The fact that his dialogue with Eve is half-interrogative and half-reflective, and shows an unusual understanding of the woman, suggests that the serpent must have brooded over his subject a long time before approaching Eve. A clever interviewer, the serpent is wise in understanding. He introduces a conflict of values that undermines personally held beliefs and awakens a desire for others once considered unthinkable.

How, then, can this apply to us as Christian communicators? I know that I have at times repulsed New Age seekers; and at other times, instead of presenting crackerjack arguments against New Age beliefs or asking good questions that undermine them, I have left my listeners shaking their heads in disbelief at *me* and probably clinging more tightly to the forbidden.

To change this, we can use some of the serpent's characteristics to God's glory. For example, the serpent misleads about the nature and character of God and man, but we can make the crooked straight. As the serpent cast doubt upon the promises of God, we can expose the unobtainable hope offered by false gods. As he was clever at innuendo, undermining the wisdom of God, we can be skilled at unseating the false beliefs of New Age wisdom. As the serpent knew how to build a relationship with someone outside his world, we can learn to develop relationships with those outside the Christian fold. It was this—the building of a relationship—that caused Eve to trust the serpent; and it will be our trustworthy relationships with New Age people that will help them to turn to the true Light. Whereas the serpent sought for himself a relationship with a human being that would result in that person's broken relationship with God, and death, we can form relationships with non-Christian spiritual seekers that will help restore them to God, and Life. And this we shall not do under our own steam but in the harmlessness and power of the dove, the Holy Spirit, replacing the serpent's congratulatory hymn, 'Glory to man in the highest', with glory to God.

As doves we will fly around, guided by the wind; as serpents when we land, we will capture the imaginations of our listeners. We will be wise in understanding as well as clear, simple and prophetic with the message of peace with God. This is what our Lord meant by wanting us to be as harmless as possible, as well as the wisest that we can be, as His witnesses. After all, when He sends us out into the midst of wolves He does not want us to have sheep-like minds! With that in mind, this book is prayerfully offered to Christians to reach the New Age world. It is divided into two parts, though of necessity some of the material overlaps. Part One will identify the intellectual/spiritual dynamics within New Age people that frustrate an effective Christian witness, to help us become wise as serpents in understanding. Part Two will introduce both time-tested and biblical ideas for outwitting these pesky dynamics, to help us to become harmless as

doves in communication. There is also a short
Inter-Mission, but it's not a rest break! It looks
at several models that are used for trying to
understand the New Age phenomenon and how
they help or hinder communication. It also
raises the curtain on a fresh and, I hope, more
desirable model.

Part One

Wise as a Serpent

1

Prologue:
Buck Fanshaw's Funeral

Mark Twain in *Roughing It* wrote an absolutely humorous scene about making a hash of communication. The incident involves a rugged fireman and mining 'rough' named Scotty Briggs who was dispatched to the new parson by a grieving Nevada mining community to make funeral arrangements for the late Buck Fanshaw, who had been a hard-living saloon keeper, bar-room brawler, foreman, miner and political aspirant. He now needs burying, and with ceremony, having been well-liked.

These early Western mining communities had 'representative adventurers', as Twain put it, from peoples everywhere, and they brought with them the language and slang of their nations and localities. Scotty Briggs and the new parson were cases in point. The former was a likable mining rough, the latter a 'fragile, gentle, spiritual new fledgling from an Eastern theological seminary, and as yet unacquainted with the ways of the mine'.

The purpose of this book is to help Christians find solutions to the baffling problems of communicating with 'New Agers'. Some will say, 'Well, that's easy enough. Just start talking.' Others, however, will understand

from experience that it is not quite so easy;
some know the ways of the mine, others do not.
And some Christians have only heard rumours
about the communication hassles, which others
have encountered at first hand. The following
extract by Twain, it is hoped, will provide all
readers with an illustration of the difficulties.
It's a different context of course, set as it is in
the old American West, yet its portrayal of the
language muddles between the new parson and
Scotty Briggs ought to be a perfect launching-off
pad for us all. Here's Twain to tell it:

> Being admitted to the presence [Scotty] sat
> down before the clergyman, placed his fire
> hat on an unfinished manuscript sermon
> under the minister's nose, took from it a
> red silk handkerchief, wiped his brow and
> heaved a sigh of dismal impressiveness,
> explanatory of business. He choked, and
> even shed tears; but with an effort he
> mastered his voice and said in lugubrious
> tones:
> 'Are you the duck that runs the gospel
> mill next door?'
> 'Am I the—pardon me, I believe I do not
> understand.'
> With another sigh and a half sob, Scotty
> rejoined:
> 'Why you see we are in a bit of trouble,
> and the boys thought maybe you would
> give us a lift, if we'd tackle you—that is, if
> I've got the rights of it, and you are the
> head clerk of the doxology works next
> door.'
> 'I am the shepherd in charge of the flock
> whose fold is next door.'

'The which?'

'The spiritual advisor of the little
company of believers whose sanctuary
adjoins these premises.'

Scotty scratched his head, reflected a
moment, and then said:

'You ruther hold over me, pard. I reckon
I can't call that hand. Ante and pass the
buck.'

'How? I beg pardon. What did I
understand you to say?'

'You see, one of the boys has passed in
his checks and we want to give him a good
send off, and so the thing I'm on now is to
roust out somebody to jerk a little chin
music for us and waltz him through
handsome.'

'My friend, I seem to grow more and
more bewildered. Your observations are
wholly incomprehensible to me. Cannot
you simplify them in some way? At first I
thought perhaps I understood you, but I
grope now. Would it not expedite matters
if you restricted yourself to categorical
statements of fact unencumbered with
obstructing accumulations of metaphor
and allegory?'

Another pause, and more reflection.
Then, said Scotty:

'I'll have to pass, I judge.'

'How?'

'You've raised me out, pard.'

'I still fail to catch your meaning.'

'Why, that last lead of yours is too many
for me—that's the idea. I can't neither
trump nor follow suit.'

The clergyman sank back in his chair

perplexed. Scotty leaned his head on his hand and gave himself up to thought. Presently his face came up, sorrowful but confident.

'I've got it now, so's you can savvy,' he said. 'What we want is a gospel sharp, see?'

'A what?'

'Gospel sharp. Parson.'

'Oh! Why did you not say so before? I am a clergyman—a parson.'

'Now you talk! You see my blind and straddle it like a man. Put it there!'— extending a brawny paw, which closed over the minister's small hand and gave it a shake indicative of fraternal sympathy and fervent gratification.

'Now we're all right, pard. Let's start fresh. Don't you mind my snuffling a little—becuz we're in a power of trouble. You see, one of the boys has gone up the flume—'

'Gone where?'

'Up the flume—throwed up the sponge, you understand.'

'Thrown up the sponge?'

'Yes—kicked the bucket—'

'Ah—has departed to that mysterious country from whose bourne no traveller returns.'

'Return! I reckon not. Why, pard, he's dead!'

'Yes, I understand.'

'Oh, you do? Well, I thought maybe you might be getting tangled some more. Yes . . . they've scooped him.'

'Scooped him?'

'Yes—death has. Well, well, well, we've got to give him up. Yes indeed . . . There ain't any getting around that, I don't reckon. Now if we can get you to help plant him—'

'Preach the funeral discourse? Assist at the obsequies?'

'Obs'quies is good. Yes. That's it—that's our little game.'

Well, the floundering *tête-à-tête* continued until the 'obsequies' were all that 'the boys' desired. And how well it captures something in principle of what many Christian conversations with New Age followers—too many of mine, at least—have been like. We may even have felt a slight pang of envy at seeing Scotty and the new parson wade through to some understanding! For our conversations may have resulted in confusion, offended feelings or further alienation between parties due to our little word wars. Yet we cannot in good conscience give up.

2

Communication Breakdown

We live in a time when it has become a priority of Christian denominations, mission organisations and para-church groups everywhere to 'evangelise the world for Christ'. Committees brainstorm innovative global, national, regional and local strategies to reach communities worldwide with the gospel. Conferences present both ministers and their congregations with the vision and equip them for the work. Programmes are developed even to reach the churched!

It is exciting to see the emphasis on world evangelisation, and this has been the reason for impressive conferences like the ones at Lausanne and Singapore, where fresh ways of reaching the world for Christ were conceived, discussed and later implemented. Yet despite all the noise and excitement about how to reach this, that and the other 'people group', there is an unfortunate silence, perhaps more of an omission, which will prove costly to us. Except for the infrequent lecture and even rarer programme, we are not preparing ourselves to reach one of the fastest growing 'worlds' within the one world, the New Age community. How, then, shall we reach the 'entire' world for Christ if we are unable to communicate with the New Age 'world'?

In becoming a world of its own, like the world of *Star Wars* or *The Lord of the Rings*, the New Age has its own authority figures and codes to live by, myths and symbols, spiritual technologies and vocabulary. It has singular ways of looking at God, human nature, the world, education, the Arts, science, industry, health care and so forth, as well as a mystical way of inner development.

We have not seen the New Age phenomenon as a 'world' of its own, I think, because New Age followers usually look just like we do, i.e. Western, and because as a community they do not live apart on a desert island. Since they look like us outwardly and live among us, it is easy to assume that they are also like us inwardly. Yet, as we shall see, they have been undergoing an intellectual/spiritual transformation that has been making them quite *un*like us inwardly and consequently foiling our naive attempts at communication.

If we begin to see the one world not all of a piece but as different 'worlds' within the one world, and if we see the New Age community as one of these inter-worlds, it may give us the kind of framework by which to consider seriously the problems of communicating with New Age followers. Missionary organisations often subdivide the one world into individual worlds. It helps them develop ways of speaking, for example, to the Jewish world, which would be significantly different from how they approached the Muslim or Hindu worlds. When Jesus commanded His disciples to 'go into all the world and preach the good news' (Mark

16:15), and later named several target communities—Jerusalem, Judaea, Samaria and the ends of the earth (Acts 1:8)—surely He knew that the different 'worlds' would have to be approached with His message in different ways.

The apostle Paul was skilled at making use of these subdivisions and in approaching the different worlds in ways that actually communicated to each one. He is explicit about this in 1 Corinthians 9:19–23, where he says that he becomes like those to whom he is sent, wherever he travels, that 'by all possible means' he might gain converts. To the Jews he was as a Jew, to those under the law he was as one under the law, to uneducated rural pagans he spoke their largely unreligious language, to philosophers he spoke their educated language. 'I do this,' he says, 'for the sake of the gospel.' He is ready to understand them as far as it is necessary to gain them for his Lord.

How large is the New Age world? How many New Agers are there, and how culturally influential are they? With no membership lists or even a coherent philosophy, such questions are difficult to answer. In every major American and European city an increasing number of spiritual seekers are becoming New Age rather than Christian, seeking the transpersonal and the transcendent through New Age perspectives. In some areas in the United States, researchers indicate that New Agers constitute as much as twelve to fifteen per cent of the population, which certainly rivals church growth programmes!

The extent of New Age influence is also difficult to determine, but some clues exist. The circulation of the popular magazine *New Age*

Journal increased from 65,000 in 1983 to 165,000 in 1989. Bantam books increased its list of New Age titles tenfold in the 1980s. Between 1985 and 1989 the number of New Age bookshops in the United States doubled to 4,000. Total sales of New Age titles exceeded 100 million dollars a year at the beginning of the 1990s.

New Age music and audio and video tapes for mind expansion and suchlike were selling at 300 million dollars a year in 1990, and in the same year corporations were spending a massive four billion dollars on New Age consultants. (Figures and statistics from *Megatrends 2000,* Naisbitt & Aburdene.)

In Great Britain, David Icke's apocalyptic revelations aside, the media has raised the profile of 'New Age' markedly. Every weekend for several months in 1989 the *Guardian* ran a 'New Age Page', which usually carried one article on a popular New Age topic or place and a shorter piece about a leading British New Ager. On March 4, 1990, the weekend London supplement of *The Times* featured a cover story on the New Age, and also that year Channel 4 ran a six-part series on the New Age that featured forty New Age leaders from around the world, including David Spangler and Sir George Trevelyan. The programmes had no guests who could provide a critical view. On August 4, 1991, the *Sunday Express* carried an article listing the names and phone numbers of New Age therapists. There are also numerous 'Healing Arts' and 'Alternative Health Care' exhibitions that are held frequently and attract thousands, the most popular probably being the

'Body, Mind, Spirit' festival held in London every spring.

As in the United States, New Age ideas influence industry and education in Great Britain. The computer giant, Digital, the South Scottish Electricity Board, British Telecom and other corporations have run training seminars for their employees that are more than cosmetically New Age. The new national curriculum sees an influx of RE methods with decidedly New Age motifs. Interestingly, the degree to which these methods now influence the national curriculum may be unlawful. The Education Reform Act of 1988, dealing with religious education and collective worship, states that 'new locally agreed syllabuses must reflect the fact that religious traditions in the country are *in the main Christian*' and that 'the collective worship in county schools must be *wholly or mainly of a broadly Christian character*' and that 'acts of worship in a term *must be broadly Christian*', (my emphases; see *Department of Education and Science Circular*, number 3/89, 20 January 1989).[1]

The above is only the tip of the iceberg in the West. As the New Age world increasingly emerges, the means by which we learn how to communicate with its followers—our neighbours, employers, fellow employees, children's teachers, health-care professionals—becomes a burning question. About the only thing resolved so far is that ways of presenting apologetics and evangelising among other kinds of non-Christians are not working with New Age non-Christians. We need, therefore, to unlearn inappropriate ways of communicating with New

Age people and develop relevant and effective
approaches.

It's not as if Christians are not trying. In fact,
it may surprise some to know that I have found
that the Number One topic of concern as I travel
and speak is 'effective communication with New
Agers'.   I have lost count of the number of
stories Christians have told me, on both sides of
the Atlantic, of failure in this area. These tales
are not only being told by novices, but by
Christians who are well-versed in the faith and
practised at apologetics or evangelisation.
People are asking, 'What can we do about this
communication breakdown?'

'My boyfriend's mother is an astrologer,' said
a girl in her early twenties. 'She's pressing me
to let her read my horoscope and compare it to
her son's, to see if we're compatible. I'm trying
to explain to her why I don't want her to do that,
but it's so frustrating because I know I'm not
getting anywhere with her. She believes we're
entering the Age of Aquarius and that the
Christian era is ending. She also thinks the
Bible endorses astrology. When I talk to her, I
think she only pretends to be listening to me,
and the last time we ended up in a big
argument. What can I do?'

'I have an aunt who's a spiritualist,' a young
man told me during a Greenbelt Festival. 'She
thinks her spiritual gifts are the same as the
ones mentioned in 1 Corinthians 12. I know
she's mistaken, and I've tried to discuss it with
her. But she doesn't see the sense of what
I'm saying, and she confuses me with her
spiritualist views of the supernatural. What can
I do?'

'I went with several friends,' said a woman in

her forties, 'to the "Body, Mind, Spirit" festival in London recently. We went to witness to New Agers, but we didn't do too well. We had read up on the New Age and had been in prayer, but the conversations we had didn't seem to do much good. I'm more puzzled than ever now. What can we do?'

'There's a psychic up the road from us,' another said. 'She likes to predict things over the neighbourhood children. The parents think it a bit of a giggle and so now she's inviting them round to have their palms read. I finally got up the nerve to talk to her about this. It was incredible! She told me that I had negative psychic fears—whatever those are—and refuses to talk to me now. What can I do?'

'My aunt,' another said, 'goes for treatment to a New Age acupuncturist. She's been telling me about body meridians and balancing her life energies. I hadn't a clue as to what she was on about, so I bought a book on holistic health. This gave me a Christian understanding of what she was saying, but even now when I try to talk to her about some of the problems, I'm not getting through to her. What can I do?'

Many stories are coming in from the increasing number of Christians who are trying their best to speak to New Age seekers. Because the number of New Age enthusiasts is steadily rising, Christians are quietly discovering friends, acquaintances, fellow employees or even family members with New Age leanings. It has been a big encouragement to all of us that we are not isolated in this particular work, but that we are part of the larger picture of evangelising the world for Christ. It is becoming more common to meet people who want to pool their resources, form small groups under church leadership and network together in their shared vision to reach New Age followers with the gospel. And the emphasis of their training, they now say, must be on communication.

As a former New Age 'insider' who is now a Christian and called to teach, I have a great desire to help us find some answers to this communication problem, and reports of break-throughs are coming in (see next chapter).

As I have understood it, we need insight in three areas. First, we must gain some understanding of New Age beliefs and practices and how they are influencing our culture. This has been our strong suit so far. Since the release of Dave Hunt's *Peace, Prosperity and the Coming Holocaust* and Constance Cumbey's best-selling *Hidden Dangers of the Rainbow* (both in 1983), Christian publishing has produced a galaxy of books on the New Age 'movement'.

However, the problem is that commun-ication still goes haywire with New Age people even after we have read the books. We remain outfoxed in conversations, not infrequently argumentative, or even speechless! It seems that knowing what these people believe is not enough.

This brings us to the two chief concerns of this book. One will take us into the area of understanding the intellectual/spiritual dynamics within the lives of New Age people, to show how they disrupt Christian commun-ication. (Insights will be offered in Part Two concerning dynamics within Christians that also contribute to this disruption.) The other area offers caring ways to outwit these disrupting dynamics.

In summary, besides knowing what New Age followers believe, we must identify prevailing intellectual/spiritual dynamics that foil a Christian witness, and then discover ways of overcoming these dynamics.

Though some of the following material of necessity overlaps, the basic plan is as follows. In Part One the subject will be identifying the dynamics that jam Christian communication frequencies, with the emphasis on becoming 'wise as a serpent' in understanding. During the Inter-Mission we pause to consider a variety of popular models for 'seeing' the New Age phenomenon. The focus here is on how these influence the manner in which people discuss the New Age; some ways of seeing the phenomenon are not conducive to effective communication. Part Two will cover overcoming these dynamics, with the emphasis on becoming 'harmless as a dove' in communication.

3

Meet Success and Failure

The Royal Pavilion at Brighton—a striking
symbol of Eastern influence in a Western nation,
with its huge oriental-looking onion domes
ballooning the waterfront—was an apt background for what had been taking place around
me there one evening in the late autumn. It was
wet and cool and the three of us were sitting
cross-legged on the thinly carpeted floor of
Brendan's two-room flat, warming by the fire,
sipping hot tea and conversing about the New
Age. The multi-coloured phantasmagorical artwork of several Eastern religious posters pinned
on otherwise bare walls corresponded to the
intellectual/spiritual confusion that hung in the
air as we talked. And we had talked for hours.

Brendan and I were new friends, and he had
invited me to his flat to talk to his friend David
about the New Age and Christianity. David was
as earnest a spiritual seeker as I have ever met,
and he was steeped in New Age thinking. The
lengthy give and take of ideas that evening
covered most of life's big questions. What is
God like? Is He impersonal energy or Personal
Being? Is life after death about reincarnation or
resurrection? Are suffering and evil the result of
everyone's bad karma or sin? Is Jesus Christ
merely a god-man akin to Buddha, Krishna and

Rama, or is he the unique Son of God? Are all religions ultimately leading to the same place but with different outward expressions, or do the fundamental ideas of Christianity preclude that? Why should the Bible be preferred over other religious books like the Bhagavad Gita?

I'm not sure how much help I was to David. Clearly the gospel did not penetrate his heart, and I probably should have prayed more ahead of time. I felt discouraged when David left after midnight to drive home. Not only because I had not been successful, but because in the back of my mind that evening another scene had been playing.

A few months earlier in June, I had visited the English L'Abri Centre to do some research. It was there that I first met Brendan, who was among the twenty other guests who had arrived to study during L'Abri's summer term. Amidst sundry activities around the manor house and grounds, Brendan and I struck up conversations and discovered our similar spiritual backgrounds. Yet I soon realised that Brendan's search had not ended; he had not met Christ, he was trying to become a Christ, which had also been one of my goals as a New Ager. He had spent a decade as a devotee of Indian mysticism and had even been on pilgrimage to India a few times seeking enlightenment. I was deeply moved by the sincerity of his search for truth. As I had done years earlier, he had given up just about everything to find it. Now here he was, a serious New Age seeker in a Christian environment, alongside me.

I was determined to use my testimony as best I could. Years earlier, before my conversion, I had been advised by a New Age teacher to read the Bible as yet another means of unearthing the esoteric wisdom of the ancients. This did not make a lot of sense to me, even at the time, but as I respected this teacher I got hold of a Bible and went excavating for a year, cover to cover. It was a long, demanding dig, and I got nothing out of it. Brendan was now in a Christian environment merely at someone's suggestion, and I did not want the same thing to happen to him. Here he was making yet another stopover in his spiritual wanderings, and so I prayed, along with the L'Abri workers, that his search would end. It did. Near the end of my two-week visit to L'Abri[1] I was privileged to help Brendan, through deep repentance, to meet the Saviour.

Back home in Brighton, Brendan had been trying to express the Christian faith to his good friend David. But as a lot of us have discovered it is not always easy for new Christians to share their new-found faith, and so Brendan had invited me to talk to David.

Having heard these two stories, you might be tempted to think that I am always level-headed in my discussions with New Agers. Don't fool yourself. I've made some terrible mistakes. Once a friend asked me to 'talk some sense' into her sister (I think it was) who believed the Aquarian views about Jesus Christ.

Do you remember the so-called eighteen silent years of Christ's life in the Gospels? To account for this missing piece of Jesus' life, several popular books within the New Age community suggest that when Jesus was twelve years old, He travelled from Israel to India, where He lived for eighteen years at the feet of gurus and through enlightenment discovered

His godhood status. He then travelled back to
Israel when He was thirty to preach not the
gospel but Christ-consciousness to the
Hebrews.[2] Well, Terri (not her real name)
believed this Aquarian Gospel, and it was a
disaster when I was taken to her home to talk
about it.

I thought I was prepared, but when Terri
hauled out books and articles to support her
position I knew that I was in way over my head.
Instead of applying some of the possibilities for
effective communication that you will read about
in the following chapters, I was reduced to
making ridiculous remarks like, 'That can't
possibly be true', without being able to say why.
I have never seen a conversation deteriorate so
fast. What Terri felt I can only imagine. I felt
embarrassed and threatened and could not
control my indignation. Within minutes I was
making heated remarks and soon we were both
antagonistic. Even when a third party tried to
clear the air, we could still feel the hostility in
the room. It was pointless to continue and I
fled, suffering an onslaught of guilt for days.

Of the three stories above, which ones were
successes, which failures? I think readers will
agree that Brendan represents a success, Terri a
failure. But what about my time with David? I
used to look at that as a failure, but I have
changed my view. The conversation lasted for
hours, as it was non-argumentative, and I
learned many things listening to David.
Furthermore, he got some clarity about the
incompatibility of Christian and New Age
answers to life's big questions. It was David's
acknowledgement of these incompatibilities, I

have concluded, that made the conversation a 'success'.

With some people, conversations like this will be enough for the time being. New Age people must come to grips with the incompatibility of the two 'wisdoms' in order to make sense of the gospel later. After all, within the New Age world it is customary to think (though they're a bit embarrassed about it) that Christianity is somehow a part of the 'oneness' of all things; albeit an outdated religion for the lesser-evolved. David, therefore, first had to see the fundamental dissimilarities and then be challenged by their significance. We could call this a pre-evangelistic conversation, and within that framework the time spent was successful. The only failure was my time with Terri.

Another occurrence that I am tempted to call a failure is when we unexpectedly find ourselves talking to New Age followers and have nothing to say. Many Christians still have not read up on the New Age and so get caught short if they happen to bump into a New Ager without notice. Suddenly an opportunity has arisen, but just as suddenly it passes. Or, in trying to be polite we may find ourselves nodding our heads in agreement with the daftest spiritual ideas.

But most likely we may keep silent because we don't know much about the New Age, or because we think it requires expert handling. The day, however, of the Christian 'expert' who handles the New Age for us has ended. That world is just too big now.

With so many opportunities arising, we want to be able to hold conversations with New Age people. And there are ways to speak effectively without first having to be an 'expert'.

This is the purpose, in part, of the 'Submarine Model' that is developed later in the book. We do not need to have communication failures even if we have not read up on the New Age. We do not need to avoid conversations because we do not know enough about it. This is a great relief, overall, as Pam and Linda discovered.

Pam unexpectedly had a captive audience 'who was dressed a trifle funny' sitting by her on a flight from San Francisco to Dallas. They had not begun the flight side by side, however. Soon after the seatbelt sign had been switched off, a middle-aged lady, beaded and fringed, with long ginger hair, glided down the narrow aisle to Pam and asked if she could sit by her, explaining that she was unhappy with her assigned seat. Pam yielded up the seat next to her and the woman settled in, rummaging through the flight bag at her feet. It then dawned on Pam that the curious aroma attending this 1960s apparition was generously escaping from the bag.

'Sorry 'bout that,' the Californian said. 'The incense bottle leaked all over the bottom of my bag.'

She then brought out a New Age music cassette and a Shirley MacLaine book, and Pam did not need a Baker Street address to figure out all the clues!

'She did not become a Christian,' Pam told me. 'But what excited me was that I was able to talk to her about the New Age during the whole flight even though I still don't know a lot about it. If this had happened to me before I became acquainted with the Submarine Model, I wouldn't have known what to say. I would have had to sit there passively for two hours listening to her preach about the New Age. What an ordeal that would have been! As it was, it wasn't easy, but I think I was able to communicate in a way that really got her thinking. Even though it was hard to bite back my words whenever I wanted to demand that she get rid of that foul-smelling incense!'

Linda is another Christian who found herself with an unexpected opportunity and was not caught unprepared. She spent much of her six-hour British Rail train journey talking to a Cypriot beauty, a university student, who was curious about the so-called white witchcraft (Wicca, at times) that was being practised in her residence.

'She was seeing,' Linda said, 'that there was a certain power behind it, but she hadn't made up her mind about what that power was. I knew I had an opening. Since I had recently read your book about astrology it was easy enough to guide her through that material to show her what kind of power her friends were dealing with. I knew from what she said as she got off the train that she had had a change of mind.'

'I'm going to explain all this to my friends at the university,' she said. 'That business is not good. We don't want to be a part of something like that.'

We can have good conversations with New Age enthusiasts. Opportunities do not have to be lost. Much of this book will help us discover how to do this.

Some may wonder, what's the point? Why not just jump right in and preach the gospel? Isn't that what Jesus, Paul, Peter and the other apostles did? Yes, but they often spent time beforehand preparing people for the gospel. In most cases, we will need to do the same with New Age seekers because they live in a world in which the gospel seems improbable, unthinkable, unimaginable. This is important. Because of what they believe, the gospel simply does not make sense to New Age people, and many of them are not being converted because of this. Should some of them make a confession of faith in this condition, they could easily backslide, not understanding the message to begin with. This means that a large part of our efforts must be spent first on helping New Age people to come into a way of seeing life in which the gospel seems probable, believable, credible. *Then* the gospel will make sense to them.

Jesus spoke of this as people who understand what they hear. In Matthew 13:11-23, Jesus taught that only those who hear *and understand* the message of the kingdom produce a crop. Those who hear but do not understand have the seed of the Word snatched away by the evil one, for there is no ground, or basis, for understanding. The effective communicator establishes grounds that help people understand what they are hearing.

Call it what you will; the task of moving these non-Christians from the improbable to the probable, from the unimaginable to the imaginable, is inescapable. It is about cultivating a certain frame of mind in our relationships. It is about presenting ideas that help make the gospel become believable in people's imaginations, so moving them closer to saving faith and gaining them for Christ in the long run. It is not difficult to do this.

The Californian, the Cypriot, David: all represent conversations no less 'successful' than the two weeks I spent with Brendan. It is a false pressure, and unsupported by the Bible, to think that every conversation with New Agers must be about giving them the gospel immediately. Not a few Christians, however, labour under this burden, and their lives are guilt-ridden because it is impossible to live up to expectations. Worse still, this state of mind generates gunslinger evangelism, i.e. New Age people are reduced to the status of mere objects—souls—to be notched on our gospel guns. Having become 'things' upon which we 'do' our evangelisation projects, they are no longer persons with whom we can have a variety of relationships. This is one of the chief complaints from New Age people about Christians. It keeps them from listening, from understanding and from opening up. After all, it is difficult to appear interested, sensitive and personable with a smoking gun in our hands.

4

Entering the Inter-World

'Son of man,' God said, 'eat this scroll I am
giving you and fill your stomach with it . . . go
now . . . and speak.'

After the repast, the prophet is then told, 'Go
now to the house of Israel and speak my words
to them. You are not being sent to a people of
obscure speech and difficult language, whose
words you cannot understand. Surely if I had
sent you to them, they would have listened.'

This selection from Ezekiel (3:1–6) seems
apropos of the Church's commission to the New
Age world but with a twist, for we are being sent
to a people of obscure speech and difficult
language, even though we all speak English.
But look at the promise: they will listen. They
will listen, that is, if we masticate the scroll,
which for us means identifying and, I think,
chewing over the intellectual/spiritual dynamics
that have created the communication barrier.
And we will now turn to identify these dynamics
for the remainder of Part One.

Inversion

In Lewis Carroll's *Through the Looking Glass*,
Alice finds everything backwards in
Looking-glass House and its countryside. The

words in books go the wrong way, seemingly straight paths have sharp corners to them, very dry biscuits are taken to quench thirst, however fast Alice runs she never passes anything, and to meet someone you walk in the opposite direction towards them! This is terribly confusing to poor Alice, and all the more so when she discovers from the Red Queen and other Looking-glass characters that they consider that their way of seeing life is normal, proper and sensible. She does try to set things right, but it's tiring. And when she has to deal with the Looking-glass perspective in her conversations, it's at best 'rather hard to understand' and at its worst 'nonsense'.

The conversations we take part in and the things we encounter in the New Age world can be just as astonishing because the perspective of New Age people is often radically different from that of Christians. Because it's similar to what Alice found, let's call it the dynamic, or principle, of inversion. Things are the wrong way round. A passage in Isaiah (5:20) reflects this, speaking as it does about 'those who call evil good and good evil, who put darkness for light and light for darkness, who put bitter for sweet and sweet for bitter'.

This principle of inversion is very bewildering within the New Age world because it brings *us* face to face with the unbelievable, the unthinkable, and I have always thought that even an initial understanding of what it is like would be invaluable for our work in that world. I found a compelling illustration of the dynamic in the book *Peace Child* by Don Richardson (Regal Books, 1974). It's in a different context—set as it is among cannibals and head-hunters—but as a description of 'inversion' it is unforgettable, as well as being helpful in preparing us for what we face.

In 1962, Don and Carol Richardson moved from North America to the western half of an island 1,400 miles long, formerly Netherlands New Guinea, now Irian Jaya Indonesia, just north of Australia. The Sawi people lived here and the Richardsons settled in to learn their language and customs. Life among these cannibals and headhunters was difficult, complicated further by warring tribes; but eventually the Richardsons had learned enough to begin communicating the gospel and Don Richardson began to meet with the Sawi men in the 'manhouse' to do just that. Though Richardson presented the gospel story carefully, building line upon line, the Sawi men just stared unresponsively day after day. That is, until the day came for the portrayal of Jesus' betrayal, when a curious amusement and excitement arose among the Sawi men.

From that moment the men were deeply interested in the gospel story, but for a most unexpected and wrong reason. Here is Richardson's account of his startling discovery:

On subsequent visits [to the manhouse] I expanded further on the life and ministry of Jesus, trying to establish His reality and relevance to their lives, but without apparent success. The Sawi were not accustomed to projecting their minds into cultures and settings so forbiddingly dissimilar to their own.

Only once did my presentation win a ringing response from them. I was

describing Judas Iscariot's betrayal of the
Son of God. About halfway through the
description I noticed they were all listening
intently. They noticed all the details: for
three years Judas had kept close company
with Jesus, sharing the same food,
travelling the same road. That any
associate of Jesus would have conceived
the idea of betraying such an impressive
figure was highly unlikely. And if anyone
had conceived the idea, one of Jesus' inner
circle of trusted disciples would have been
the least likely to choose such a course.
And yet Judas, one of Jesus' disciples, had
chosen to betray Him and carried out the
dreadful act alone, without any of the
other disciples suspecting his plot.

At the climax of the story, Maum
whistled a birdcall of admiration. Kani
and several others touched their fingertips
to their chests in awe. Still others
chuckled. Then the realisation broke
through. *They were acclaiming Judas as
the hero of the story!* [his emphasis] Yes,
Judas, the one whom I had portrayed as
the satanically motivated enemy of truth
and goodness! A feeling of coldness
gripped my spine. I tried to protest that
Jesus was good. He was the Son of God,
the Saviour. It was evil to betray Him.
But nothing I said could erase that gleam
of savage enjoyment from their eyes.

What do you do? The Sawi admired Judas!
An unthinkable principle of inversion influenced
their way of seeing. How do you put the thing
the right way round? For Don Richardson it

meant discovering why Judas, not Jesus, was
the hero. In private conversations with one or
two Sawi men, Richardson dug up the appalling
fact that treachery was highly esteemed among
the Sawi men. It was therefore natural for these
men to admire a betrayer, especially Judas
whom they saw as the archetypal quisling.

'The Sawi honoured cruelty,' Richardson
wrote. 'Their highest pleasure depended upon
the misery and despair of others. *Judas was
the super-Sawi!* [his emphasis] And Christ, the
object of Judas' treachery, meant nothing to the
men in the manhouse. My task was to reverse
the situation totally.'

Unbelievable? Unthinkable? Yes. And
though Judas may not be the hero of the story
in the New Age world, we will be encountering
unthinkable perspectives there, each of which
results in its own fundamental difficulty in
communication that must be overcome. Part of
our work, then, will be similar to Richardson's:
to reverse the situation. He wrote:

But how could one man and his wife
reverse the worldview of an entire people,
a worldview which had been entrenched in
their collective psyche for perhaps a thousand years? I wanted to win *this*
generation of Sawi. And I wanted to win
them on their own ground and by their
own fireplaces. If the gospel could not win
men like Mahaen, Kani, Hato and Kigi, it
was not the message it claimed to be. I
was game, but I was also stymied. I didn't
know how to tackle a cultural enigma like
this. I headed home for lunch groaning
inwardly, 'Lord, in all of time and space,

has Your message ever encountered a
worldview more opposite . . . to the gospel?
And has anyone ever faced a
communication problem bigger than this
one You've assigned me?'

Does this sound familiar? I have wondered
before God, groaning over exactly this. Yet one
man and his wife in the wisdom and power of
God cracked the code. We serve the same God.
Shall He not also enable us to solve the
communication riddle we face?

The Closed Mind

At least the Sawi men were willing to listen. But
what about New Age people who do not want to
listen to us? One meets them. And here we
encounter the dynamic of the closed mind.

When my wife and I lived in Paisley,
Scotland, we liked to take the train to
Edinburgh for a break from our hectic
schedules. Strolling through the beautiful and
nearly year-round gardens along Princes Street,
visiting museums, or simply seeing sights like
Edinburgh Castle, we found time to relax. And
after meandering around, we had a habit of
stopping in the Waverley Market for a cup of
coffee and something sweet!

Many of those times were slightly marred
for me, however, by the sight of a numerologist
who worked the Waverley Market. He had been
granted permission to set up a small table,
folding chairs and a poster that announced
numerology readings. For more than a year I
saw him set up in the same conspicuous spot

inside the Waverley Market, where he would be dispensing numerology charts, giving readings and collecting small fees from a steady stream of punters. Nearly every time I was there, he was there. Whether coincidental or not, I don't know. But the more I realised the number of people he was influencing, the more grieved I got, until one day I summoned up enough nerve to speak to him.

I waited off to the side until he had a free moment. I knew I would need to be brief, whatever I said, because the interested would begin queuing up again. As I was waiting I pondered what I would say and how to do it in the short time I figured I would have. Since I had some copies of *What Your Horoscope Doesn't Tell You* with me in my briefcase, I decided that it was probably best just to get a book into his hands. 'It won't take long to do that,' I thought, 'and then he can read it at his leisure, and discover what we don't have time to discuss here.'

I walked up and carefully asked if I could have a quick word with him.

'What about?' he said.

'I used to do readings for people similar to what you're doing. I've got a different perspective on it now and was wondering if during your break here you might like to hear about that.'

"No. I'm not interested.'

'Could I give you a book, then, that you could read in your spare time?'

'No.'

'Oh, well, why not? The book's free.'

'Because I know what I'm doing. I've been

doing this for twenty years, and it's not what people think.'

'But I've got a book here in my briefcase I'd like to give you. Wouldn't you like it?'

'No,' he said with the finality of a judge.

I took the hint, rose from the chair and said a polite goodbye. Similar experiences have taught me that to stay and press harder for a hearing when up against a closed mind usually degenerates into a heated argument. Even though I was being as circumspect as I knew how, the numerologist had shut down the avenues of approach. I had not used any religious language or words such as 'occult', 'New Age' and 'Christian', as these might easily make him lose interest in what I wanted to say and deter him from accepting the book. I had not even told him it was my book! In plain English, this guy was closed. I had encountered the closed New Age mind.

It's ironic. New Age people claim to be very open-minded. And indeed they are open-minded to virtually anything and everything *except* to traditional Judaeo-Christian perspectives. Agonising though this may be, we must allow them their choice; unwise though it may be, they are free to make it. Arguing will probably entrench them deeper in their New Age position and so further alienate them from the only true Hope. When we get the cold shoulder it may be best to disengage ourselves from the conversation, as graciously as possible. A closed mind is a shut door. This is not our fault. We have not failed. If someone does not wish to hear us, that is the choice we must allow them to make.

Yet even walking away from a shut door

graciously can be redemptive. The person may respect you for allowing him the freedom of his choice. This might seem inconsequential, but not when the God of grace can work with it. It may just be that in walking away graciously, rather than in a huff or staying to argue, you make a favourable impression on the New Age seeker. It may even have been the first favourable impression he has ever received from a Christian. This, then, could pave the way for you to have a conversation with the person later, or perhaps with another Christian at another time. Let us never underestimate the redemptive potential of our actions.

5

The Storm of the Irrational

There is the story about the absent-minded professors who were gathered for a leisurely day in the country. When invited by their host to spend the night because a storm had arisen, they went home to get their toothbrushes!

It's amusing, yet one cannot help but wonder what in the world was going on in their minds. We may face similar bewilderment during some of our conversations with New Age enthusiasts. It needs to be seen as 'irrationality', which, due to the nature of the beast, is hard to pin down. Never mind how real it is, or how annoying; it is by nature ambiguous and therefore incapable of being nailed down by airtight definitions. At least by me. Nevertheless, storms of irrationality have been known to blow in unexpectedly and make shipwreck of an effective Christian witness to New Age people. Consequently, we need to take a look at it as best we can.

I have sailed into these storms more than once. On one occasion it happened during a live interview on BBC radio's *Head On* programme as I was going head-to-head (indeed!) with *Daily Express* astrologist Marjorie Orr. I had been seated with a presenter in a soundproof studio

in Glasgow, Orr was in a BBC London studio.
The programme had begun with me trying to
reason with Orr about glaring contradictions
within the rationale of astrology. We were at
variance within minutes.

The subject of the supernatural eventually
came up, and I mentioned that that was one of
the things which was wrong with astrology at its
deepest level, because of the frightening supernatural experiences it could give people. I cited
one of mine as a case in point.

'I would kindly like to suggest,' Orr said,
'that it was Mr Strohmer's psyche that produced
these things, rather than the astrology itself. I
mean, astrology certainly comes out of the realm
of the irrational, but that's no reason to be
frightened by it.'

When I then tried to reason with her about
this, she tried interrupting me and shouting me
down several times (maybe she thought she was
in the House of Commons!). I had to
concentrate very hard to drive through her
agitation and finish what I had to say. The
presenter tried switching the topic 'to more
practical matters', but unsuccessfully. Orr was
speaking of irrelevancies, and I tried to pin her
down to the question and our need for
a reasonable discussion of the matter.

I don't think Orr liked hearing about the
necessity for rational thinking. She caught her
breath and said that 'the rational' was the real
problem, 'similar to what we have at the
moment with Islamic fundamentalists' (who
were that week making world headlines by
pronouncing their death sentence against
Salmon Rushdie for his 'blasphemous' book
Satanic Verses). I wasn't happy about being

placed alongside such infamy, and the presenter saw the illogic herself and rolled up her eyes in disbelief. Orr would not be stopped now. She rattled on explaining 'the irrational' in terms of Mrs Thatcher (then Prime Minister) living out the Athena myth.

This must have been enough even for the presenter who quipped that she wasn't convinced that Mrs Thatcher sprang from the head of Zeus, and then she promptly ended the 'interview'. I have a suspicion that even the BBC presenter was tired of dealing with the irrational during this 'conversation'. Yet no doubt the dust-up that morning was great for the programme's ratings!

The Bible challenges people: ' "Come now, let us reason together," says the Lord,' (Isa. 1:18), and the picture is from the law court, i.e. the arguing of cases, frank confrontation and the use of evidence and good and sufficient reasons. This is what Job would have liked in his case (Job 23:7)!

Part of the trouble in storms like this is that the irrational has little or no tolerance for the rational. It takes issue with reasoned argument, especially the kind which discloses its inconsistencies. In extreme cases the irrational gets behind the wheel and then bullies the rational into taking a dusty seat at the back of the bus. Also, irrationality creates an intellectual/spiritual climate in which New Age people begin to feel comfortable bedding down with contradictory beliefs and values. Such people may not only appear diffident when a reasoned analysis discloses inconsistencies, they may even be proud of them, for in the New Age world the rational is understood to be a

hindrance to reaching enlightenment, expanding
consciousness and spiritual evolution. This will
be understood by Christians who have heard
New Agers say, 'I don't care if that seems
illogical to you. We must escape the confines
and limitations of rational, black and white,
thinking. Our society has placed too much
emphasis on the analytical left side of the brain.
It's time to develop the intuitive, creative "right
brain". We must get beyond the rational.'

Now according to the New Age way of
thinking, in order to 'get beyond the rational', a
person must first have let the irrational subdue
the rational. A striking yet typical illustration of
this curious process is found in *Dancing in the
Light*, Shirley MacLaine's best-selling second
New Age autobiography.

MacLaine has travelled to 'a very evolved
spiritual community' in Santa Fe, New Mexico,
to visit Chris, a woman who 'is a very
experienced acupuncturist in psychic therapy'.
MacLaine writes that she will receive 'psychic
therapy' sessions from Chris, who (like
MacLaine, we are told) has her own 'spirit
guides' who will assist her during the sessions,
in which MacLaine will be 'administered past-life
recall treatments through . . . acupuncture'.
The sessions take place daily, with MacLaine
resting in deep meditation while lying face up on
an acupuncture table with 'needles quivering
from various areas of [her] body'. Here is an
example of how the process of restraining the
rational occurs and must precede these 'therapy'
sessions.

'Now relax,' said Chris. 'Let your mind go.
Don't evaluate, and don't let the left brain judge

what you are thinking. Give your right brain more space. As a matter of fact, don't think.'

As MacLaine submits she feels her mind 'drift away from its own consciousness . . . into blankness'. It then occurs to her, 'I lay there wishing there were words in the English language which could more aptly describe the experience . . . the whole process of measure-ment and evaluation was an exercise in futility unconsciously designed to keep us in the muck and mire of our own limited thinking.'

The rational mind, however, was not created to be set aside but to think, and whenever a meditation technique attempts to outwit this the rational mind fights back. MacLaine discovered this the moment the 'spirit guides' began giving her mental pictures of her supposed past lives. She slipped and began evaluating.

'It's nothing,' she says to Chris.

'No,' said Chris. 'Wait a minute. Something is happening. Stop judging and evaluating what you're getting. Leave your mind out of this. Just get out of your intellectual way.'[1]

And what happens is that the more MacLaine 'gets out of her intellectual way', the more the irrational 'pictures' come into her mind.

The above is typical of the way in which a New Age way of seeing develops an intolerance for things rational. This may seem unthinkable to Christians, and we will talk more about this during the Inter-Mission. For New Agers the promised goal makes it all seem worthwhile. For irrationality, it is said, holds the key to upward spiritual mobility, the way to discover one's godhood. The sickly sweet fruit of the wrong tree still tempts.

In *Understanding the New Age*, Russell Chandler quotes psychologist Maxine Negri about obtaining godhood, New Age style:

> 'One only has to rid oneself of the limitations imposed by the human brain's left hemisphere's reasoning which Western culture, by way of its technological advances, holds in such high esteem. The pathway to godhood lies not in the left hemisphere's logic but in the right hemisphere's intuitive knowing and creativeness.'[2]

The inevitable results, however, run in the opposite direction: further decline into irrationality, and this intellectual/spiritual dynamic plays havoc with Christian communication. By denying the rational, the New Age adherent permits the irrational to reach a place of ascendance where there will be a marked intolerance for things rational and reasonable, like the gospel message.

Yet this is not the end of the story. It only identifies a condition. There is a symptom of this condition that needs bringing to light, and that is the contradictoriness of certain presuppositions and beliefs that are held by many New Age seekers, who may even be unaware of them. The contradictory nature of the presuppositions can present a troublesome roadblock to effective communication. Yet when identified and properly handled they can be used to help the New Ager pause and consider.

In his book *Confronting the New Age*, Douglas Groothuis discloses both the problem and how it can be handled by recounting part of a conversation between an East Indian Christian, Vishal Mangalwadi, and a Hindu:

Vishal: Is . . . universal consciousness personal or impersonal?

Hindu: It is impersonal and infinite.

Vishal: Is personality higher than impersonality?

Hindu: Of course!

Vishal: Then why do you want to become lower and merge into impersonal consciousness?

Hindu: Well, no, personality is actually lower than impersonality.

Vishal: Why do you then use the term evolution? You should say that we devolved out of the impersonal. Then you should really respect this grass on which we are sitting. Being impersonal, it is higher than us, and you should not walk on it.

Hindu: This is confusing.[3]

I frequently point out another example during my seminars. The 'universal consciousness' cited above has many shades of expression within the New Age way of seeing life. For our purposes, we may simply deal with the presupposition that the ultimate nature of the universe is an invisible spiritual energy which is *impersonal*. After doing some teaching on this, I then move on to discuss another prominent New Age belief, karma and reincarnation, a non-biblical view of the next life. 'Karma' is simply an old Sanskrit word meaning 'deeds', 'works', or 'actions'. 'Reincarnation' means 'to come again in the flesh'. The belief is that at the end of each lifetime a person's good and bad deeds are weighed in a sort of cosmic scale of justice and the balance between them determines the quality of his next life. Mother Teresa, therefore, is doing quite well, but Hitler is in a lot of hot water!

Invariably during a seminar someone will say, 'But you've just told us that in the New Age view the universe is ultimately an impersonal energy. How then can an impersonal energy make value judgements about good and bad deeds?'

Obviously it cannot, and part of our efforts as effective communicators will be to help the New Age seeker discover such inconsistencies of belief.

André Kole has a humorous though astute illustration which clearly sums up what we are up against here. He calls it 'Fire Engine Logic', and it's a story about why fire engines are red. 'Fire engines are red because they have two firemen. Two firemen have four feet. Three feet from four feet leaves one foot. One foot is a ruler. Queen Mary was a ruler. Queen Mary ruled the seven seas. The seven seas have fish. Fish have fins. The Finns were conquered by the Russians. Russians are red. Fire engines are always rushin'. And that's why fire engines are red.'[4]

This, I think, epitomises many New Age presuppositions. Christians usually wonder how on earth New Age seekers can be satisfied by this illogical position. But there are reasons for this which are quite significant as far as understanding the communication breakdown. Here I am thinking not only of irrationality but of prior personal and cultural conditioning.

By 'personal conditioning' I am thinking of the many years during which non-Christians live making bad, unwise or immoral choices. Thus they become accustomed to existing in a state which is by degrees increasingly inconsistent with the way God made the universe and made them as moral and rational beings.

And then there is the 'neglect of rational thought', as *Reader's Digest* put it, saying that children today 'can't apply reasonable thought to everyday situations' and the problem is similar with adults. *Reader's Digest* asks:

> How do Americans come to neglect rational thought? The answer is complicated, but one explanation is depressingly obvious. Thinking is hard work, demanding rigour and discipline. But those virtues went out the window when we let children in the 1960s and 1970s 'do their own thing'. Television reinforced this by encouraging children to sit passively with their minds on idle. [And] in too many classrooms too little was demanded.[5]

By 'cultural conditioning' I have in mind what Dr Francis Schaeffer called the 'escape from reason' that is characteristic of our age, as it seeks to free itself from the box of philosophical rationalism in which it has been suffocating. Rationalism became entrenched in the West during the eighteenth and nineteenth centuries, a period during which Western man was dismissing the knowledge that God could act in human history and speak to him. Rationalism holds that by reason and human intellect alone man is capable of discerning all that can be known. It therefore takes issue with religion and fundamentally rejects the claims of faith. The increasing knowledge of the sciences helped stir popular support for rationalism. This meant that both God and the Bible had less and less authority in the mind of Western man, who then had only his reason to turn to and to depend on. This brought a tremendous change in the thought-forms of Western culture in the area of how people came to *know* things about man and the universe. It was during this period that the secularisation of our culture and society advanced momentously.

Several decades ago, however, people began admitting to the deficiencies of rationalism and a great disillusionment set in. The limits of human reason were becoming only too evident. Rationalism had left man without meaning, without a way of coping with the problems of life's big questions, e.g. about God, human freedom, morals, immortality and so on. This provoked another radical change in the thought-forms of Western peoples, who shook off rationalism (not completely but to a great extent) to search for meaning in an escape from reason. 'The worship of science and the rational to a great extent [was] thrown over for a revival that specifically value[d] the emotional and the non-rational.'6 They sought for that which would 'transcend' reason in order to discover the meaning of life.

Yet where did they escape to? God? No.

To them He is dead. There was no point in looking 'outside' to God. This left them with two choices. They could look for life's meaning either in something in the universe or within themselves. In our day, this search for meaning has usually meant 'going within'. Thus people are swinging from reason alone to intuition alone as the Source for spiritual insight. Rationalistic man is being replaced by intuitive man. The flight from reason prepared the way for a kind of gut mysticism.

The language of the intuitive, therefore, is in no short supply in the New Age world. Terms that contextualise it include: right brain, self-exploration, going within, centring, stilling, meditation, grounding, enlightenment, inner self, Higher Self, self-realisation, mystical experience, altered states, cosmic conscious-ness, transcendence, psychoactive drug experience, the irrational, the non-logical and the non-rational.

Now there is some justification for the swing from reason to intuition. There are limits to human reason and there is an intuitive dimension to man. People are reawakening to something that is true about themselves, which was suppressed by rationalism. We must not dismiss this but redeem the truth of it in a Christian context, or a whole aspect of what it means to be human may be lost.

Christians should submit the intuitive, as they do all else about themselves, to the Lordship of Jesus Christ, and within this context the intuitive does not stand against reason but has a proper relation to the world of the rational. Also, under Christ's lordship it can be renewed. The problem is that non-Christians make an idolatry of the intuitive when they divorce it from reason and God in Christ.

New Age seekers look to the intuitive for that 'final experience' which is so big that it answers for them the question of life's meaning and provides them with spiritual enlightenment. Yet the New Age adventure with the intuitive will fail because all answers and mystical experiences are strictly relative to the person who receives them.

Here is another area of the communication headache posed by the irrational. Mystical experiences are ineffable. They cannot be explained. This means that New Age people can usually live contentedly with themselves and others even when their experiences, views and lifestyles are personally or mutually contradictory. Nothing is absolutely true for them. So truth is merely whatever happens to the seeker, whatever he or she happens to like intuitively. If you sweep away reason and rationality from life's big questions, you no longer need to be responsible for truly knowing if you are right or wrong. You just leap into your experience.

New Agers have no way—no Book, no God, no absolutes—by which to verify an answer or a mystical experience as 'final', or even true, because no certainty about anything exists in intuition alone. Everything is relative to the individual. Thus the search for life's meaning and for enlightenment will go on *ad nauseam* and never be experienced. It will be pursued even on the death bed, which is exactly what happened to long-time LSD experimenter Aldous Huxley, who on his death bed invited Timothy Leary to help assist him in taking LSD in a last desperate attempt to receive the 'final experience'.

Final Observations

There are two kinds of irrational, namely, that which merely *looks* irrational and that which *is* irrational. By the use of the term 'irrational' in this chapter, I do not mean that which only looks so to the one perceiving it. Such would be the case if the thing under consideration simply did not seem possible to someone. A long time ago I asked my grandparents what they would have thought as teenagers—this would have been before the first World War—if someone had told them that a man would be walking on the moon during their lifetime. 'Such an idea was unthinkable,' they replied. 'It was preposterous. We would never have believed it.' Yet it happened in their lifetime. What *seemed* irrational to them eventually became possible.

This is not what I mean by irrational. I have in mind that which is by nature irrational because it stands against, and is contrary to, the way God has ordered the universe and the way things ought to be; therefore it will *never* be true. I also have in mind the anti-rational, as the demonic world is thought to be. Perhaps it is when the demonic realm interferes with the human realm that things turn irrational, which may provide a clue as to why 'the irrational' as a spiritual/intellectual dynamic within the New Age world can pose all sorts of communication difficulties. The advantage we have, however, is that even the New Age person, because he or she was created in the image of God, has certain

God-given inner characteristics by which to apprehend and understand truth. All is not lost.

Also, in saying that New Age seekers trust in the irrational, I in no way mean that they are thoroughly irrational. For instance, they realise that the bills must be paid and so they work. They don't leave their car windows down when it's raining. They will not break the law if they want to stay out of prison. One plus one still equals two, at least in their cheque books! In some areas they live rationally. Indeed many New Age people seek a balanced development of intellect and intuition, seeing the two as complementary.

Yet for some, their intuition may have become the only criterion for 'critical' thinking. It is not that New Age people lose their critical or rational faculty *in toto*; rather, this faculty may be framed by intuition alone, which then becomes their single means of discriminating right from wrong, especially in the area of life's meaning. The individual is then left with his or her own private interpretation or meaning of things, apart from any outside authority; except, perhaps, for the New Age world itself. An individual may therefore look for insight from a spiritualist minister, or a transpersonal psychologist, or even a 'spirit guide', but his rational analysis about how to process the information and apply it, or ignore it, may be framed entirely by his own personal, intuitive New Age way of seeing life.

Thus Christians will find New Age people discussing values and standards, but not often in the way we are used to. For example, some New Age spokespersons argue for 'setting standards' in 'channelling' to stop what they consider abuses. Now how could they 'set standards' apart from using their critical faculty to discriminate between 'good' and 'bad' channelling? Their reasoning, however, will be framed by their own personal intuition on the subject. Helen Palmer, a New Age psychic with strong leanings towards channelling and transpersonal psychology, states it clearly, 'The task remains yours to evaluate what you receive in terms of your own experience, your inner world and the world at large.'[7]

Also, in communicating what is reasonable and rational we must not give the impression that the Christian faith has Reason as its core principle or God. Let us not be seen as rationalists. This is important for two reasons. One is that some New Agers recognise a glaring contradiction within Western Christianity; that we will fight tooth and nail to affirm the miracles of the New Testament but deny the supernatural today. Thus they see the Church as rationalistic today and they're not interested. The other thing we want to be careful of is not to disagree with New Agers that there are some very real limits to human reason. The mind certainly is limited. What we want to do is help the person see that reason and rationality have a much higher and consistent place in the ultimate scheme of things than he or she may have thought. We want to help the person see that when the Christian looks outside himself to God in Jesus Christ, for meaning and salvation, it is not an *un*reasonable or *non*rational mysticism. This does not mean that suddenly there are no more question marks; rather, though much mystery and paradox remains, we know that it is ultimately resolved in the person of Jesus Christ. And so we can rest spiritually, knowing contentment amidst the very real limitations of our human reason.

This significant distinction may be worth mentioning to New Age followers. Whereas New Age enlightenment stands opposed to reason and rationality, due to its subjective reliance on intuition, Christian salvation rests consistent with the world of the rational when it looks outside to a supernatural God as He is known in Christ Jesus.

Let us, therefore, be wise when working in the New Age world. We will meet people in whom the irrational is to be desired. Most of them will have been led towards it by both personal and cultural conditioning. And as an intellectual/spiritual dynamic, the irrational (usually occultic in nature) plays havoc with Christian communication.

6

The Calm of Passivity

Closely allied to the escape from reason into intuition, and its attendant the irrational, is the intellectual/spiritual dynamic of passivity of mind. It is another communication foiler in the New Age world, and is probably easiest to understand in the context of meditation. In fact, it is difficult to separate passivity of mind from New Age forms of meditation. They are like halves of a pair of scissors; if you had only one half you would wonder how the thing worked.

It is the rare New Age adherent who does not practise some form of meditation (which includes visualisation), and therefore it is likely that we will meet New Age enthusiasts who have become accustomed to degrees of passivity. In so far as it hinders our Christian witness, an understanding of how it develops will give us an advantage. Also, as we saw with irrationality, passivity of mind is hard to define conclusively. But we will make an attempt here.

New Age passivity of mind may be understood by analogy with the inactivity of the body and the sensory isolation that usually precedes the individual's entering a meditative state. The person deliberately separates himself for a short time, often about twenty minutes, from people and daily activities. A quiet room is recommended, where one can be alone.

External sources of stimulation, including sensory ones, should be eliminated or kept to a minimum to avoid distractions. Emphasis may also be placed upon maintaining a specific posture to keep body movements to a minimum.

By these means everything about the person becomes still and quiet—except for the activity of the mind, which is 'noisy' with all kinds of thoughts. However, with the body at rest and the senses largely inactive, the mind can be made to follow suit. To 'still' the mind, one's attention is focused for as long as possible on a single object such as the flame of a candle, or the picture of one's guru, or perhaps a sound called a mantra, or a colour, or a symbol like a mandala. Concentrating on one object, source or idea helps push all other thoughts aside. This is essential for achieving stillness (passivity) of mind. It is a prerequisite for entering a meditative state. Because it restricts awareness to a single source for a definite period of time, 'focusing' acts as a sort of quietening device for all other thoughts, pushing them aside.

This active restriction of awareness to a single source and the withdrawal of attention from conscious thought is the common element in most forms of meditation.[1] It's no secret that meditation has always been on a collision course with conscious rational thought. Because the exercise of meditation does not involve reason, 'stilling' the conscious mind of thought (passivity) is unavoidable before a meditative state can be entered. The meditator, therefore, becomes involved in a process of restraining, subduing and inhibiting the rational faculty and conscious thought.

To the New Age person, meditation is the

obverse of rational thought, not being concerned with intellectual but intuitive knowledge which is frequently called inner knowledge, or self-knowledge. Meditative techniques and styles, including yoga, necessitate a shift away from conscious rational mental activity to 'intuitive knowing' and are designed to produce a corresponding alteration in consciousness by 'going within'. One is supposed to shut down perceptions of the external world and tune into the internal, and it is a meditational axiom that this cannot be accomplished actively, only passively. Passivity therefore becomes the passage to temporary suspension of conscious thought while in a waking state, a key for entrance into New Age meditation and intuitiveness.

Some meditators, like the ancient mystic St John of the Cross, are militant about forbidding conscious thought. St John of the Cross, it is said, demanded of meditators that the soul must 'strip and void itself' of all 'forms and manners of knowledge', including memory.[2] This tyranny of passivity over conscious thought offers New Age meditators a goal which is variously described as: an open mind, emptying the mind, a blank page, a clear state, the void, emptiness, ignoring thought, silencing the mind, turning off the active-verbal mode and suchlike. However it is stated, the effect is a vow of mental silence, and however this is interpreted it equals passivity of mind.

Let us now move the discussion from the theoretical to the practical. Imagine thirty participants—ordinary persons, university students, single parents, secretaries, businessmen, taxi drivers, some unemployed—gathered in the conference room of a suburban hotel. We

are in the middle of a weekend 'Mind
Development' course, which I later discovered
was very similar to 'Silva Mind Control'. It is a
bright Saturday afternoon and for the next
session the thick tan curtains have been drawn
across the floor-to-ceiling windows. Some of the
fluorescent lighting is now being switched off as
we listen, keenly attentive like students before
exams, to Tom, a forty-five-year-old, silver-
haired retired Marine, who is our instructor for
the weekend.

'So that you won't distract your neighbour,'
he said, 'for this next session separate your
chairs about three to four feet apart.'

We slid the cushioned, straight-backed
chairs apart and reseated ourselves. Tom then
gently asked us to become quiet.

'Get as comfortable as you can, too,' he
said. 'That's it. Now relax. Take several deep
breaths, slowly, and relax. Now I want you to
close your eyes and try to relax even more.'

It grew very quiet, and as Tom's voice, deftly
modulated, became the only sound in the room,
it began to occupy our thoughts fully.

'You're doing fine,' Tom continued. 'Try not
to let yourself be distracted by anything. Even
try to let the sound of the air-conditioning
disappear. Now you'll begin by focusing your
attention on a single area of your body when I
name it. Follow my voice. Try to block out all
other thoughts. We'll start with the toes.
Concentrate upon your toes.'

After a brief pause he said, 'Now focus on
your entire foot.'

A short pause, and then, 'Now concentrate
on your calf.'

About thirty seconds later he continued,

'Now on your knee. Try to see it in your mind's eye. Ignore all other thoughts which arise.'

A pause, and then, 'Now move the focus from your knee to your upper leg. Try to forget about the other body areas as I lead you on to the next one. Hear only my voice. Focus only on the area I mention. Try to keep your memory out of this, as well as thoughts about tomorrow.'

A longer pause, and then, 'Now concentrate on your hip.'

This procedure continued until we had covered the entire anatomy from toe to head. It took about half an hour.

'Continue with your eyes closed as we move to a deeper level. Remain relaxed and place your hands on your laps, palms up. Now rest your thumb-tips lightly on the tips of your index and middle fingers. That's it. Try to remain as comfortable as you can. I'll pause momentarily to let you get used to this new position.'

Tom's voice was compelling but without coercion, which produced a desire in me to obey it, perhaps because of my dislike of being forced into something. I decided to follow the voice into the next level, whatever that meant.

'Now I want those of you who can,' Tom continued, 'to move with me beyond relaxation and into meditation. To accomplish this, you will need to quieten your minds of all thoughts. This will be difficult for some of you at first. So to help you, without opening your eyes, I want you to recall the symbols I had on display during the previous session. Some of those symbols will have impressed themselves on your mind. I want you now to focus your attention on the one, and one only, which now comes to mind. It will be a different one for each of you.

Push all other thoughts away and concentrate on the one symbol. See its colour, its shape, its lines. Try to discover its meaning for you. But remember to block out all other thoughts. I'm now going to leave you in quietness to experiment with this for several minutes. Meditate on your symbol.'

I do not recall hearing any noises in the insulated and dimly lit room as I practised this, my first ever contact with meditation, which occurred more than twenty years ago. After several minutes Tom spoke again.

'Now with eyes still closed, I want all of you to take your minds off your symbol and gradually become aware of this room again. Hear its sounds. Feel the air-conditioning. Now slowly open your eyes and become fully conscious of this room. Good. Some of you had trouble stilling your minds. Don't be too con- cerned about it. You will soon be able to master it. You may stand up and move around now. We'll take a short break, and then come back and talk about your experiences in a moment.'

From the comments which followed, it was evident that many of us did a poor job shutting down our conscious thoughts whilst trying to remain awake. If someone wasn't thinking about the coming summer holiday, it was the unpaid bills, or the fight with a spouse, or roses, or the dental appointment, or the recent funeral . . . Tom knew we would have trouble 'stilling'. After all, the mind has been created by God to think. Attempt to shut it down and it fights back.

'Your stories,' Tom said, 'sound so familiar. I used to have the same difficulty. But there are ways around this. So if you're willing, we'll pick up where we left off before the break. Get comfortable in your chairs again, and I'll give you some tips to help you quieten your minds. Then we'll try practising them. After you have mastered them, which may take a few weeks, you should be able to move in and out of meditative states easily. But this is not something I can do for you. You must learn to do it for yourselves.'

During the next session, Tom instructed us in the use of various mental techniques, i.e. 'quietening devices', by which to outwit conscious thought and still the mind. This is not the book to take you through the slough of details describing them. They entail 'imaginative' use of symbols, sounds, objects, colours, Zen koans, breathing exercises, even crystals, and with practice these become mental trigger mechanisms by which to outwit conscious thought and slip into meditation.

How, then, is the use of this technique able to counter an effective Christian witness? The answer lies in its *aftereffect*. After years of using meditation, the New Age person has been party to a shift of consciousness from the rational mode of receiving spiritual knowledge, to receiving from the intuitive, mystical mode. This means that he is less interested in 'comprehendible' spiritual knowledge and more interested in the incomprehensible, the ineffable. Meditative passivity has actually *reduced* the range of sources of spiritual knowledge available to that person. It has become a narrower band, and a kind of spiritual antenna signals the person to receive things New Age, but there is no longer much of a frequency or 'carrier wave' to receive things which are not New Age. This transformation produces a temper of mind which increasingly guards itself against non-New Age spiritual answers. Such a person has a heightened resistance to whatever he perceives as spiritually foreign to the meditative, mystical, intuitive way of life.

What happens then when a Christian talks to a meditator about 'comprehendible' spiritual knowledge? The meditator sees it as outside the range of what he has been conditioned to accept. Refusals to listen to Christians are therefore not uncommon. There may even be antagonism to the Christian message.

There is one other aspect of this dynamic which needs mentioning here, and that is the potential for demonic activity in the meditator which will impede Christian communication. The continual practice of New Age, i.e. Eastern, meditation produces an 'open' mind through passivity. We need to ask the question: to what is the mind open during states of passivity? It may be open to new ideas because prejudices have been cast off, which in itself may not be wrong. The danger, however, is that the meditator's mind sooner or later opens to contact with the spirit world. This is certainly no secret in the New Age community, though its adherents would not admit that the nature of their 'spirit guides' is demonic. A host of spirit 'entities', with names such as Mafu, Ramtha, Lazaris, Seth, John, McPherson, Raphael and Michael, have been popularised by several film stars and leading New Age 'channellers'. Yet even ordinary New Age meditators may have their own personal 'entities'.

I ended up with several myself, having been taught how to contact them in the subsequent

'Mind Development' sessions that followed the one described above. I was told that in deep meditation my mind would open up to powerful forces and voices in the spirit realm, and that these spirit beings live in a 'belt in the air' which surrounds the earth (echoes of Ephesians 2:2?). Through meditation I could contact them. The object was to discover their individual names and characteristics and find out in what areas of my life they could be of help. I was taught how to contact these spirits by using visualisation techniques to construct a spiritual room, or workshop, in my imagination, which would be the place of communion with the 'spirit guides'. I merely had to invite them in. And the more 'open' I became the easier it would be to receive them.

I submitted to this for reasons that are common to most meditators. The 'spirit guides', I had been taught, were not demonic but former human beings who had lived many previous lifetimes. They had reincarnated so often that they were now spiritually evolved; they no longer had to return in their earth suits any more because they had paid off all their bad karma with good karma and were therefore entitled to be highly evolved spirit beings. If I contacted them, they would instruct me and entrust me with all the esoteric wisdom that they had gained during their, possibly thousands of, incarnations. In this way my spiritual evolution would advance by leaps and bounds. This is a common deception in the New Age world.

When a regular pattern of contacting 'spirit guides' develops, a meditator can become oppressed, possessed or in some way influenced by demonic powers, which can impede

communication with him. This was my
experience more than once when I was a
meditator. And I was clearly delivered from the
evil spirits which I thought were 'spirit guides'
the evening of my conversion to Christ. The
wise communicator will want to be alert to the
possible problems, and I have made some
suggestions in Part Two.

Summary

The way of seeing the intellectual/spiritual
dynamics that I have described in this and the
previous chapter have helped me a great deal,
though I do not claim that it is etched in stone.
I hope that the following illustration will help
readers to whom the idea is new. It ties both
chapters together.

God created the rational mind to think,
reason and analyse. New Age irrationality,
however, slips into the driver's seat after
relegating the rational to the back of the bus.
The rational mind, however, dislikes the
passivity and scrambles its way back into the
driver's seat time after time. Quietening devices
are then instituted—to outwit the rational mind.
Eventually, New Age meditators are conditioned
to accept passivity of mind as a way into the
intuitive, mystical mode of perceiving life and of
receiving ineffable mystical experiences. This
becomes a chief vehicle of spiritual development
à la New Age, and along the way irrationality
rationalises the illogical and the adherent then
feels comfortable bedding down with
contradictory beliefs and values.

The Genesis of Deception

The Bible is a book with many literary images. They are important because they embellish the realities that they represent with depth of meaning. Take the Holy Spirit as an example. Some images in the Bible, especially as used by Jesus, depict the Holy Spirit's nature as personal. Other images do not, i.e. fire, dove and wind. Each image of the Holy Spirit has its own nuance which contributes to a fuller understanding of the third Person of the Trinity.

Now this holds true throughout the Bible; its literary images ornament the things they are naming with significant features that we would otherwise be unaware of. In this chapter we will look at one particular biblical image, that of the 'serpent', which is one of the ways the Bible depicts certain clear characteristics of the 'hidden things of darkness' (1 Cor. 4:5, AV). Other images may be more difficult to understand, such as the dragon mentioned in the book of Revelation. As a rule, the dragon image represents multinational or international evil. Then there is the devil. Why is the devil not given the image of a dragon in Matthew's Gospel? Simply because it is not international

evil but temptation that the Bible wants to
convey here.

Another image of darkness is found in the
book of Job: Satan, or *the* Satan, as the Hebrew
has it, signifying an enemy or accuser. In the
first two chapters of Job we see Satan levelling
accusations against Job. Here the Bible
enlarges our understanding of the hidden things
of darkness by showing us a characteristic we
can liken to a prosecuting counsel. From it we
get the familiar biblical doctrine that Satan is
the 'accuser of the brethren'.

Now this is merely hermeneutics simplified:
the dragon, for international evil; the devil, for
temptation; the Satan, for accusation.
Associated, overlapping or parallel features are
often found among the images. Let us,
therefore, not be simplistic about this. Yet
neither let us ignore discussion about the
hidden things of darkness because we may have
been nettled by the raw handling given them by
some people. At times it is necessary to do some
study in this area.

So now we move from Revelation to
Matthew to Job to the beginning of the Bible,
where we read about 'the serpent'. As a rule,
the image of the serpent portrays deception and
the treachery of the deceiver. It reminds me of
old pirates who sailed under false colours in
order to get alongside merchant ships without
arousing opposition; but once alongside they
hoisted their true colours, the Jolly Roger, and it
was too late for their prey.

'Deception' is a strong word and ought not
to be used lightly; nevertheless, it brings us to
another intellectual/spiritual dynamic within
the New Age world that can cripple Christian

communication. And the Bible is certainly not silent about deception and its ramifications. In fact, in the image of the serpent, deception is the first characteristic of the kingdom of darkness that is mentioned in the Bible. Here is a working definition we will use; it has many implications for us as communicators, and it is what I take to be its chief feature biblically: deception is about the deliberate misrepresentation of facts or truth to purposely lead someone astray.

Let us look at the biblical setting and see how it relates to our work with New Age people.

Now the serpent was more crafty than any of the wild animals the Lord God had made. He said to the woman, 'Did God really say, "You must not eat from any tree in the garden"?'

The woman said to the serpent, 'We may eat fruit from the trees in the garden, but God did say, "You must not eat fruit from the tree that is in the middle of the garden, and you must not touch it, or you will die." '

'You will not surely die,' the serpent said to the woman. 'For God knows that when you eat of it your eyes will be opened, and you will be like God, knowing good and evil.'

When the woman saw that the fruit of the tree was good for food and pleasing to the eye, and also desirable for gaining wisdom, she took some and ate it. She also gave some to her husband, who was with her, and he ate it. Then the eyes of both of them were opened, and they realised [not that they were 'like God', but] that they were naked [quite a distinction]; so they sewed fig leaves together and made coverings for themselves (Gen. 3:1–7).

Note that deception begins with the deceiver's introduction of facts or truth into the conversation. These are then later distorted, perhaps when a degree of fascination in them is expressed by the listener, in the hope that the listener will then act in obedience to the distortion. In an effort to see how deception led the primary human family astray, let's do a little time-travelling. Can you pretend with me that you are secluded in Eden's lush, beautiful foliage watching the incident unfold?

To clarify some of the points, let us pretend that Eve is 5'10" tall and adorned with long dark hair. Here she is, then, a beautiful tall brunette standing alongside a certain tree, and she appears to be talking to it. No, wait a moment. She is not talking to the tree but to the serpent.

Notice that the serpent does not open the conversation with a bold-faced lie, saying, for instance, 'You're lookin' good today, Eve. I always did like short blondes.' This sounds silly, but, after all, he is the father of lies (John 8:44), so why not begin straightaway with an outright lie? Obviously, if the serpent had begun by lying, Eve would have brushed him off immediately. If he could not get even the simplest facts right, she would not have bothered to listen further. But if he starts with certain facts or truths he can appear credible and so *hold* Eve's attention. Thus he begins with something that Eve knows to be *true* about herself: God has been speaking to her about the trees. And around this fact the serpent will then camouflage his deception at the point in the conversation where Eve is becoming fascinated by his hidden (occult) spiritual knowledge.

Still with me in Eden? If so, let's supplement the conversation and imagine the following exchange between Eve and the serpent in an effort to get a fuller understanding of the nature of deception.

Serpent: Afternoon, Eve. Don't be startled. No need to be afraid. Here, over here. Yes, I am a bit difficult to see, but don't let that worry you. Lovely weather today, eh? By the way, I hear that God has been talking to you.

Eve: What!? Who said that? Who's speaking?

Serpent: Oh, there's no need for introductions. It's not important who I am. What's important is that I know who you are and that God has been talking to you. God talks to me too, you know. I also know what He's been talking to you about . . . the trees, right?

Eve: That's right. But how do you know God has been talking to me? I don't recall seeing you around here before.

Serpent: Like I said, it's not important who I am or how I know these things. What's important is that I do.

Eve: Well, you've certainly got your facts straight.

Serpent: Good. But that being so, I'm more than somewhat puzzled about your well-being. If God is so good, as you believe, why has He withheld spiritual advancement from you?

Eve: Now you're puzzling me.

Serpent: What I mean is, why has God forbidden you to eat from *any* tree in the Garden? Sounds as if He's withholding some higher good from you.

Eve: No. There you're mistaken.

Serpent: Oh?

Eve: You're right in saying that God has been speaking to us about the trees, but you're wrong in thinking that we can't eat from *any* of them.

Serpent: Sorry, I probably wasn't paying attention when I should have been. But I really would like some clarity on the point, then. Sure you've got it right?

Eve: There's no doubt in my mind about that! God said we could eat from all the trees in the Garden. Except one, that is. In fact, it's this tree right here!

Serpent: Imagine that. What a coincidence! Still, I think it's harsh of God to forbid you to eat from such a splendid tree.

Eve: Not in the least. He doesn't want us to die. And if we eat from this tree we will die.

Suddenly, the *coup de grâce*.

'You will not surely die,' the serpent said to the woman. 'For God knows that when you eat of it your eyes will be opened, and you will be like God, knowing good and evil.'

Before Eve had had time to collect her thoughts, the serpent had shown himself a master of innuendo and undermined what God had said.

Eve: There must be some mistake!

Serpent: No. Not in the least. There's no doubt about it. I'm not kidding. I'm deadly serious. Trust me. I've got my facts straight, right?

And the rest is history. Fascination with the forbidden is too much for Eve to handle and the way of the curse is substituted for the way to blessing.

Here, then, is an unmistakable process: the deliberate misrepresentation of facts and truth to lead someone away from what God had said. The initial introduction of facts (one, God has been speaking; two, about trees) catches the listener's attention and then holds it and gains credibility for the speaker. As the listener becomes more interested, the speaker can then distort the truth in the hope of soliciting the listener's obedience to what is now a lie. This is the process of deception. Through the subtle and *mis*leading use of facts or truth, which in and of themselves cannot be disputed, disobedience to God and obedience to serpentine enlightenment is realised. If the speaker has got his facts straight, the listener is likely to assume that the interpretation of those facts will be right. Trust is gained and the hidden knowledge is then adopted for guidance.

Let's now leave Eden and return to the present to look at a sample of this dynamic in a New Age context. The following illustration is from Shirley MacLaine's best-selling book *Dancing in the Light*. The excerpt is taken from a lengthy conversation that MacLaine says she had with a 'spirit guide' called 'John', who speaks through channeller Kevin Ryerson.

MacLaine (to 'John'): I guess my first question is, is there a real need on our earth for spiritual enlightenment? I mean, would it decrease human suffering if more people understood the spiritual dimensions of themselves?

John: That is correct. The collective consciousness of the entire human race manifests the reality of your earth plane. The influence of the mind of man creates disturbances in nature and of course in your human activities.

MacLaine: You mean the mind of man can influence nature, like earthquakes and flooding and things?

John: That is correct. Gravitational influences and planetary harmony are affected by the minds of beings on every planet. You are experiencing natural disturbances on your planet because the consciousness of the human race needs raising.

MacLaine: Is that why spiritual enlightenment is necessary?

John: Yes, the mind of man is more powerful than nature. You are suffering from your state of mind, which is influencing the patterns of nature on your plane.

MacLaine: Okay. With all the bad stuff that's happening in the world today, would you say there is a negative force operating here that is equal to the God-force? I mean, is evil a part of God also?

John: You are speaking of satanic influences?

MacLaine: Yes.

John: The concept of Satan as interpreted in your Bible had its origins as follows: Adam and Eve stood symbolically for the creation of souls. They were created originally as pure spiritual soul energy, as everyone was. When they became captivated by the material plane, or the earth plane as you know it, they found themselves incarnated in the bodies of the lower primates because they were seduced by the attractions of physical existence. Because of their fall from grace, they activated the law of karma. Their spiritual and divine origins were only dimly remembered because of the confined restrictions of their physical bodies. The struggle back towards original divinity is what your Bible means by Satan . . . What you term as Satan is merely the force of your lower consciousness as you engage in the struggle to return and know God, which was your origin. The feeling of what you term evil is the struggle with self.

MacLaine: Well, how could we have gone so far wrong about this subject?

John: The struggle for self-knowledge would not be a struggle if one loved God with all one's heart and soul and one's neighbour as one's self. For one's neighbour is one's self. But mankind set up the dualities of good and evil in order to judge others rather than to discover self. Therefore, it was even possible to make war on one another. Out of a lack of knowledge of God came the concept of evil. But when mankind understands that it itself is a collective being representing the

God-force, it is impossible to make war on
the self. Is this to your understanding?
MacLaine: Yes.[1]

This piece from *Dancing* is indicative of a
galaxy of occult ideas that fill MacLaine's New
Age autobiographies, which have influenced
millions. It also takes us to the source of many
New Age ideas and beliefs, i.e. the countless
spirit-channelling sessions (channelling being a
sort of quantum leap from the old spirit-medi-
umship phenomenon) that now dot the New Age
map. Topics will vary from the big questions of
life's meaning to small mundane matters. We
might be tempted to dismiss it as just so much
bilge. Yet what the 'entities' are saying is being
ingested and acted upon because lie is blended
with truth in the spiritual chalice from which an
increasing number of New Agers are drinking.
As Christian communicators, we will want
to help the spiritual seeker unscramble the
truth from the deception, so let us examine the
exchange between MacLaine and 'John' to see
the similarities with what occurred between Eve
and the serpent. It begins for MacLaine, as it
did for Eve, by becoming interested in forbidden
spiritual knowledge, which places her on the
threshold of deception. 'John', then, loads the
conversation with facts and affirmations by
which he gains credibility and keeps the
dialogue running. Throughout the conversation,
the facts and truths are distorted, and, like Eve,
MacLaine reaches a point where she has no
further answer or response (Gen. 3:5, 6); she
has been brought to an acquiescence in the
forbidden knowledge.
The conversation opens with the facts of

human suffering, pain and the spiritual
dimension of man (things true enough), and
soon includes the question of evil. These 'John'
does not deny but affirms. In fact, he loads the
conversation with Bible words: Satan, Adam and
Eve, fall from grace. 'John' may have pitched
the conversation in this direction because such
images would carry obvious connotations for
MacLaine as they connected with her childhood
Christian (such as it was) memories. 'John' has
got his facts and he has got a listener, now he
can distort them as much as he wants.

Earthquakes and floods become the result
of low human consciousness. Suffering
becomes merely a state of mind. Satan becomes
the struggle within human beings to get back to
original divinity, and it is implied that Satan is
an equal opposite to God. And I admit I am
slightly impressed by 'John's' craftiest sleight-of-
mind in the passage. Right on the heels of the
truth that one ought to love God with all one's
heart and one's neighbour as one's self, 'John'
tells his listener why: because 'one's neighbour
is one's self'. This, however, is sheer monism.[2]
(I wonder if 'John' in some curious way inspired
the popular Beatles' line, 'I am he, as you are
me, and we are all together'?)

The image of the serpent also gives us an
instructive point about how mediumship and
channelling hooks listeners. It is as true today
as it was in Eden. There is an element of truth
in what New Age adherents hear from the 'spirit
guides'. This is an important principle because
it means that some New Age beliefs may be only
partially false. I will have much more to say
about this in Part Two. This is because a lie or
a deception would have no power to fascinate

and *mis*lead people on its own. It would have no power to solicit obedience in an epistemological vacuum. A lie or a deception derives its power because there is such a thing as truth. It is not the other way round.

As Christian communicators, we will want to be conscious of the dynamic of deception when we are in conversation with New Age seekers. We will want to be informed and sensitive to the truth behind the distortions. In Part Two, we will try to discover ways to rectify the distortions and thereby redeem the truth of the matter. The habit some of us have had of throwing out the baby with the bathwater has been about as helpful as a screen door on a submarine. Deal with the dirty bathwater by all means. But let us not flush the truth out with it.

8

Identifying Distortions

'Get your facts first,' Mark Twain wrote, 'then you can distort them as much as you want.'

This and the next chapter look at several areas where truth becomes distorted in the New Age world in such a way as to hinder Christian communication.

We have touched upon the phenomenon of channelling. It provides New Age enthusiasts with communication from a 'higher power' that acts as a spiritual authority figure. Channelling also helps the seeker break free from the strictures of reason and rational explanations. These and other features of the phenomenon are meeting some spiritual needs, at least temporarily, of New Age seekers. Thus famous channellers like J. Z. Knight, Kevin Ryerson and Jach Pursel can pack auditoriums in city after city, with people who are longing for 'a tender word to come and tell them who they are'. Channellers and their 'spirit guides', therefore, take the place of prayer, counsel, comfort and the authority that people ought to be receiving from the *Holy* Spirit.

Yet the New Age is meeting another spiritual need, and that is by offering answers to life's big questions. We will now look at what the New Age has to say about some of these big questions and see how distortions of truth occur. Please note that the following material will barely scratch the surface and is meant merely to get us thinking from this point of view. The Recommended Reading list at the end of this book includes titles and brief reviews that cover these topics more thoroughly.

• God. Most New Age people take the truth of God's existence seriously. Unlike atheists and agnostics, New Age people are convinced of a reality called 'God'. But then, all who grapple with this big question must come to some conclusion about 'God's' nature. Is God a He or an It? A personal being or an impersonal energy or force? Is He or It good, evil or some combination of the two? The answer to these questions will influence how we relate to Him or It. The Bible reveals that though God is Spirit He is also personal in nature. Though the New Age 'way of seeing' assents to the truth that there is 'God', it then distorts the nature of God, who becomes strictly 'It', an impersonal energy or life-force. It is the 'God' typified by the Luke Skywalker mentality in *Star Wars:* the Force be with you. In the biblical view, God makes moral demands and is known through the person of Jesus Christ. In the New Age view, 'God', being impersonal, makes no moral demands and can be accessed and utilised like electricity by anyone who knows how to plug into it. In another New Age view, God is that which is both good and evil, darkness and light. Or, in another, beyond good and evil.

• Death. New Age seekers also take the truth of death seriously, and they grapple with its nature and meaning. The Bible, of course, teaches that death is the judgement of God upon the human race as a result of our sin. Also, death is seen as an enemy that is faced once. Christ defeated it through His resurrection, and believers in Christ are passed from death to life.

In the New Age world, death is redefined as a 'transition' from body to body through thousands of lifetimes, i.e. reincarnations. It is not thought of as an enemy but more like a succession of invisible archways through which one passes between periods of physical existence, wandering the long and winding road of spiritual evolution in search of perfection, enlightenment, the discovery of one's status as a god and so on. Death is therefore seen as the result not of sin, or as an enemy, but of one's bad karma, which can be paid off, sooner or later, by accruing mountains of good karma during future incarnations, of which there may be thousands.

• The Universe. Concepts about the nature of the universe abound within the New Age world. The Bible teaches that the universe and its countless material 'things' are real and not illusory. They are real because the Reality who created them is real. Perhaps we could call God 'Creating Reality' and material things 'created reality', which might help us understand that both are real but not the same reality. Furthermore, the Bible teaches that when God created 'things' He created them distinct from Himself and also from one another. We may take as examples: day/night; land/water; the inanimate/the animate; a mineral kingdom, a vegetable kingdom, a human kingdom, an angelic kingdom. We also learn that within the vegetable and animal kingdoms, things are brought forth 'after their kind', which is another mark of distinction. In other words, separately created realities are distinct from each other and not a part of God. This does not mean that there is not an interconnectedness to life, which we will see shortly.

In what may be the dominant New Age presupposition, the universe is scrambled up with 'God' to become the distortion: pantheistic monism.[1] In another view, the universe and its things are thought of as an illusion, not necessarily in the sense that they are non-existent but 'unreal' the way a dream is unreal. This ancient view from Hinduism has been adapted to the Western New Age way of seeing. In Hinduism, one encounters millions of gods, but there is also an important trinity representing three aspects of 'The Supreme': Brahma(n), the creator; Vishnu, the sustainer; Siva (Shiva), the destroyer. In this metaphysic, the world is the Dream of the creator, Brahma. Thus the things of the world, including individual souls, are parts of the Dream.

Now there is an element of truth in this dream metaphor that is close to a biblical view, for there would be no world without Brahma and Brahma's existence does not depend upon the appearance of the world. However, Hinduism parts company with the Bible with ideas that in the Dream World, the senses are deceived by *maya* which prevents us from realising the dream nature, or illusory quality, of the world and the universe. Also, the human mind is said to be deceived by *maya* into attributing much more reality to the world than it possesses.

• Oneness. There is an interconnectedness and interdependence, or wholeness and unity, to the things of creation. Yet Christians know that the unity is only found in God through the Agent of His creation, Jesus Christ in union with the Holy Spirit (see Heb. 11:3; Col. 1:17). In no way, however, do you lose the reality of the existence of the things that God has made or their fundamental distinctions (see 'Universe' above). A true interdependence would mean, for instance, that you could quite rightly talk about the dependence of the butcher upon the cow for his livelihood; the cow upon the grass for its continued life; the grass upon the soil for its existence. It is an interdependence in which the grass 'takes up' from the soil the minerals it needs and the cow 'takes up' from the grass the nourishment it needs, and the butcher takes from the cow what he needs. The most striking example is our dependence upon dust for our physical bodies. There is, therefore, a kind of interconnectedness and interdependence, amongst the distinct things of God's creation.

The New Age way of seeing distorts the biblical picture of unity. It relies heavily on Eastern religious wisdoms. In these views— chiefly expressed in Hinduism, Buddhism and Taoism—one certainly loses the distinction between things and their realness and that, then, becomes the Oneness. The world is said merely to be seen as separate objects (and events), not because it is a fundamental feature of reality, but because we have so categorised it to help us deal with everyday life. This is why most leading Eastern mystics are uninterested in explaining things and much more intent on intuitive experiences, whereby things lose their distinctions and they perceive the Oneness of all.

We have room for one example. *Maya* is one of the most difficult words in Hinduism to understand. Earlier, it was seen that *maya* prevents the senses from recognising the dream nature of the world. It is also said to prevent the recognition that reality is one and indivisible because nothing else really exists except Brahma. *Maya,* therefore, is generally understood (at the least) to be the quality of illusion, or the illusory structure, of the empirical world that makes the One appear as many independent 'things'. When a person perceives he is a part of the Dream, which he may do intuitively through ascetic practice, contemplation, meditation, yoga and so on, oneness with Self, i.e. with all else, is the deception. This is the Oneness that New Age seekers reach for, and it is a far cry from the answer to Jesus' prayer in John 17.

• Jesus Christ. Interest in the person and nature of Jesus Christ runs high within the New Age world. The Bible reveals that Jesus Christ is God the Son, the Incarnate One, Lord and Saviour, and it discloses many other characteristics which mark Him off as uniquely different from any other religious teacher or holy man.

Within the New Age, Jesus is seen as one of several special holy men who have walked the Earth. He is considered an 'ascended master', 'christ', or 'avatar', i.e. one who attained perfection and divinity through enlightenment. Here Jesus is immortalised in a select constellation of spiritual teachers such as Rama, Buddha and Krishna, who were considered godmen. There are many variations on this theme. Gnosticism, theosophy, anthroposophy, the 'I AM' movement, Unity, George Trevelyan, David Spangler, Annie Besant, Benjamin Creme, Levi Dowling, Matthew Fox and a host of other schools and teachers have produced distortions about the person and nature of Jesus Christ. The New Age world may lift Jesus higher than most mortals but not nearly high enough.

• Man. The nature of what it means to be human is another big question addressed in the New Age. The Bible teaches that we have been created by God, and that we are finite and limited in potential and power; also, that we are beings separate from God. Having been created in the likeness of God, who is personal, we are each unique in that we are *persons* and not mere animals or things, or illusory souls in a dream state.

Within the New Age way of seeing, human nature is exalted to the status of God or as being part of God, or in some sense Divine. In *Dancing in the Light*, a 'spirit guide' tells Shirley MacLaine that 'You each need to become masters of your own souls, which is to say, the realisation of yourselves as God.' This belief is taken from Hindu pantheism, updated and adapted. Thus many spiritual seekers now believe in their unlimited self-potential. Alternatively, in 'Deep Ecology's' biocentrism, each living organism has the same level of value and uniqueness, which makes human beings, as far as worth goes, on a par with animals or a Brazilian rain forest.[2]

In the New Age world, therefore, Man is unique, which is true. But in that world, Man is unique not because he is made in God's image, but because he is God. That is the distortion.

• Union with God. The Bible reveals that man is separated from God because of his sin, and that he is utterly unable to save himself from the consequences of this. Union with God, as the Bible teaches, is more of a reunion. Man is reconciled to God through the Cross of Christ as his moral guilt is removed, and this access to God is through the Cross.

New Age views about man's connection with 'God' are many and varied and difficult to state succinctly. Gnosticism holds that one's union with the Supreme Creator is achieved through escape from this present material world, which is said to be evil, into life in the sphere of pure spirit. Hinduism holds that Brahma(n), the all-pervading 'God', is not separate from the world, so man is never really 'separate' from 'God'. Some adaptation of the gnostic and Hindu views are found throughout New Ageism. In the former, access to God is attained through knowledge (*gnosis*). In the latter, one reaches God through karma (good deeds) and the metaphysics of reincarnation. Either is thought to liberate one from the limiting, confining world of time and physical existence and release one into the invisible world of the eternal and infinite. In these and other nonbiblical views, one is never really separate from God. We have merely forgotten our true state; we are unaware that we are already divine. It is therefore merely a matter of 'going within' in an effort to receive that special intuitive experience which ends all doubt about being part of God.

These and other views dot the New Age map, and what they have in common is that they are all doctrines of self-salvation in various forms. They are all Cross-less forms of salvation. This, of course, is incompatible with the biblical doctrine of salvation, which is the gift of God through the Cross of Christ.

• Suffering and Evil. The Bible teaches that these are in the world because of man's sin and disobedience to his Creator, and because the mystery of iniquity is at work, i.e. Satan and his demonic host's interference in human affairs. In the New Age community, there are several schools of thought on this. Suffering and evil, it is said in one view, are merely perceived as such. If people would change their perception, there would be no suffering and evil. This is the chief motif of *A Course in Miracles*, which is a high-profile book of channelled material in the New Age community. Another view makes suffering and evil a matter of ignorance. If people were enlightened that 'All is (also morally) One' then the problem would be solved. Or, as in gnosticism, matter is seen as evil, with people suffering in contact with it. Or, as in the view of karma, suffering and evil result from everyone's bad karma. In yet another school of thought, that of Zoroastrian dualism, suffering and evil are regarded as the result of the perpetual conflict between two equally powerful and opposite principles or gods, e.g. darkness and light.

• **The Supernatural.** The supernatural world is a frequent topic between Christians and New Agers. The Bible teaches that the supernatural has two distinct realms (not two sides of a coin, as may unwittingly be thought), and that God is the ultimate authority over both. These two realms are two angelic kingdoms; one comprises angels, the other devils. The former obey God and co-operate with Him in fulfilling His purposes, even in human affairs. The latter have disobeyed and rebelled against God and in so doing have become demonic. They have been thrust from God's presence and work against the purposes of God, even within human affairs. We are not taught in the Bible to contact angels, though they may be sent by God to contact us at special times. We are strictly forbidden to develop any kind of relationship with the demonic realm.

The New Age generally sees the nature of the supernatural as one realm comprising innumerable 'spirit guides', 'ascended masters', 'entities', 'forces' and so on, whose natures, with rare exceptions, are not considered evil or demonic. New Age seekers are often encouraged by many means—meditation, visualisation, guided imagery, sensory deprivation tanks, the use of crystals or pyramids, and more—to contact 'spirit guides'.

• **Supernatural Experience.** If a person actually has a supernatural experience, the Bible reveals that it will have originated from one of two sources: God through Jesus Christ, in which I would include the sending of an angel; or the demonic realm. It is important to realise that both sources are *personal* in nature.

Many New Age seekers are eager for supernatural experiences because they are dissatisfied with the prevailing reductionist philosophies so rampant in the West, in which the supernatural world and mystical experience are said to be virtually nonexistent, or the product of delusions. In the New Age world, however, the *source* of the power is mistaken, which in turn affects how the seeker understands the *nature* of the experience. The source of the power, which produces various mystical experiences, is thought to be the *impersonal* life-energy or god-force, and this is the case whether the mystical experience originates from the seeker's lone use of crystals, pyramids, meditiation and so forth, or if it originates through the intermediary of a guru or a 'spirit guide'.

This *mis*understanding has far-reaching ramifications. Since the ultimate source of mystical experience, according to the New Age, is *impersonal*, supernatural experience is off-limits to no one. *Anyone* who is willing to employ the various New Age 'psycho-spiritual technologies' can tap into this supernatural force and receive an experience. The whole thing becomes like a kind of massive metaphysical DIY store, chock-a-block with mystical experiences and available to whomsoever wills.

As the biblical teaching about the power source and the nature of 'spirit guides' is not believed by New Age seekers, and because they do at times have mystical experiences, they must have some explanation for them. The foregoing explanation is convenient because it accounts for the source and the power without having to involve the seeker in moral choices.

• The Ultimate Goal of Life. The Bible teaches that the whole of creation is moving towards a climax, a consummation, a goal, which means that life has a purpose. It is not meaningless but caught up in the purposes of God. The creation then is not, as some have been tempted to think, ultimately subjected to the law of entropy. If it were, then life would be ultimately meaningless. The Bible, however, asserts that the overriding law of the universe is one that includes purpose, aim, goal, and therefore a meaning in terms of the future. Thus nothing in the whole of creation, whether seen or unseen, can escape God's ultimate purposes.

But what are the purposes of God for us, for life and for the universe? The goal is not an ideal or even a state such as the kingdom of heaven, which, though important, is not comprehensible enough to be the ultimate purpose. The Bible identifies the goal of life and creation as God, but even more specifically as a *Person*, Jesus Christ (Rom. 11:36; Col. 1:20; Eph. 1:10). Everything, the individual as well as the whole creation, the seen as well as the unseen, will be 'summed up' in Jesus Christ.

Now because of the present situation with sin and evil, this 'summing up' is seen as a rescue operation in which all things are 'reconciled' in Christ (Col. 1:20). That is to say through reconciliation in Christ everything gets organised and ordered into its proper place at the end; also evil and wickedness and sin and self-will go into their proper non-place, so to speak. This is reconciliation. 'The idea is that there are elements in creation which have become disjointed, alienated, disordered and meaningless in relation to Christ. And in relation to Jesus Christ they are going to be restored to order and meaning and a proper inter-relationship.'[3] Also—and this is amazing to consider—Christians are not merely moving along with the flow of the summing up; they are a part of the 'machinery' at the end which directs the flow, because Christ lives in them.

This is a far cry from any teleology I have seen formulated in the New Age. In fact, as far as I am aware, there is no ultimate purpose envisaged in the New Age way of seeing. Yet this is not surprising because much of New Age spirituality takes its cues from Eastern religion, which does not understand the world in terms of purpose. As someone rightly said, there is 'movement and change without involving the idea of purpose'.[4] It seems then that *ultimate* purpose has no place in the New Age world. What one finds in its place are almost countless expressions of individual purposes. This may shed some light on the popular New Age platitude 'we create our own realities', which provides New Age seekers with a way out of meaninglessness by allowing them to assign at least a personal, individual, relative meaning to movement and change. Being made in the image of God, New Age seekers cannot escape the God-given drive for 'purpose', and so they will have to create purpose for themselves.

This they do in almost countless ways, and

so the goal of New Age seeking becomes: to escape the confines of the material plane; or to move through the metaphysics of reincarnation up the ladder of spiritual evolution; or to process endless cycles of creation, life and destruction; or to become subsumed with all other personalities into the impersonal force of cosmic life-energy; or to live in a state of bliss in *this* life; or to expand consciousness, become enlightened, realise one's godhood status; or to transform self, society and the world. There are probably as many goals as there are New Age seekers, who, like so many others, desire to be the architects of their own futures, creating their realities as they go.

About the only goal which seems similar to that of the Christian's, at least in its language, is that of transforming self, society and the world. But the New Age idea of transformation derives from a spirituality that is incompatible with God's divine purposes, which means that it is not directed towards the purpose or end for which all things exist.

Some readers may wonder how the above survey could help them, since the folk they talk to are merely 'dabbling' in New Age thinking or practices, such as astrology, tarot, the I Ching, meditation, yoga or crystals. Yet these people are dabbling with derivatives, or the fruit, of the above distortions. And most likely, they may never have thought of the false beliefs behind what they are into. If a friend ever says to you, 'What's wrong with such and such?' then you are being given an opportunity to use the information in the above survey, which shows some of the spiritual soil out of which New Age practices grow.

Conclusion

I want to stress that the above survey only scratches the surface of several New Age positions on these matters. There are many, many more aspects to these complex topics.

For example, Eastern views of reincarnation have been greatly modified by the New Age. There is a marked dissimilarity between the depressing Oriental and the flowery Western anticipation towards reincarnation. In the East it is seen as a lamentable fact of life, an overwhelmingly dreary burden to be endured. It is called *samsara:* the eternal cycle of birth, suffering, death, rebirth. In the idiom of the West, *samsara* means 'more hard times'. Yet in the alchemy of Western, especially American, positivism and New Age optimism, the believer's attachment to *samsara* becomes bright and sunny. (Shirley MacLaine nearly gave *Out on a Limb* the title *Many Happy Returns*.) For bored Westerners who continually run out of new toys, *samsara* becomes a sort of cosmic playground, in anticipation not only of more and better lives but of reruns through 'past-life recall'.

So let the Christian communicator be wise. There are areas within the above topics that have not been covered, and these may come up in conversation with a New Age person. Know your limitations. What I have tried to do is to reveal areas that will often come up for discussion with New Age people and to show the principle that these areas are distortions of truth. Nevertheless, we do not need exhaustive knowledge of New Age beliefs in order to become effective communicators. This will become clear as we develop the 'Submarine Communication

Model' in Part Two. I find this a great relief. I do not need to be an expert on the subject. In Part Two we will learn how to use effectively in our conversations the ideas we have discussed here. I would also again direct the reader's attention to the Recommended Reading list.

9

Predicting Problems

Another common communication headache is
the New Age person who thinks that astrologers,
psychics or 'seers' like Nostradamus have the
ability to predict the future. This widespread
deception gets many people involved in the New
Age. There seems to be no stopping the
influence of palm or crystal readers, clairvoyants, mediums and others who claim to offer
their clients a knowledge of the future.
And there is an intellectual/spiritual dynamic at
play here that can frustrate Christian
communication.

Here is a typical illustration of how the
error flourishes and how the dynamic frustrates
communication. Roger and Rose have had a
stormy marriage in which they have raised three
children, who are no longer living at home. The
cement of this marriage has been an earlier
decision by the parents to put off getting a
divorce until the children were grown and
independent. Roger, however, now refuses to
initiate divorce proceedings because he has
discovered that his father-in-law will then cut
him out of a sizeable inheritance. Rose is at her
wits' end because of her husband's marital
infidelity. Yet she is reluctant to initiate divorce
because of her father's intolerance of it. It
would be far easier on her if Roger would simply

leave and make it 'official'. After several more months of misery and bewilderment, Rose decides, 'I may have to take the risk and file for divorce myself, even if Dad misunderstands.' She then rings up a solicitor and goes for an initial consultation, but afterwards still leaves things up in the air.

A few weeks later, Rose attends a 'psychic house party' and her friends needle her into getting a reading. After some small talk with the psychic, Rose consents. The psychic examines Rose's palm and asks, 'Have you raised several children?' (Like Eve, a fact gets Rose's attention.) She raises an eyebrow and confirms this for the psychic, who continues by saying, 'I'm also wondering if you're not bewildered about a very important decision you're trying to make.' When she hears this, Rose thinks of her visit to the solicitor, and with a tentative smile broaches the subject with the psychic. They chat for several minutes and finally Rose sighs, 'I just don't know what to do. I'm so confused. Do you see anything ahead for me?'

'Its not my place to give you advice about your marriage,' the psychic replies, 'or to make decisions for you. But I do see a man in your future. An interesting man. He's tall and attractive and has a full beard. He understands you. I think he's a businessman. Does this sound like your husband?'

'No, it's not Roger,' Rose responds.

But she has 'seen' enough. She rises, thanks the psychic and moves off to talk to her friends about the reading. Afterwards, she cannot shake off the fact that her husband is short, clean-shaven and works as a car mechanic. She is a little confused but also a little interested.

A week later a friend named Ann is talking to someone at the school where they both work. 'I have a friend named Rose,' Ann says, 'and we went to a psychic house party last week. A psychic told Rose that she had three children and that she was going to get a divorce. Well, Rose does have three children and she told me she was thinking seriously about getting a divorce. How did the psychic know that?'

Time passes. Two years later a divorced Rose is having lunch with Ann and mentions that she wants to consult a psychic.

'Whatever for?' Ann asks.

'Remember that psychic reading I had a couple of years ago?'

'Yes.'

'Well, that psychic told me that I had three children, that I would get a divorce and that I'd be loved by an understanding man. She said he would be a tall business man with a beard.'

'I remember now. I even told Martha about it. So why the sudden interest in seeing a psychic again?'

'Now that I'm divorced, I'm wondering what's ahead. I mean, how do I meet this man, anyway?'

Do you see what has occurred? Rose and Ann have put words into the psychic's mouth. The psychic had actually said (and in the form of a question, which leaves a non-embarrassing way out if wrong), 'Have you raised *several* children?'. Yet when Rose tells it it has become *three* children. The psychic had also said, 'I'm wondering if you're not bewildered about a very important decision.' Yet when Rose tells her friends about this part of the reading, it is, 'The psychic told me I would be getting a divorce.' The psychic had also said, 'I see a man in your future . . . ', but when Rose tells it, it is, 'The psychic told me I would be loved by . . . '

It is essential for the effective communicator to see what is going on here and help people like Rose to recognise it. What the psychic actually said was either ignored or forgotten. Rose has taken specific incidents from her life and tucked them into the psychic reading as if they were the psychic's actual words. The original statements were ambiguous, equivocal and merely suggestive, yet they became *specific* events in Rose's mind by association, which becomes the story she tells. This sleight-of-mind occurs frequently to the undiscerning, who then think that future events have been foretold.

Without thinking—this is the problem—the average person is not aware that an astrologer, psychic, palm reader or even a Nostradamus merely makes clever use of ambiguous language. Expensive, glossy, full-colour books are printed about Nostradamus' 'prophetic' quatrains in an effort to reveal how he predicted twentieth-century events in the sixteenth century from a bowl of water! Yet his 'predictions' are ambiguous and can, and have been made to, mean almost anything. Whether it is a Nostradamus or a local psychic, people have a penchant for placing words and events into the mouths of 'seers' and then telling friends that something specific was known or foretold.

The most frequent way in which people get tripped up like this is through the vague and ambiguous advice of newspaper or magazine horoscope columns. Let us say that Gillian is sipping her morning coffee and reading in the paper under her sign Aries: 'Expect domestic troubles this week'. Two days later, Armageddon erupts: with her teenager, Ian, who storms out of the house, drives off with the family car and is not heard from for two days. While playing bridge the next month with friends, Gillian complains, 'A few weeks ago, Ian and I had a terrible row. I don't know what I am going to do with him. He drove off in my car and was gone two days, It gave me and Colin a horrible fright. But what's really amazing is that my horoscope that week predicted the whole thing!'

Again, words were put into the horoscope's 'mouth'. Like psychics, horoscope columns employ ambiguous language which may be interpreted in many specific ways, and then astrology is credited with the power to predict the future. What is 'really amazing' is that people are so gullible. Unfortunately, in this way astrology has gained a reputation for 'accuracy' over the years that in itself is quite amazing. And the extremes people will go to to bolster its reputation for accuracy can get comical. I am reminded of one of Don Quixote's humorous incidents. This famous knight errant had his share of hallucinations, to say the least, but on occasion his discernment was striking. Take for instance the time he was educating the ever-faithful Sancho about the illogical conclusions people draw from astrological forecasts.

'I know of a lady,' Don Quixote tells Sancho, 'who asked one of these horoscope-casters whether a little lap-dog bitch she had would fall with pup and bear, and how many pups she would have and of what colour. To which Master Astrologer replied, after he had cast the figure, that the bitch would fall and bear three puppies, one green, one scarlet and one speckled . . . And what happened was that two days later the bitch died of overeating, and Master Astrologer gained a reputation in the town of being a very accurate caster of a horoscope, a reputation which they mostly have.'[1]

The wise communicator will want to help the person to see the ambiguity of a psychic prediction and how specific events are later made to refer to it as if that was what was originally said. This way of ascribing specificity to ambiguity is rife within the New Age world, and it is often used as 'proof' that astrology, numerology, crystal readings, psychics and so on have future-telling power. For people who are unwilling to trust in God and His grace day after day no matter what happens, this can be an appealing aspect of the New Age. It gives them the hope of being able to know about tomorrow. The future, however, comes only one day at a time.

There may also be another dynamic at work in psychic readings. I have in mind here what is called 'cold reading', which also gives New Age practices a semblance of a power far beyond that of mortal man. I am not going to go into great detail about this. An excellent job has been done on this in Dan Korem's book *Powers: Testing the Psychic and the Supernatural* (IVP, 1988). What I will do here is mention how some principles of 'cold reading' could have been employed by Rose's psychic.

In *Powers*, Korem lists six principles of cold reading: one, the Barnum effect; two, identifying the psychological profile of the client; three, observing physical features and micro-expressions; four, accessing specific information; five, loading the language; six, the educated guess. The first is about general comments that can relate to whoever is sitting for a reading. It is a kind of 'stock sketch' of personality which is sufficiently ambiguous so that the client could easily apply his specific characteristics to it. The second is about 'partially pinpointing [the client's] personality type', e.g. choleric, sanguine, phlegmatic, melancholic, introvert or extrovert. If the psychic reader is familiar with the characteristics of each 'type' and has seen a few hundred clients he will probably be able to identify a client's personality type quickly. And if he also knows the person's occupation, the psychic would not find it difficult, for example, to 'predict' the client's likes and dislikes. Using the third principle of cold reading, the psychic looks 'for clues that can be detected primarily by three senses: touch, sight and hearing'. The look of the skin, or something said by a client which he does not recall later, or feeling the resistance or yieldedness of the client's hand when touched, or the sight of clothes, body posture and so forth all help to assist the psychic with his readings.

The fourth principle actually includes eavesdropping or doing research on a client ahead of time. The fifth 'refers to statements that can be interpreted in more than one way'. Korem says that when this technique is combined with the others, it can give the appearance of infallibility. The sixth principle is

the educated guess and is based upon knowing
percentages, for example, of the most common
jobs held by different personality types, or the
most common forms of recreation, and so on.

The psychic who did Rose's reading could
have used many of these principles. For
example, at the psychic house party before the
readings began, everyone present could have
been mingling and chatting about this and that,
including the psychic, who could have heard
Rose mention her children. Later during the
reading, the psychic may then have identified
Rose as a phlegmatic temperament (often prone
to indecision) and noticed that she was very
unhappy or uneasy. The psychic would have
known that the divorce rate is high today and so
decided to risk an educated guess in that
direction, but without mentioning the subject
directly, which would leave the psychic a way
out, such as to move the conversation into
another area, if Rose did not take the bait.

The principles of cold reading are used,
whether consciously or not, by astrologers,
psychics and other 'seers'. When I used to give
horoscope readings to people, I found myself
using them without having been taught them. I
picked them up through common sense. There
is always a bit of small talk going on between a
psychic and a client before a reading. I used to
listen for people to mention areas of interest that
they had, or how their jobs were going, or what
special problems they faced. I frequently did the
readings in their homes, where I would pick up
further clues. Many of the readings I did were
for hippies, rock musicians and their wives and
1960s counterculture people in general. I was
one myself and so knew the ins-and-outs of it.

This meant that I could drop a whole category of information from the readings which I did for such folk and never needed to worry about getting it 'wrong' therein. I never needed to mention the things that concerned a 'normal' lifestyle (except perhaps in a negative light!) because most of my clients were not living it. In keeping my readings confined to the categories of a countercultural lifestyle, and by including any titbits I had overheard, I could usually keep the interest of such folk, some of whom returned for more readings.

So it is not only specificity substituted for ambiguity but also cold readings that give certain New Age practices and their spokespersons a semblance of having the power to predict the future. We can use this information in our discussions.

I am often stopped at this point by Christians who ask, 'Are you really saying that psychics can't see into the future? What about the devil? Can he see into the future?' The answer to the first question is yes, and to the second, no. As I understand biblical theology, the devil cannot see specifically into the future. He is not omniscient, like God. He cannot know a person's free moral choices before they have been made. He cannot know if God may intervene in a certain situation. He cannot know the 'time and chance' which happens to us all (Eccl. 9:11).

The analogy of a chess match between two chess masters has helped me to understand the only manner in which I believe it is possible for the spirit world to have even a slim knowledge of the future, and that *only* of the immediate future. After each chess master has made several opening moves, he is expert enough to know what probabilities exist for his opponent's up-coming moves for the next few plays. There are only so many subsequent combinations of moves, and each chess master will know what those are, following, as they do, as consequences of the prior moves. Because each chess master will know what these are, he will, shall we say, have specific insight into the future. This anticipation of probabilities seems to me to be the only way a psychic or the spirit world can see into the future, very short-sightedly at that. And it still boils down to making an educated guess, for even the chess master cannot know with certainty which one of the chess men his opponent will move next.

This principle applies either to a cold reading or to a psychic who is actually receiving information from the spirit world, which could have been the case with Rose's psychic reading. The Bible is clear that evil spirits exist, that they are knowledgeable, and that they are able to communicate what they know to people who have the means of getting in touch with them. From what I understand, both from the Bible and from my experiences as a former astrologist, the psychic acts as a kind of satellite dish, receiving information from the spirit world to send to a client. If the 'familiar spirit' is privy to some facts about the client, as was the serpent with Eve, it could feed this information to its spokesperson, who in turn would reveal it to his client.[2]

With Rose, the psychic could have been receiving impressions from a spirit about 'children' and 'divorce'. The former has nothing to do with a prediction; it is merely a fact used to get Rose's attention. The children already exist. The latter, at the time of the psychic reading, was not yet a fact but an educated guess based upon a fact: that Rose had gone to see a solicitor about divorce. It is history, and the spirit could have known it. The probability, then, was there for a move towards divorce. The psychic could have had this 'impression' and hedged it within the ambiguous statement about Rose's bewilderment concerning an important decision.

I want to stress that this ability to perceive probabilities and make educated guesses about them is the only way I can see either a human being or a spirit having the 'power' to tell the future. In either case the seeing into the future boils down to a guess, however educated. In no way could it be called a prediction, even if the thing came to pass; for that only meant that the spokesperson guessed right. Neither the psychic nor the spirit are omniscient. It could even have occurred that, sometime after the psychic reading, Roger and Rose became Christians and God healed their marriage. So we also have the sovereignty of God to consider.

Biblical prophecy is of an entirely different nature, resultant as it is from an omniscient God, the One with the power to accomplish what He says He will. Biblical prophecy, therefore, is about predicting events of which there are *no* apparent probabilities, the occurrences of which depend upon innumerable contingencies involving the history of things and the volitions of persons who may not even exist yet. Other characteristics of Biblical prophecy are that it announces suitably ahead of time the event it foretells; it has a particular and exact agreement with that event when it comes to pass; no human wisdom or foresight could produce it; it has a moral element to it (this is always missing from New Age 'prophecies'); and it is delivered by someone under the inspiration of God Almighty.

Clients of astrologers and psychics, however, as well as the general public, are often oblivious to all of this, and the Christian communicator will want to rectify this.

10

Darkness as Light

We have been addressing a number of questions about irrationality, passivity, deception, distortions of truth and other intellectual/spiritual dynamics that can foil an effective Christian witness to New Age enthusiasts. These are people just like you and me, and they have not become enmeshed in these dynamics by taking some premeditated giant step. Quite the contrary. The progression is much more like the slow, almost imperceptible swelling of the pregnant womb. As Jeremiah says in chapter 17, verse 9: 'The heart is deceitful above all things and beyond cure. Who can understand it?' That is to say, who can see what is happening? Deception is like that.

This should give us some compassion for New Age people. Indeed, I think that if we Christians examine our own non-Christian pasts we will see that we did not set out intentionally to go astray. I know that I did not. It was a gradual process, and it had its genesis in my determination to search for Truth and the meaning of Life. Now this holds true for most New Age seekers; they begin with a good enough motive, but having little or no interest in a biblical way of seeing they then move into the wrong paths when looking for spiritual answers.

I used to think that some of the

conversations I have had with New Age seekers
were just so much silly hair splitting, but now I
see the sense of them. It has occurred to me
that error begins like two persons diverging
along slowly widening lines from the point of a
very acute angle. Each person began at the
same point with the same motive, but a different
way of seeing life informed each person's search.
Person A began his walk along the line of truth;
person B began his walk on the line of error.
And because it is a very acute angle, there may
be a span of time in which both persons appear
to be in agreement, as if they were walking
side-by-side on the same path. It is not until
the lines of the angle are extended far enough
that the incompatibility of each person's walk
with the other becomes obvious. The disparity
existed with the first steps but may have gone
unnoticed until some distance down the road
precisely because there was no 'silly hair
splitting' at the start.

This brings us to another intellectual/
spiritual dynamic that can frustrate
communication, and I would like to illustrate it
from a statement by Jesus Himself. It is a
rather puzzling statement for those of us who
live twenty centuries this side of Calvary; the
Master's meaning being obscured through the
veil of ages. It is found in Matthew 6:23, where,
almost as an aside, Jesus declares, 'If the light
within you is darkness, how great is that darkness!'

Now this is not a question; it's an exclam-
ation, a cry filled with emotion. Today He might
have exclaimed, 'Don't be surprised that people
who walk in darkness write books called
Dancing in the Light!' What's Jesus talking

about here? How can people be walking the path of New Age occultism and think that it is the 'light'?

We can ferret out the Master's meaning from a nightly phenomenon with which we are all familiar. That is, if you are like me when it is time to go to sleep at night! You change your clothes for bed, slip in under the duvet, perhaps read for a while, and then you switch off the bedside lamp and close your eyes. The room has been plunged into darkness and you fall asleep. But what would it be like in the room if you were to keep your eyes open immediately after switching off the light? Would you be able to see anything? Not likely. (I'm assuming there's not a street-light outside your window!) But if you were to keep your eyes open for several minutes, what would happen? Of course, we have all experienced this; it gets a bit lighter in the room and you can 'see', not clearly, but enough to detect the shadowy appearances of furnishings, picture frames and so on. It's dim, but if you had to dash suddenly from bed to answer the telephone in another room, as you sprang from the bedroom you could now avoid smacking your shin on the lower dresser drawer that accidentally got left open. Try hurrying from the room immediately after switching off the light and you might not be so fortunate!

This illustration may help us grasp the Master's meaning in Matthew 6:23. And I ask the reader to forgive me for a little literary playfulness here. To highlight the subtlety of the process, I led you slightly up the garden path in the previous paragraph to enable you to appreciate the ease with which New Age people get tripped up. Take a moment to reread the previous paragraph to discover where I 'deceived' you. Some readers may have noticed it already. Look at the wording carefully. I'll wait here for you . . .

So, what mischief did I make? It is in the phrase 'It gets a bit lighter in the room.' Of course, it does not get any lighter in the room; it merely *appears* to get lighter. What would actually happen, of course, is that your eyes would become accustomed to the darkness, which slowly begins to look like light. Those who 'walk around in the darkness' (1 John 2:11), have had the 'eyes of [their] understanding' (Eph. 1:18, AV) acclimatised to a shadowy world that gets mistaken for light. This is a strong delusion. So much so that Jesus cries, 'Look how great it is!', which may be an echo of Isaiah 5:20, where the prophet speaks of the misfortune upon 'those who put darkness for light'.

Let's extend the analogy further. I suppose everyone, at one time or another, has been startled awake from a nightmare and opened their eyes in the darkness only to receive a good fright from what they thought was in the room with them. They saw an indistinct shape and perhaps mistook it for an intruder. Later it became something to laugh about. 'How silly we were,' they tell friends, 'to think that the coat extending from a hanger over the wardrobe door had broken into the house!' Sadly, this state of affairs exists within much of New Ageism, but with this significant difference: *it never becomes clear what the object really is*. If people are not in a covenant relationship with the Light of the World, the light of day never comes to them, and they walk around in a shadowy world in

which they know that *something* is there, but
just what it is is never clear. The real truth
about it is unknown.

And as it cannot be denied that they are
seeing something, explanations are offered.
Thus, God becomes an impersonal energy; man
becomes God; death becomes a door to many
future lives; evil spirits are mistaken for 'spirit
guides'; sin becomes bad karma or merely one's
perception of evil, and so on. It is only in Christ
that the truth of these matters is clarified in the
light of day.

For those who walk in darkness, the things
of creation, and God Himself, are seen 'out of
character'. Darkness shrouds a proper
understanding, evaluation and interpretation of
what is seen or discerned; the coat always
seems to be an intruder. This condition, though
it does not develop overnight, may not go
completely unnoticed by the person. When I
was becoming a New Age adherent and was
taught, for instance, that reincarnation followed
death, or that the 'spirit guides' were not
demonic, I recall being slightly startled.
Something about those explanations seemed
suspect, at least initially. I do not think that I
could have articulated why that was, but it
certainly was how I felt early on. Some sort of
'early warning system' within me sounded when
I opened my eyes in the darkness.

This did not disturb me for long, however,
because my continued fellowship with New Age
teaching rationalised the disquiet, and the eyes
of my understanding acclimatised to the darkness. The longer I trafficked in the shadowy
world, the more accepting and established I
became in its way of seeing. Eventually, a fully

justified rationale existed in my mind that the coat was an intruder, and there were few doubts that I was wrong. The New Age rationale led me on like this until several years had passed and I became a Christian.

Changing the Nouns of the Game

I believe that this principle of 'darkness as light' accounts for the New Age penchant for renaming and redefining many of the 'things' of life and reality. This is an important area; one in which we shall need to work hard within our conversations with New Age thinkers as they become more and more outspoken about it.

'Use the language of diplomacy,' Anne Carson advises in her book *Spiritual Parenting in the New Age*. She goes on:

> Say *prayer*, not *magic* or *spell* . . . Say *ceremony*, not *ritual*. This way, I can tell my aunt that we had a blessing ceremony for our infant daughter under the auspices of a Dutch Reformed minister, leaving out the invocation to the four elements, the sprinkling of corn meal and the bestowing of a spirit name.

Most of all, Carson urges, fudge on the word *pagan*. 'Using the word *pagan* tends to make people think that you are a) an atheist, b) a flake, c) joking.'[1]

This is what I call 'changing the nouns of the game'. It is a deception that often strips occultic or mystical connotations from the New Age world by substituting the old offensive terms

with new nonreligious, psychological or
scientific-sounding ones. 'Therapeutic Touch' is
a case in point. This popular health care
technique has been popularised by Dolores
Krieger, R.N., Ph.D., who teaches it chiefly to
nurses throughout the United States. Upon
researching it, I discovered that Therapeutic
Touch is virtually the same thing, almost step
by step, as what I learned as 'psychic healing' in
the early 1970s.

Other examples of changing the nouns of
the game are numerous. 'Centring', 'grounding'
and 'stilling' are a few of the new names for
Eastern meditation. 'Astrograph' is slowly
becoming a euphemism for astrology, and
'channeller' is already locked in place for the old
'spirit medium'.

This only scratches the surface of the
semantic distortions spreading throughout the
New Age. They present a whole range of
problems for the Christian communicator which
we will look at in Part Two. What needs saying
here is that changing the nouns of the game in
no way changes the nature of the game. No less
a pillar of New Age psychological thought than
Carl Jung was unequivocal on this point.

Jung (1875–1961), a complex man, became
disillusioned with Christianity at an early age
and went deeply into occultism several times.
He also became an authority on alchemy,
gnosticism and religious myth. But his *pièce de
résistance* is his 'Analytic[al] Psychology', which
is the name he gave to his life's work as a
psychologist and psychiatrist, to distinguish it
from Freud's 'Psychoanalysis' and Adler's
'Individual Psychology'. Through this
psychology Jung made some contributions that

may merit further study in a biblical context, for example his theories of personality types and his elaboration of the universality of symbols. He also brought needed adjustments to what at the time was the highly rationalistic and reductionist field of psychology. He placed much more emphasis on human responsibility and choice. He warned against the dangers of arid dogmatism. He saw religion positively—as a necessity, in fact—and bore witness to the supernatural realm. Yet in this latter area Jung did much mischief.

To develop many of the concepts and categories of thought for Analytical Psychology, Jung changed the nouns of religion, spiritualism and occultism into those of psychology. He gave as his reason for this that as a psychologist he needed to use the terms of his own discipline and not borrow those of the theologian. We can understand this, but nevertheless it has obscured the demonic nature of some of Jung's 'unconscious contents'. For example, one of the terms Jung popularised was 'archetype', the nature of which is difficult to pin down in Jung's voluminous writings. In short, archetypes are about the universality of symbols of the human race *and* the 'unconscious dynamisms' or 'activating points' behind the symbols and images. Of these unconscious dynamisms, Jung wrote that they had a life of their own, purpose, and that they could be composers of dreams. In his autobiography, Jung discloses the name of four 'archetypes' which appeared and spoke to him during seasons of deep occult experimentation.[2] He also writes about the days in which his 'whole house [was] filled as if there was a crowd present, crammed full of spirits.

They were packed right up to the door, and the air was so thick it was scarcely possible to breathe.'[3] Jung took copious notes whenever any spirits were in contact with him. And he frequently called these spirits 'the dead' or 'unconscious contents', and his contact with them his 'fantasies'.

Late in life, Jung had this to say about such times:

> [T]hese conversations with the dead formed a kind prelude to what I had to communicate to the world about the unconscious.[4]
> Today I can say that I never lost touch with my initial experiences. All my works, all my creative activity, have come from those initial fantasies and dreams which began in 1912 . . . Everything I accomplished later in life was already contained in them . . . [5]
> It has taken me nearly forty-five years to distil within the vessel of my scientific work the things that I experienced and wrote down at that time.[6]

Though he used a psychological vocabulary for speaking about demons, Jung felt that people were stupidly gullible if they thought that changing the nouns of the game in any way changed the nature of the game.

> I did all in my power to convey to my intimates a new way of seeing.[7]
> [If] by employing the concept of archetype, we attempt to define more closely the point at which the daimon

grips us, we have not abolished anything.[8]
The concept of them as demonia is
therefore quite in accord with their nature.
If anyone is inclined to believe that any
aspect of the *nature* [his emphasis] of
things is changed by such formulations,
he is being extremely credulous about
words. The real facts do not change,
whatever names we give them . . . [T]he
change of a name has removed nothing at
all from reality.[9]

But the real mischief is that Jung did not
believe that the nature of the demonia were
demonic and evil in the biblical sense. Jung
could not deny that he was seeing and
encountering something, but since he had
rejected Christianity he was walking in darkness
as to the right explanation for what he was
experiencing. He thought that the demonia had
a kind of neutrality or dualistic nature, and this
led Jung to conclude that they could be either
the gravest danger *or* the most redeeming power.

This is a fatal attraction for many New Age
enthusiasts today, who see Jung's archetypes in
terms of helpful 'spirit guides'.[10] This is only one
of the disastrous ramifications of seeing the coat
as an intruder. As Christian communicators,
we will want to help these spiritual seekers come
to some understandings about their spiritual
eyesight. This may take some work on our part,
but with God's help, as we endeavour to become
wise as serpents in understanding the problems
of communication, we can get through to New
Age people. We can offer them the truth, and
then it is up to them. God has placed within
every person, perhaps as a feature of His image,

a capacity for recognising the truth. This is a part of what it means to be human; were it not so, how could we ever recognise the truth of Christ—or any truth, for that matter—and accept Him? Even those who walk in gross darkness can therefore recognise the truth. Whether or not they accept it is another story. The task, then, of the Christian communicator is to express the truth about God and Life in a way that makes sense to New Age people. We are called to untangle the lie from the truth and to make the crooked ways straight.

Summary

To help readers sustain their knowledge of the intellectual/spiritual dynamics that frustrate Christian communication in the New Age world, here is a list of those characteristics in brief, summarised from Chapters 4 to 10.

- The principle of inversion. Things are the wrong way round, as Alice saw in Looking-glass House, or as the Richardsons discovered with the Sawi men who saw Judas Iscariot as the hero of the gospel story.
- The closed mind. Here is the person like the Waverley Market numerologist, who was absolutely 'not interested'.
- The irrational. This dynamic has little or no tolerance for reason or for the rational. It conditions the spiritual seeker to feel comfortable about holding to contradictory beliefs and values. It gives a context in which to receive intuitive mystical experiences.
- Passivity. This widespread dynamic is

found in New Age meditators. It trains them temporarily to suspend conscious thought while in a waking state, which in turn opens them up to the spirit world.

• Deception. This is the deliberate misrepresentation of facts or truth in order to purposely lead someone astray. (Also see: distortions of truth, Chapter Eight.)

• Assigning too much power to the spirit world. Here people think that psychics, mediums, channellers, astrologers and so forth have power to predict the future.

• Darkness as light. The non-Christian spiritual seeker lives amidst a shadowy world that is mistaken for light. In this world, the person knows that 'something' is there, but the real truth of the thing is unknown to him or her.

• Changing the nouns of the game. This involves renaming and redefining reality according to a New Age way of seeing.

As far as I know, these areas encapsulate most of the communication problems Christians will encounter in the New Age world. After the Inter-Mission (it's not really a rest break!), we will discover how to reckon with them.

Inter-Mission

11

Models or Muddles?

Two Christians were arguing and the subject was a hot one. Jenny was saying that we must not overreact to the New Age phenomenon. To this Tim responded, saying, 'Yes, but . . . ', and the exaggerations which then shot from his mouth clearly betrayed overreaction. Jenny then tried a different tack. She said to Tim that we had to be careful not to throw out the baby with the bathwater. Here the *tête-à-tête* heated up because Tim, evidently, saw nothing of value about the New Age. Jenny then said that Tim might change his mind about this if he had a heart-to-heart talk with some New Age seekers. But when Jenny suggested that she and Tim have lunch with a couple of New Age adherents she knew, Tim was turned off by the idea.

Later, Tim had great doubts about Jenny. 'Maybe she's not even a Christian,' he thought. 'Maybe she's a New Ager.' As he was feeling suspicious of Jenny, she was praying, 'Lord, forgive me for upsetting Tim. Help both of us to see the situation more clearly, so that we may reach New Age people with the gospel.'

This rupture between Christians occurs more often than you may think. The discomposure and variance that this rift has produced is evident in most of the audiences I meet. It happens chiefly because we do not really

understand one another's positions, although
we think we do. Ask yourself, could you express
'Jenny's' position to her in a manner that would
convince her that you really understand it? If
not, what right do you have to think that her
perspective ought to bow to yours? This pride
holds us at arm's length from brothers and
sisters in Christ, and we find ourselves unwilling or hesitant to learn from them. If Christians
themselves cannot have dialogue with one
another about the New Age, how will we be able
to hold effective conversations with New Age
seekers?

Both Tim and Jenny are Christians, so the
real problem lies elsewhere. It is found, as
Jenny prayed, in the crucial area of 'seeing'.
Tim and Jenny 'see' the situation somewhat
differently. It is *not* that one sees it biblically
and the other nonbiblically. Rather, each has
different *biblical* 'categories of thought' for
analysing, evaluating, interpreting and
understanding the New Age. The way Tim sees
it, he fears that Jenny's view is a compromise
that will open floodgates of deception and
demonic activity into the Church. Yet if Tim had
not got so uptight, he could have discussed this
with Jenny and discovered her firm stand
against occultism. He would also have had his
mind set at rest when he learned from Jenny
that she was uncompromising in essential
biblical beliefs. When he had settled such
questions, Tim would have been in a position to
learn from Jenny. She had been hoping to
communicate to Tim a biblical perspective that
she finds helpful.

This is not to say that Jenny's view is
flawless, or that she can say to a member of

Christ's body, 'I have no need of you.' We all approach this topic as disciples, i.e. as learners. Unfortunately, experience teaches that the 'Tims' of Christendom usually refuse to learn much from the 'Jennys', while the latter tend to underestimate and even disregard the former. But there is a more serious consequence. Experience has indicated to me that the 'Tims' outnumber the 'Jennys' in the work of trying to reach New Age people with Christ's gospel. This may mean that the majority of workers in the New Age world have a manner of communicating which is not as conducive to that end as it could be.

It is not that Tim does not try. He does, and he does his best. Yet he finds New Age people argumentative or dismissive of him. It would probably surprise Tim to learn that New Age seekers see him as uncompassionate, prejudiced, shallow, hypercritical, even boring or threatening. In a word, irrelevant. I realise that we may not like the case put so plainly, but how are we ever going to be able to break down the stone walls which separate New Age people from the gospel if we do not first know what they may be thinking of *us*, the messengers of the gospel? Worse still, in many cases there is justification for the ways in which New Age people describe us. Talk about a communication barrier! Tim may never have seen himself in this light. When New Age people brush him off, he may think they are rejecting Jesus and that he is suffering for the gospel. In a sense this is true. But it is probably more to the point that they are rejecting the messenger and that he is suffering because of his own mistakes. Tim may not be the best 'epistle' to be read by people that he

could be. Feeling discouraged, he may now
pass up opportunities to be around New Age
people, and the Lord has one less minister to the
New Age world.

Much of the problem, here, centres around
how we 'see' the New Age phenomenon. How we
see it not only affects our evaluation of it; it also
greatly influences how we communicate with its
adherents. Of course, how we see the New Age
is largely the product of how we were taught to
see it. One difficulty here is that we may have
accepted *carte blanche* some untenable and
specious arguments, opinions and conclusions.
That is to say much of 'what we think we know'
about the New Age has not emerged from what
we ourselves have researched, investigated,
thought and prayed through. Rather, we have
taken for granted the arguments, opinions and
conclusions of the one or two Christian books
we may have read on the subject, or what our
friends have told us about the New Age. Many
of us may have given very little personal
thought, if any, to what is actually being taught
in Christian books on the New Age.

Another difficulty is *how* it is being said.
An unhelpful spirit or tone may have rubbed off
on us as we read certain books. Frankly,
speaking as a former 'insider', I have to say that
several widely read Christian books on the New
Age are so wide of the mark that New Age
people would not recognise themselves in the
pages. You could never give a book like that to
most New Age seekers. There is also an arrogant
tone to some of these books, suggesting that 'If
you don't agree with my evaluation down to the
last jot and tittle then you, too, are part of the
problem, Christian or not.' I have seen this

contribute to an attitude in Christians that builds a barrier between brothers and sisters in Christ who see the New Age differently. Maybe the authors are not aware of this. But brothers and sisters, we cannot afford to be closed to each other. We need to learn from each other.

The shrill tone, the emotional hyper-ventilating and the mischievous use of selected facts leave us a long way from being equipped to reach the New Age *person*. Then there is the sensationalism which surrounds some books. This often produces in many readers an *un*healthy fear of the New Age and its people. All this results in Christians being generally alienated from the very people they should have been equipped to help.[1]

We may, then, need to make some significant adjustments in the way we 'see' the New Age. It will require humility about what we think we know of it and its people. Somehow we have got to overcome any personal arrogance we may have and repent of it. This should result in a big stride towards mutual understanding and co-operation among us as Christians and enhance our communication with New Agers.

I once heard someone say, 'Humility of mind produces a teachable spirit.' I like that. In his book *The Practice of Godliness* (Navpress 1983), Navigator Jerry Bridges clearly puts the case for developing humility of mind in the context of modifying our views:

> We evangelicals are not noted for our humility about our doctrines—our beliefs about what the Bible teaches in various areas of theology. Whatever position we take . . . we tend to feel our position is

airtight, and that anyone holding a different view is altogether wrong. We tend to be quite impatient with anyone who differs from us . . . It is one thing to be persuaded that what we believe is correct as we understand the Scriptures; it is quite another to believe that our views are *always* [his emphasis] correct. Twice in my life I have had to make significant changes in my doctrines as a result of additional understanding of the Scriptures . . . We must remind ourselves that God has not made our minds, or even a particular church, the depository of the sum total of his teachings (pp. 93–4).

Although Bridges is writing to a different audience and in a different context, may we not say 'Amen' to this? I think this will require, at the least, setting aside attitudes like that of one high-profile Christian who, in a letter I have on file, accuses a respectable Christian book on the New Age as being 'atrocious', 'abominable' and 'monstrous' and demands its withdrawal from bookshops. I do not say that everything in the book in question, or in this book either, is the gospel truth. Only one Book is that. But if this brother really has a leg to stand on, I wonder if the best the way to use it is to kick the authors of the book in question in the groin. It is one thing to see an issue differently; it is quite another thing to see it differently in humility of mind.

If we want to have a united witness to reach New Age people with the gospel, we shall have to start going the extra mile, or two, with our brothers and sisters in Christ who may 'see' it

differently from the way we do. And it will have
to be done in love, truth and sincerity. I have
had to make significant adjustments since
becoming a Christian in how I see the New Age,
yet still I do not think that I have the best appre-
hension of it that it is possible to have. I see
through a glass darkly.

It is never easy for me when going through
significant changes of perspective. It grates
against what I think I know. It means my
thinking has been found wanting in certain
areas. Changing is difficult because the found-
ations, structures and ideas of what we believe
to be true are not so easily reorganised. One
reason for this is that they usually sit
comfortably within the views represented by our
group, congregation, denomination and so on.
And as someone has said, if we suspect that by
changing our perspective we may run afoul of
the opinions of our group, we may be unwilling
to do so.

There is a real blessedness, however, in
running the risk (humbly!) because it opens one
to new biblical horizons and fresh possibilities.
There are, then, other biblical perspectives
besides ours, other Christian ways of seeing
something. We may want to make some
adjustments. We owe it to each other, to New
Age people and to our Lord to really listen to the
reasons other Christians have for holding to
their various views. We may discover that their
perspectives are more biblical than we thought.
Humility of mind will keep us teachable and it
will grace us with a godly pliability. Being
intractable may be the fruit of a stubbornness
whose root is idolatry (1 Sam. 15:23).

It really is silly how uptight and defensive

we can get about this, considering that adjustments of perspectives have been taking place in us since childhood. Children may for a season think that babies are bought at hospital, or that gifts arrive on December 25 from Father Christmas. Someday, however, these views change with the discovery and acceptance of a 'better' way of seeing. And we would think a teenager quite odd who held to childish views that had run their course.

Please note: in saying that we may have an occasion to change a perspective I am not suggesting that we compromise sound doctrine or the gospel, or that we relinquish orthodoxy. I merely wish to encourage us to be willing to reorganise our perspectives if there are good and sufficient reasons to believe that our thinking has been found wanting. I have a love/hate relationship with myself whenever some facts or truths present themselves to my way of seeing and so require a change in perspective. A friend of mine once had a professor tell him, 'Jeff, if the facts don't fit your theology, change your theology.' However, I dislike doing this because it shows up some inadequacy in my thinking, often in an area where I thought my understanding was sufficient. On the other hand I like changing because I realise I have therein been blessed to know more of the mind of the Master, and yet again comes the force of 1 Corinthians 8:2: 'The man who thinks he knows something does not yet know as he ought to know.'

What really ruffles me, though, are not so much the times when a Christian's influence modifies my view, but when it happens as a result of talking to a New Age person. It is difficult eating humble pie then, I can tell you!

Yet if we have a fundamental respect for the truth, we will relinquish our pride and change. Will we not receive correction from whatever source it comes? It strikes me as amusing, the sudden and unlooked-for change of perspective Balaam must have gone through after hearing the truth of the matter from a donkey! (See Num. 22:21–33.) So, if we come across a New Age person who complains about the fragmentation of society and longs for community, or who speaks out for a health-care system which would include the spiritual dimension of man, or who assesses the dangers of long-term environmental abuse, or who takes issue with the Western Church for being rationalistic, how can we turn a deaf ear? It is all true.

When the New Age person is right we will want to agree. We need this humility of mind before God and our fellow man in order to become effective communicators. As Christians, we are in a covenant relationship with, and a respecter of, the Truth Himself. Therefore we ought to be glad and rejoice whenever *anyone* points out that which is true. We can agree with it. This does not mean that we may be able to agree with the person's *full* evaluation, analysis, interpretation or solution suggested for each matter. He may, for example, define 'community', 'holistic health care', 'the supernatural' and so on differently from the way the Bible does. This is an entirely different matter. So we may have to say, 'Yes, you are right about such and such, but your definition is amiss, therefore your response is inadequate.'

How, then, should we 'see' the New Age phenomenon? Actually, there are several ways of seeing it, with some being more helpful than others. A person's 'model' for understanding a highly complex social and religious phenomenon, like New Ageism, cannot be taken lightly and it will greatly influence at least three areas:

- how we use or misuse the Bible to interpret the New Age
- how we deal with it or ignore it in our own lives
- how we speak to others about it (or see no need to)

I want us to look at the third point here.

The Christian's model for understanding the New Age may be a bridge or a barrier to the communication process. Some models easily short-circuit effective communication. Take the 'fad' model. To someone who has invested years of time, study, effort and money into New Age spirituality, it is certainly not a 'fad'. The Christian who labels it as such has no communication bridge into the New Age world.

Another example of a communication barrier is the 'demon-monger' model. It lumps the whole New Age world and all of its people together as promoters of occultism. If this is a Christian's model, how can there be conversation with those New Age people who have no interest in occultism? Talking about demons may indeed make such people frightened—of us!

The view that the New Age world is thoroughly occultic is far from exact. Clearly, occultism runs throughout the New Age landscape, and I am not 'soft' about this problem. I have understood and experienced occult deception and demonic bondage at first hand. Nevertheless, the occult is but one realm of the New Age world. Have you ever run your hand over the coat of a dog whose hair is wadded in large mats? The New Age phenomenon is somewhat like that, a tangle of complexity, diversification and even contradictions. Some of the strands are non-occultic, and if our model is the 'demon-monger', how can we communicate with New Agers who are uninterested in the occult? Even when the 'demon-monger' model is used in the context of occultism, it generally compounds rather than eases the communication difficulties because it lacks a certain tact.

There is also the 'conspiracy' model. This has been a fairly well-received Christian way of seeing the New Age. In many ways, the 'conspiracy' model sees the New Age as a tightly organised global collusion to install a totalitarian one-world government that would establish its own world religion to usher in the Antichrist. I do not make light of this model, or even say here that it is totally wrong, but perhaps 'ad-lib co-ordination' or '*laissez-faire* co-operation' is a better way to describe the corporate efforts of some New Age leaders.

One problem with the 'conspiracy' model is that it oversimplifies. It is like the tale of the three blind men who reported their encounters with an elephant. One had come upon a leg, and so reported that the elephant was like a stout tree trunk. The second man had experienced the elephant's trunk, and reported

that the elephant was a long flexible tube. The
third man felt an ear, and said, 'You're both
wrong, it's like a massive leathery leaf.' It is the
oversimplification of the New Age phenomenon
that has contributed to the sensationalism
surrounding it. Christians have been taught
that it is an occult conspiracy and they get
worried. And, again, the sensationalism
generates an unhealthy fear of the New Age
among Christians, which tends to keep us at a
distance from the very people we are called to
reach. (From counselling many Christians who
have had this unhealthy fear, I have been able
to identify what I think is the core problem: they
have failed to understand and appreciate that
their inheritance in Christ includes authority
over the powers of darkness. I will say more
about this later.)

An understanding of the 'mystery of
iniquity' (2 Thess. 2:7 AV) may be helpful here.
When the Bible speaks of Satanic or demonic
evil working itself out in human affairs it uses
the image 'mystery of iniquity'. This means that
there are many silences on God's part, to us,
about how and when Satan's purposes are going
to be fleshed out in the earth. It's a mystery.
There are some things we are not going to know.
In this, we must be content.

Another failing of the 'conspiracy' model is
that it does not help Christians to speak to the
New Age people who are opposed to one-
worldism. To have a one-world government,
there must be a *centralisation* of global political
power, either in the hands of one person or an
élite group of world governors. Many New Age
leaders, however, argue strongly for
decentralisation, being fully aware of the

totalitarian dangers inherent in a sovereign global federation of political powers. Decentralisation seems to be especially liked by 'Green' New Agers (I do not say all 'Greens' are New Age). The Christian who sees all New Age people advocating a one-world government or religion may be hard-pressed for anything to say to a 'Green' New Ager. All in all, the 'conspiracy' model, when it comes to the communication process, is a rickety bridge.

One's model, therefore, determines the 'categories of thought' that are brought to a conversation, and these in turn influence communication because they limit or expand the scope of what can be said to New Age people. Two other Christian models are worth mentioning. One is to see the New Age as a 'philosophically united confederacy'; the other is to see it as a 'meta-network', i.e. a network of networks. Both of these are more to the point and therefore more user-friendly; they carry some solid 'bridge-building' equipment.

There are also the models that the New Age uses to describe itself. One is that of a 'paradigm shift in consciousness'; another, that of 'personal, social and global transformation'; another, that of a 'quantum leap in the spiritual evolution of the planet'. These, and others, conceptualise how New Age people see their world, and they shape the categories of thought from which these spiritual seekers discuss the New Age, both amongst themselves and with 'outsiders' .

Several models have also arisen from secular points of view. It may be helpful to consider the progression of secular labels that have been put upon spiritual trends during the past two centuries. In the late eighteenth century, notoriety about the so-called new 'mind-powers' arose when Anton Mesmer popularised a healing technique he called 'animal magnetism'. Though it had a stormy history, it caught on under the name 'mesmerism' and later 'hypnotism'. During the mid-to-late nineteenth century the interest in spiritualism revived, led by the now discredited Fox sisters. This kept the interest in latent mind-powers alive in the media, as did the Society for Psychical Research.

Also in the nineteenth century, 'mind powers' and 'mental healing' received further secular recognition as an increasing number of small independent groups met to discuss 'new revelations'. People such as Phineas Parkhurst Quimby, Mary Baker Eddy (Christian Science) and Charles and Myrtle Fillmore (Unity) caused quite a stir. Just before the turn of the century this rising spiritual mix was given the name 'New Thought'. The 'New Thought' movement is one of the seedbeds in which part of what we call 'New Age' was planted.

By the mid-twentieth century the 'New Thought' model was no longer able to carry the weight of explanation needed to describe, analyse and interpret a growing trend, and the label 'Human Potential Movement' largely displaced it. This became the new secular model for identifying the supposedly latent but vital forces of untapped human potential—but without reference to any kind of 'God'. The label quickly became a Western buzz-phrase and rallying point, depicting the ideology of people who believed in sheer human ability to transform self and society. It, too, is another discernable seedbed of today's New Age phenomenon.[2]

From 'mind powers' to 'New Thought' to 'Human Potential' to what? To the mid-to-late 1960s and the 'Age of Aquarius', which is an astrological motif about the supposed dawning of two thousand years of peace and harmony on the earth. Then after regrouping in cultural backwaters during most of the 1970s, the Age of Aquarius was quietly relaunched in the 1980s as the 'New Age Movement', which has become today's most ubiquitous model for trying to understand the phenomenon.

The 'movement' model for depicting the New Age is the most familiar one, both to Christians and non-Christians. Yet is the 'movement' model big enough to hold all the information we now know about the New Age phenomenon? Is it truth-full enough to carry the weight of explanation, evaluation and interpretation that is now needed to characterise the New Age? Perhaps it was, once upon a time. But given the New Age's wide-ranging sweep and deepening penetration throughout virtually every cultural discipline today, the 'movement' model seems *passé*. A 'movement' usually depicts one particular ideology, its agenda and the accompanying group of activists who labour to promote its goals, generally within one strata of society—for example, the student or civil rights movements of the 1960s. Perhaps it was once fitting to use the 'movement' model as a label for the New Age, but today, with its complexities, diversification and even contradictions, the 'movement' model seems behind the times and therefore not conducive for constructive conversation.

If we want to discuss 'movements' it would be nearer the mark to speak of the movements within the New Age world. Gaia consciousness, goddess worship, myth revival, holistic health care, earth stewardship, transpersonal education, new age business management and others are all designations that can be properly identified and discussed as 'movements' within the New Age world.

So where do we find a model that can do justice to the facts about New Age today? Is there, in fact, a way to see the New Age as a whole? If so, the model will be foundational enough to carry the weight of all the New Age's complexities, diversification and contrariety, and not only today but also tomorrow. So far it has been rather like trying to explain the size and weight of the Great Pyramid of Egypt from the foundation of a beach house. Furthermore, we need a model that will give us not only a faithful understanding of the whole New Age phenomenon, but also an effective way by which to communicate the gospel to its adherents.

I am not sure that I know the answers to such questions, but in the next chapter I am going to try to suggest a model that seems to be comprehensive enough for the task we face. So if you are ready, we will plunge in.

12

Wisdom in the Marketplace

Have you ever wondered what motivates people
to do what they do, or what accounts for the
decisions they make?   Take voting as an
example. In the United States, some people vote
Democratic, others Republican. In Great
Britain, the choices range from Conservative to
Labour to Liberal Democrat to Green. People
can be quite inflexible about their political
alliances. Or take the question of education.
Many parents send their children to state
schools. Other parents cannot stomach that
idea and place their children in various sorts of
private schools, and yet other parents believe in
home schooling. Why do people make the
various choices that they do? What is it that
influences people in different directions, not only
at the voting booth and in the choice of a
classroom but across the spectrum of life?

Also, have you ever wondered why some
New Age seekers seem to be capable of doing
such apparently silly things at times? 'Silly' to
Christians, that is. I'm not thinking of the more
understandable things like having a horoscope
read, or meditating, or visiting a psychic. I'm
thinking of things that seem unthinkable,
unimaginable, to a Christian, such as sitting

cross-legged inside a custom-built pyramid in order to sharpen your senses, or immobilising yourself in six inches of water while in a state of trance within the stark blackness of a sensory deprivation tank, or wearing electronic 'mind massagers' or 'brain machines' around the eyes and ears that flash psychedelic light patterns on to the retina to an accompanying sound track. This would be unthinkable behaviour for Christians but not for many New Age adherents, for whom it would be as sensible as voting for their favourite political party.

Or take the 'laying on of stones'. Some New Age seekers like to have crystals, and the right ones, in the bath with them. Others like to have crystals, and the proper colours too, as earrings or jewellery to wear for healing or consciousness raising. Others, however, lay small colourful crystals and stones of diverse sizes and shapes on various areas of the body. The person, usually in a meditative state, will be stretched out flat on her back, arms slightly extended from her sides, palms up. Small crystals will have been placed upon the forehead, shoulders, upper chest area, the open palms, the navel area, and perhaps at selected points along each arm or in a straight line from the navel to the neck. Why does the person do this? To the Christian it seems unthinkable, even foolish. But don't worry, New Age people return the favour. They generally consider our Christian practices as unthinkable and foolish, e.g. prayer, the Lord's table, confession of sin, preaching the gospel. Why is this?

The answer is found, ultimately, in each person's wisdom. Yes, superficial reasons for various behaviours—peer pressure, experimentation, amusement—could be cited, but these are not our concern here. The deeper answer for the choices we make is found in the kind of wisdom for life that each of us has.

'Wisdom' is the subject of Paul's first letter to the Corinthians, chapters 1 and 2, where he speaks not only about the futility of man's wisdom but also about the blessedness of God's wisdom. This latter point is occasionally overlooked or dismissed by Christians. Not *all* wisdom is futile. There is the wisdom of God as it is known in Jesus Christ, which is the 'message of wisdom' Christians speak, and there is futile, worldly wisdom. The passage, therefore, teaches that all people have a wisdom for life, be they atheist, agnostic, humanist, a bar-room brawler, a mother of four, a prime minister or a New Ager. And when you become a Christian and are in Christ your wisdom changes radically. You become a part of a wisdom that the world does not know. The point of the passage is Paul's contrast of the two wisdoms.

But what is wisdom? In his thought-provoking and ground-breaking book *Wisdom in the Marketplace*, English theologian and philosopher John Peck brings out its biblical meaning in a contemporary way. Writing as someone who teaches both Hebrew and Greek, Peck states that in the Bible 'Wisdom is a word about the sort of sense you make of creation in order to live in it effectively (and it will affect what you think is effective living too).'[1] Or, 'Wisdom is a way of seeing life and behaving in it.'[2]

Wisdom, therefore, is not mere head knowledge. According to the Bible it brings theory and practice together—it is a way of making sense *and* living, a way of seeing *and* behaving. Perhaps it could be said that wisdom is applied knowledge, and this seems to be how it is used in the Old Testament. In the book of Exodus, for instance, whenever God gave wisdom to a man or a woman, that person was both a teacher *and* a craftsperson (hearer *and* doer). These people not only taught others how to make the priestly garments, the tabernacle curtains, the altar, the laver, the utensils and so on; they also got their hands dirty doing it. In so doing, they were said to have God's wisdom, which brings belief or theory and practice together. (See Exodus chapters 28, 31, 35 and 36.)

I do not want to be so presumptuous as to speak for the apostle to the Gentiles, but this is probably what Paul meant in the passage in his first letter to the Corinthians. Paul was steeped in Old Testament understanding. His is a Hebrew mind. He knows that wisdom relates theory to practice. So he says that non-Christians make sense of the creation and live in it according to human or worldly wisdom, and that Christians see life and behave in it according to the wisdom of God in Christ.

Now the apostle is quick to recognise that between different wisdoms there will be communication difficulties. This is implied in his statements that different wisdoms look like 'foolishness' to one another (1 Cor. 1:18, 20 and 25). One wisdom looks at the beliefs, values, assumptions, practices and lifestyle of another wisdom and ridicules them. But the other wisdom returns the compliment!

Perhaps you can see what I am leading up

to. I promised you a model for understanding the New Age phenomenon. This is the 'wisdom' model. New Age people, like everyone else, have a way of making sense of the creation in order to live in it effectively. They have a way of seeing life that influences their actions. That is, they have a certain 'wisdom' for life.

Christian writers on the New Age such as Douglas Groothuis, Elliot Miller, Vishal Mangalwadi, James Sire, Brooks Alexander and several others have spoken of this in terms of a 'worldview'. Ronald Enroth, for example, has said that 'Rather than a cult or a movement, the New Age is a philosophy, a worldview, a way of defining reality.'[3] Now the idea of 'worldview' is very similar to what the Bible means by 'wisdom'.

Let's see this in action with the laying on of stones. The person who does this is usually a meditator, who sees the universe as a sort of uncircumscribed metaphysical supply depot of invisible and impersonal spiritual life-energies that can be tapped into through meditation. This is a part of the New Age meditator's wisdom, and it influences behaviour. The person meditates in the hope of accessing the spiritual life-energy and generating inner peace and harmony, enlightenment, healing and so on. What, then, is the purpose of the stones and crystals? Crystals are laid on the body as a kind of spiritual power booster, to amplify the desired effects between the meditator and the cosmic energy. The procedure may perhaps be likened to the difference in reaction time and intensity between the oral and the intravenous administration of a drug.

The idea is that the crystals enhance the

body's ability to tap the healing potential of the
life-energy. The scope of what is promised by
way of getting rid of 'dis-ease' is quite amazing.
Crystal therapy purports to: eliminate repressed
memories, resolve mental conflicts, change
attitudes, cleanse the body's 'auric energy field',
sharpen psychic powers, direct telepathic
messages, replace sadness and depression with
joy and enthusiasm, provide transpersonal
experiences and much more. Crystals are also
said to store memory, to be programmable by
the human mind, and to teach. This is another
part of New Age wisdom and it influences
behaviour. Why meditate under one's own
steam if crystals will energise the process?

Here is a typical way in which this example
of New Age wisdom is expressed by an expert in
the field. Katrina Raphaell has been working
with crystals for twenty years. In her book
Crystal Enlightenment (Vol. 1, Aurora Press
1985), she describes the transforming properties
of crystals and healing stones:

> Now with the knowledge of the healing
> power of stones, the physical, psychic and
> emotional bodies can be healed and
> aligned with the source of life energy-
> spirit. Crystal healing, through the art of
> laying on stones, is one of the most
> advanced and effective methods of
> cleansing the aura, releasing suppressed
> traumas, and connecting a person
> with his/her own source of truth and
> power . . . Crystals and stones assist in [a]
> self-empowering process by increasing the
> amount of light present in the aura which
> stimulates and activates the more

powerful subtle realms of being. In the practice of crystal healing, the stones become crystallised light forms that are placed onto vital nerve centres, chakra areas and plexus points on the body. The stones act as a catalyst to perpetuate and integrate more colour and light into the subtle energies of the human aura. This increased energy frequency serves to dissolve and dissipate the dark shadows of suppressed or unreleased pain that cloud the aura, confuse the mind and dis-ease the body. The crystals can neutralise this negative charge and energy is released from the mental-physical blockages. The transforming power of the stones recirculates that energy to its source, to be used for conscious purpose. It is then the responsibility of the individual receiving the healing to let go of the old and receive the new energy, using it to recreate a positive identity based in self-love and truth. This then becomes the foundation upon which dreams are built and visions lived (pp. 32–3).

It may sound convincing to someone whose wisdom is becoming New Age, but according to biblical wisdom it's certainly not the foundation upon which dreams are built and visions are lived. Christians who are steeped in biblical wisdom look at all this with amusement, though the meditator is absolutely serious about it because it is a part of her wisdom; just as the Christian is absolutely serious about, for example, prayer. The problem is, Christians are going to have to learn how to overcome the gulf of foolishness between the two different wisdoms in order to communicate effectively in the New Age world, where the marketplace is teeming with oddities. And this will only occur through our increasing understanding of the 'different' wisdom and through learning how to communicate with New Age people in a way that makes sense to them. (This is the purpose of Part Two.)

We may find ourselves talking to people who visualise world peace, globe-trot on goddess pilgrimages, access their 'past-lives', cleanse their auras, bond with their zygotes, eat macrobiotically, make friends with their tarot, search for their soulmates, undergo vision quests, achieve shamanistic communications, practice psychic self-defence, endure rolfing, recount visits with UFOs, consult transpersonal psychologists, arrange preconception contracts with their children, meditate on the fixed stars, and so much more in the New Age world.

In one way or another these activities are either derived from or engulfed by New Age wisdom. More seriously, so many New Agers are sincerely searching for so much: answers to life's meaning, life after death, spiritual power, personal/social/global transformation, love, healing, ecological stability, (w)holistic health care—concerns that we all share. These, too, are part of a New Age wisdom. New Age seekers are trying their best to make sense of life and live in it as effectively as they can, as Christians are—but quite unlike Christians, New Age people do it outside the context of the wisdom of God in Christ. Thus the communication problem runs both ways, as the New Age person also shakes his head in disbelief at

Christian values, practices, lifestyle.

At the outset of this chapter I posed questions that now have an answer. It is one's *wisdom* that influences what is thought and the choices that are made. I also mentioned that wisdom brings together theory and practice; yet it also relates inner development to outer behaviour, or 'interior matters' to a person's 'outer realities'. You will remember the difficult radio interview that I had with astrologist Marjorie Orr (see Chapter 5). Orr has gone through a process of inner transformation in which an interior dynamic of irrationality now influences her outer behaviour. Irrationality is part of New Age wisdom, and this played havoc with that interview. Thus one's wisdom is also a kind of invisible inner generator of outer actions. We will see in Part Two how to get past such communication barriers.

Christians therefore, have a certain wisdom for life, and New Age people do too. The former is God's as found in Jesus Christ; the latter is worldly, of man. In the two wisdoms, the basic assumptions about God, man and the universe are very different. This poses great communication problems. *Foolishness* is the bridge that must be crossed between the two wisdoms in order for effective communication to occur.

13

Acquiring Wisdom

The thing to remember about wisdom is that it is chiefly about people. Wisdom does not sit in a hermetically sealed tin next to the tomato sauce. *People* hold wisdom, and we are mysterious, complex and different from one another. What makes the 'wisdom' model feasible and convincing for understanding the New Age phenomenon and its adherents is that it seems to be able to handle all the complexities, diversification and contradictions that people and their beliefs are.

One of our Christian failings has been the rather simplistic way that some of us have looked at the New Age and by implication its people. We have believed that we understood the phenomenon, whereas we have only grasped one or two aspects of it. Yet it is a highly complex and greatly diversified mosaic. Now there may be ways to *simplify* the evaluation of a complex phenomenon, but there is a great difference between the simple and the simplistic. To treat a person and his wisdom simplistically is to invite disaster into the communication process.

Wisdom accumulates in people from childhood. People, therefore, are not born with New Age wisdom any more than being born in a chip shop gives you a potato head. Wisdom is not a characteristic of birth; it is acquired whilst growing up and throughout adulthood too. John Peck writes that wisdom is much like a language we pick up as we go along, by hearing, by imitating, through others correcting us.

> Long before we go to school to 'learn English' from textbooks we are already using it with considerable fluency. By that time it is so much second nature to us that when we begin to study it from books, the way it comes to us as a subject looks strange, like algebra. We develop in the wisdom of our culture in the same way . . . We do not formally learn our wisdom. We absorb it as we go along.[1]

By adulthood, one's wisdom generally includes an unlikely collage of ideas, beliefs, values, habits and practices that have been accumulating from many and diverse sources throughout one's life. This is because we absorb it from a host of diverse and at times inharmonious sources: family, friends, neighbours, associates, books, teachers, ministers, newspapers, television, films, music, videos, cult(ural) heros and others. This explains the diversity and the many incongruities in the New Age world and person, and the 'wisdom' model gives us a means by which to speak to that diversity and incongruity.

In the West, absorbing wisdom has generally meant that a child takes on board values and beliefs that are materialistic, rationalistic and naturalistic. In simple terms, this is what it means to become 'secular'. This, then, has been the wisdom of the West for a long time. What is occurring in our day is that an

*incoming, cosmopolitan spirituality that is
unbiblical is informing and transforming existing
secular wisdom, and this in turn is creating a
'New Age' wisdom*, a wisdom in which
nonbiblical kinds of spirituality are informing
existing 'secular' ways of looking at life and
behaving in it. This means that the New Age
people to whom we shall be speaking will have a
wisdom that includes the cosmopolitan
spirituality as well as secular ideas, values,
beliefs, assumptions and practices. This
process of the transformation of secular into
New Age wisdom is so important, and influences
communication in such far-reaching ways, that
we need to understand the transformation as
best we can. For me it has been very helpful to
approach it from a historical perspective.

Slowly in the 1950s and with increased
momentum in the 1960s, Westerners rose
satiated from the table of secular wisdom and
stepped back to consider the feast in a new
light. What is that gnawing hunger within us,
they asked one another? What appetite is the
current banquet unable to satisfy? It was not
long before it became clear that they were empty
in spirit. There was a spiritual hunger. As a
result, many secularists who had once believed
that they could reach their fullest potential
without spiritual sustenance began to admit
that the well-being of the human race could not
be produced without it.

But let's go back a bit further. Under the
sway of eighteenth- and nineteenth-century
enlightenment thinking, the 'unseen', i.e. the
spiritual, the supernatural and the religious,
became the butt of public jokes everywhere in
the West. The 'unseen' became unthinkable, at

least in the minds of those professing themselves wise, and by the late nineteenth century large numbers of influential Westerners belittled religion and spiritual concerns. 'The unseen' became unthinkable largely as a result of the philosophy of materialism, which was a controlling force of enlightenment thinking. The dominant principle of materialism is not, as is frequently thought, an excessive regard, or penchant, for acquiring more and more possessions and wealth. This is but a fruit of the philosophy of materialism, because it sees physical well-being, worldly possessions and affluence as of very high value. The dominant principle of the philosophy of materialism is that 'all that is seen will explain all that is'. Generations cut their intellectual teeth upon this presupposition, and so removed spirituality, the supernatural and religion from being much of an influence in public life, in such areas as education, art, science, politics and economics. The unenlightened could entertain themselves privately with religion—or superstition, as it was usually called—if they liked, but the wise saw it as a security blanket that they could do without.

Physical matter, with its movements and modifications, is the only reality in the philosophy of materialism. The entire universe, including thought, feeling, mind and will, was said to be explainable by physical or natural laws. Science and technology seemed to confirm that this was a comprehensive principle for all of life, and a secular wisdom and the culture it produced arose to the glory of materialism.

Yet after nearly two hundred years of trying to bury a ghost—such is the exercise in futility demanded of human beings by materialism—

droves of secular folk today are admitting defeat. Spiritual denial cannot be maintained. People can for only so long deny a God-given aspect of their nature before it turns to taunt them. And so such people are now confessing that 'all that is seen *cannot* explain all that is'. They feel that there must be more to life than meets the eye, and that the philosophy of materialism is not comprehensive enough to explain all of life. They wonder whether there is a spiritual dimension to life.

The spiritual pioneering began in awkward fits and starts with the rebellion of the Beats in the 1950s against a society whose 'mind is pure machinery, whose blood is running money, whose love is endless oil and stone, whose soul is electricity and banks!'[2] The road (the search) was their symbol, and while travelling it the Beats offered marijuana, meditation and drugs as vehicles for spiritual enlightenment. Allen Ginsberg, Gary Snyder and Jack Kerouac were three famous and articulate mouthpieces for the Beats, and they influenced many teenagers and others in the direction of Buddhist enlightenment. Though the media either castigated or made comic relief of them, their energy brought early ecological consciousness into the sixties rebellion, and their spoor was followed by countercultural heavies such as Bob Dylan and Jim Morrison, as their spirituality trickled into the West.

Then in the 1960s, the beat intensified as the 'Age of Aquarius' dawned. By the end of the decade millions of young people had created a counterculture that was a no-holds-barred search for spiritual food. This spiritual revival would have taken Western culture in the direction of a biblical reformation if the young people who pushed it had done so in the context of Christian spirituality. Yet not being Christian, the 'revivalists' looked for beliefs that would not be morally demanding and yet have the appeal of things spiritual. Having been raised man-centred rather than God-centred, bending the knee before a holy God was unthinkable to the secular sixties generation. Thus a generation of Aquarians rather than Christians was raised up.

I was one of the burgeoning multitude that embraced this spirituality without morality. I first became acquainted with it in 1963, as a teenager, when researching for a massive term paper on an Eastern religion called Brahmanism. By 1968, I was trading my short hair, Oxford shirts, continental trousers, pointed leather shoes and generally clean-cut look for bell-bottoms, long hair, a Fu Manchu mustache and the generally disarrayed look of someone on the road. And it is no secret that Buddhism, Hinduism, Taoism, occultism, mysticism, TM, LSD, marijuana, hashish, Carlos Castaneda, Alan Watts and his Zen, Baba Ram Dass, Paramahansa Yogananda and countless other sources and people formed a kind of cosmopolitan spirituality that people like me enjoyed immensely. It gave us spiritual answers and did not interfere with our permissiveness.

This cosmopolitan spirituality included virtually anything and everything 'spiritual' *except* that which was Judaeo-Christian, and by 1970, I was well on my way to being one of its spokespersons. I became an astrologer and a meditator, I contacted 'spirit guides', was a

vegetarian and trained in psychic healing. But I
did not completely lose all of my secular values,
especially at first when I still clung, for instance,
to nice clothes, new cars, money in the bank
and so on as high values.

This was the Aquarian counterculture, and
as its spirituality was travelling through Western
culture, informing and transforming what it
could, it was the genesis for transmuting secular
wisdom into New Age wisdom within our young
lives. But what about transforming the rest of
society? Why remain in cultural backwaters
with the greatest thing since electricity and
sliced bread? Surely there must be millions of
others, in education, health care, politics,
science and business management, who are also
dissatisfied with the prevailing materialist
philosophy. Why not transform them, and
transform society in the process? Good idea!
We can have a new culture, a new age.

The mandate, therefore, to 'turn on, tune in
and drop out' was reversed: Aquarians cut their
hair, shaved and planned for the future—no
mean feat for existentialists! They traded their
Indian guru clothes and tie-dye for a more
conservative look and re-entered university
where they graduated with various degrees and
Ph.D.s. They took respected and influential
positions, married, had children and began
amassing finances and networking with the like-
minded. And as they did they were influencing
secular culture with the cosmopolitan
spirituality. Now this was not a human
conspiracy orchestrated by Aquarians *en masse*.
It was the changing *Zeitgeist*, and the more
people there were who had burned out on

secularism, the greater the potential for moving the changing *Zeitgeist* along.

By 1980, it was becoming normative to be 'spiritually attuned'. This was not, however, limited to New Age people, for in the 1970s the Jesus Movement had won tens of thousands of converts to Christianity. Unfortunately, millions of others became interested in the spirituality now called 'New Age'. But then, most of it was not really 'new'; it was a revival of ancient wisdom, pre-Christian faiths and pagan traditions, the old occult, Eastern mysticism, meditation and the like. It was marketed as 'new' because these beliefs and practices had been updated to late twentieth-century thinking and language. This has been accomplished by 'changing the nouns of the game' in order to present formerly taboo-sounding beliefs and practices in a euphemistic language that won't offend most people. It is also called 'new' because it claims that many of its beliefs and practices have the support and even the ratification of science. This spiritual renaissance is documented in glowing terms by best-selling New Age writer Marilyn Ferguson in her landmark book *The Aquarian Conspiracy*, which was published in 1980.

The past few decades, therefore, have seen 'secular humanists' being transformed into 'cosmic humanists'; 'cosmic' because they are now spiritual in orientation and 'humanist' because they are still man-centred. For the first time in a *long* time a nonbiblical spirituality on a massive scale is informing and transforming secular culture. A New Age wisdom is arising.

The Admixture

Yet this is not the whole story, because it is not ideas but *people* we are talking about. The effective communicator will seek for clues about the degree to which a particular person's wisdom has turned 'New Age'. This will help you in approaching the person and in knowing what topics may be best for conversation.

Let's draw an analogy from the artist's palette. Let the red paint represent secular wisdom, and let the blue paint be the incoming cosmopolitan spirituality. Mix a bit of the blue with the red and it produces purple, i.e. a New Age wisdom. Yet it will not be purely purple because many streaks of red and blue will be mixing it up here and there, still on their way to a purple coloration, or perhaps even resisting it. Thus besides discerning what is purple, we want to be wise in knowing that the wisdom of the people we talk to will also comprise hues, tints and shades of the old and the new. Even the most serious New Age adherent, if a Westerner, will have been so thoroughly secularised that it is not possible for him or her to have a purely 'purple' wisdom.

If you are having difficulty believing this, take yourself as an illustration. As a Christian, are you thinking and living out of a purely biblical wisdom? If you are tempted to say 'Yes', it means that you are thoroughly consistent with the Father's will in everything you think and do, day in and day out. The New Testament, however, would not speak of the need for the Christian's mind to be renewed if we received the gift of a thoroughly biblical wisdom at conversion. This means that there are still some humanistic or pagan or materialistic or other nonbiblical beliefs and values influencing our thoughts and behaviour. These areas need renewal. There is only one Person who thought and lived a purely biblical wisdom, and He got crucified for it! If you would like to know how biblical your thinking is, ask yourself how close you are to getting crucified.

We shall, then, meet people who have various shades, or intensities, of the new wisdom and this will affect how we speak to them. Remember the Waverley Market numerologist from Chapter Four? His is a very 'purple' wisdom. Compare him to your friend or neighbour who has for the first time encountered the New Age, perhaps at a 'Mind, Body, Spirit' festival. We could think of this as the first dab of blue in the red. Or, you may find yourself in conversation with someone who has been practising Wicca for a couple of years. This person may have several dabs of blue mixing with the red, with the purple beginning to influence more areas of her life. The effective communicator will want to become sensitive to the intensity of purple coloration, and in Part Two we shall discuss appropriate responses.

There is yet a further matter to be taken into consideration. The person may have had an upbringing which included religious beliefs, values and practices as well as secular ones. The wise communicator will take this into consideration. A Christian only needs to start chatting with New Age people to discover that not a few of them will have had a Christian denominational background, or Jewish, or some other religious influence on them. This may have been in the distant past, merely long-forgotten Sunday school memories, or it may be something that carried a lot of weight until recently, until some final straw . . . , and now the person sees much more hope in the New Age. Or, you may engage people in conversation who say they are Christian but who obviously hold to New Age beliefs and values and practices, and this can be very confusing.

Immediately after the Nancy Reagan 'Astrology in the White House' exposé broke in May, 1988, I was invited to do a number of media programmes. During two of these, one on radio and one on television, I debated with a prominent astrologer who unabashedly claimed to be a Christian. This created a context that was completely different from any of the other programmes I did during those months. Frankly, I would think twice about appearing in this unusual context again, for it meant engaging in two battlefronts concurrently. For the other programmes it was sufficient to have good reasons and a biblical apologetic for the case against astrology. In these two pro-grammes, however, I also had to have a case against the idea that someone could be both an astrologer and a Christian, and that case had to be both convincing and sensitive. I found it tiring to wield the sword in both directions. It was difficult to know when the astrologer would change direction and where I would have to pivot to when he did. The double context and short time-frames left important areas unresolved for the audiences.

My point in mentioning this incident is to show that New Age people may have religious as well as secular beliefs that are undergoing transformation by the cosmopolitan spirituality. Yet if those religious convictions are Christian this may be a real boon to us, as it may give us something solid to appeal to.

Just before we move into Part Two, I would like us to see several examples of how the philosophy of materialism has dissatisfied secular people. This will help us identify areas where the cosmopolitan spirituality has capitalised on that dissatisfaction and so influenced people in the direction of New Age wisdom. (It may also be a motivation to some enterprising Christians to research mouth-watering biblical answers that are better than the cosmopolitan spirituality ever could be, and present them to secular or New Age people at the points of their dissatisfaction.) We will only concentrate on one area of damage done by materialism, that it is reductionist in nature; i.e. it reduces, or diminishes, all of life to physical matter as the only reality.

Here is an example of a growing secular dissatisfaction in the realm of health care. The domination of the philosophy of materialism over medical science has reduced health care to that which treats chiefly physical ailments and symptoms. This is because materialism has reduced the human being to a composite of minerals valued at the price of a couple of fish dinners. Materialism played upon the minds of many of those who nursed us and it taught them to view us as flesh, blood and bones only. Thus most doctors see their patients as living organisms of physical or natural laws that have been collected and understood from centuries of anatomical research.

I do not want to make light of having X-rays taken and needles jabbed and scalpels inserted and drugs administered into this 'living example of physical laws'. This saved my life once. But when little or no treatment can be offered outside this health care system by its professionals, and when it turns thumbs down to credible areas of chiropractic and osteopathic procedures, and when massive amounts of research have revealed that sixty to eighty-five per cent of the symptoms we take to the doctor may be psychosomatic in nature, and when more and more people are realising that there is a spiritual dimension to themselves which affects the body, then a hue and cry arises for a health care system that includes treatment of the whole person.

Today we hear people saying, 'Hold on, all that is seen *cannot* explain all that is us. There is more to us than meets the eye, and we need a health care model that understands our spirituality'. The result is holistic health care and alternative or complementary medicine.

It must quickly be said that not everything that goes on under the umbrella of 'holism' is wrong, though much of it is. But I will share with you an observation. In almost every seminar on holism that I conduct, I find myself engaged with two different kinds of Christian health-care professionals. There will be those who see no good in holistic health care and alternative medicine and there will be those who argue tooth and nail for it. The first group seems unaware of the growing body of scientific research that may one day give validity to some areas of 'holism'. The other group, if I may speak frankly, seems overly positive about 'holism' because scientific enterprise, rather than biblical wisdom, acts as a final authority for them in the area of health care 'alternatives'.

Though the Bible ought to be the final authority over health care, what has tended to happen is that some Christian doctors and nurses have not evaluated 'holism' through the wisdom of the Bible. Therefore they may not understand the unbiblical spiritual ramifications of much of the holistic and alternative therapies that they are endorsing. The idea, then, is not to evaluate and critique 'holism' solely by the scientific enterprise; neither is it, as the first group has a tendency to do, to chuck out the baby with the bathwater; nor is it to fully embrace 'holism' because we now understand the failings of Western health care. Simply put, the idea is not to critique the East with the West or the West with the East; rather, it is to evaluate what comes to us from *both* camps from the point of view of the Bible. This, I think, must be part of the task, though it is a monumental one, of Christian health-care professionals. The Church needs them to do some biblical thinking, speaking and writing about the spiritual ramifications of 'holism'. Too many people, Christians too, are in bondage to 'holism' because many of its beliefs, values and practices are spiritual idolatries.

Another example of reductionism is in the area of nature and the environment. Materialist thought saw no point in treating the earth carefully; the earth was reduced to 'simply a stockpile of raw *materials*'[3] that we are free to plunder. Modern-day piracy no longer has to go to sea to satisfy its greed, and as a result havoc is wreaked upon the ecology—ecosystems are being destroyed, animals are becoming endangered or extinct, chainsaws run amuck in rainforests, chemicals contaminate water supplies, energy sources diminish, the air of the cities grows foul, nuclear waste (deadly for centuries or longer) cannot be disposed of, titanic oil slicks float on the oceans and wipe out shoreline marine life, and the threat of widespread skin cancer arises from Chernobyl-type nuclear disasters. Is it any wonder that in the face of these and other environmental nasties people are looking for a non-materialist view by which to respect the planet and find a solution? This is what gave rise to the various attempts to arrive at a spiritual understanding of nature and the environment such as Green ecology and the Gaia hypothesis.

Again, it is not entirely rubbish. Of all people, Christians should be on the leading edge of the earth-stewardship movement. After all, we have been commanded to care for God's good earth (Gen. 1—3). In this respect the Christian Ecology Link in England, as well as up-and-coming organisations in other nations, is trying to find the connections between ecological beliefs and the Christian faith.[4] Christians like these could become effective communicators to non-Christian spiritual seekers.

The vast and important field of education is another area of great secular dissatisfaction. In the United States for the past hundred years, non-private education has been largely about indoctrinating school children in what the State deems important. This has been politely called by the euphemism *socialisation*. Now if the State is secular and greatly influenced by the philosophy of materialism, it becomes necessary to remove any and all references to religion or spirituality from your state schools so that the schools can become secularised themselves. Religious values in general, and Christian values in particular, place limits upon the amount of loyalty one can have towards the State. If you want to raise up citizens loyal to the State, you remove, usually through government legislation, religion and spirituality from your schools and so make education a process of indoctrinating children in what the State deems important for greater loyalty to it.

But in America this process of socialisation has contributed to the social disintegration of the State's student bodies. There is great disrespect for teachers; a police presence is needed in some city schools to restrain and discourage theft and violence; an unyielding alcohol and drug abuse problem exists even among pre-teen school children; high student absenteeism and drop-out rates increase, and much more. 'Piecemeal reform of education is hopeless,' shout New Age educators. 'The whole basis of education is our problem. It is based on a set of assumptions which is no longer valid. We need a complete redesign of the way we teach our children.'5

It is not surprising that parents and teachers are now listening intently to the incoming cosmopolitan spirituality for advice about transforming education. Here we have room for just one example. When New Age intellectual Jean Houston (adopted daughter of anthropologist Margaret Mead) spoke to five thousand secular curriculum developers at a national education conference in Florida in 1989, the gist of her speech, in no uncertain terms, was that the solution to the educational crisis was to establish a 'world curriculum' that would incorporate spiritual motifs from around the world, ancient and modern, into every subject. Houston received several standing ovations during her address. Here is a case where disgruntled secular educators are getting a few dabs of 'blue' mixed into their old 'red' way of seeing. They have seen that conventional secular education has failed and are looking for help from a spiritual direction. It will be difficult, however, to establish spiritual motifs from the world's religions in America's state schools because of the First Amendment appeal to the separation of Church and State. It will be interesting to see how these educators proceed with Houston's model. At the least it will entail placing these motifs in an inoffensive non-religious language to bypass the First Amendment barrier.

Things are very different in Great Britain, where religion and spirituality, especially Christianity, are legally welcome in state schools and sit happily under the protection of national legislation. Yet in Great Britain the cosmopolitan spirituality of the New Age is now up on its own two feet and taking great strides throughout the national curriculum (see Chapter 2). As long as these religious values and spiritual practices, whatever names they are given, further the aims of the State and produce increased loyalty to it, they will probably be allowed to stay. Either side of the Atlantic, however, it behoves Christians, and especially Christian educators, to meet secular people at the points of their dissatisfaction with reductionist education and offer them biblical answers and alternatives.

To quote the writer to the Hebrews, 'What

more shall I say? Time would fail me to tell about' scientists, business managers, politicians, economists, film makers, writers, celebrities, young people, office workers, postal clerks, sales people, your neighbours and all the other secular persons who now realise that there is more to life than meets the eye. Dissatisfied with materialism, it is no longer unthinkable for them to look for answers and alternatives from the cosmopolitan spiritualty. Yet in closing this chapter I would like to emphasise that though their wisdom is turning 'purple', the wise communicator will want to keep in mind that it nevertheless has a lot of 'red' remaining, and this will affect how they are approached and spoken to with a Christian message.

Even those who are thoroughly dissatisfied with materialism will not discard it *in toto*, empty the house and move in the new cosmopolitan spirituality the next day. Transforming a worldview does not work like that. Too much in the 'old' way of seeing will continue to support them and commend itself to them; after all, they spent perhaps decades deriving meaning, value, purpose, cohesion and integrity from the philosophy of materialism, and this is not so easily got rid of. It is somewhat like asking the person to give up an arm or a leg. (The 'tenacity of the old' affects Christians after conversion as well. The reason we at times have such difficulty with the renewal of our minds is that there is still much in the 'old' way of seeing and living that commends itself to us. Perhaps our Lord had something like this in mind when He mentioned that no one pours new wine into old wine skins.)

Because of the 'tenacity of the old',

Christians may find themselves engaged with elderly New Age people, for example, who may still hold to many of the ideas and values of early twentieth-century secularism, such as Darwinian biological evolutionary theory, Freudianism or perhaps even socialism. Persons raised in the 1940s and 1950s may still retain ideas and values from 'Human Potential' thinking. Folk raised in the 1960s may still be influenced by the ideas and values of the political Left, or humanistic psychology, or illegal drugs. And even younger New Age seekers may cling to 'me first' values and the 'can do' individualism of the 1970s, or values clarification, self-help endowments and so on.

This is all about *people*, and the 'wisdom' model of the New Age is about people. Though we may consider them New Agers, they will carry with them many secular, or even religious, values, principles and ways of doing things. Thus the wise communicator knows that he or she does not have to speak to the person only about 'New Age' things. There are other ways to win these spiritual seekers to Christ. In speaking a Christian message, the communicator may discern that it is more effective to speak to some of the old 'red' bits within the mix.

And it can be quite a mix. The 'me first', 'can do' individual may acquire from the cosmopolitan spirituality an even stronger sense of optimism and confidence about demonstrating human capabilities, as a once *limited* self-potential turns into infinite potential and expression through pantheistic monism. Similarly, ex-Aquarians turned New Age can retain access to altered states of consciousness (ASCs) through a host of available 'psycho-spiritual technologies' that act as trigger mechanisms for exploring new spiritual territory, and thus be free of the legal ramifications and social stigma of hallucinogenic drug use. Or, without fear of too much ridicule, biological evolutionists can cook up theories of spiritual evolution, spiced up from centuries-old Hinduism, Buddhism and Taoism to meet Western tastes. Or those therapists and their clients who are disgruntled with Freudian, behavioural or humanistic psychologies may now opt for New Age versions of Jungian depth psychology or transpersonal psychology, where one learns how to integrate one's 'dark side' into the personality, or how to lift the veil over human problems to reveal traumas and repressions, i.e. bad karma, even from one's supposed past lives.

And the beat goes on. Migration from tradition and materialism towards the new cosmopolitan spirituality is evident throughout the secular landscape. The rational is downplayed. New choices displace initial misgivings. Old 'limitations' are broken through. Inner discoveries feel irrevocably right. Former taboos now line the High Street. Mystical experiences become the way home. Consciousness expansion and exploration provide the fuel. From psychic house parties to cutting-edge physics, impossible dreams become possible. Whether 'the mind's true liberation' is dawning is doubtful. What is clear is that a New Age wisdom is rising in the ascendant of Western culture to become the most prominent constellation of its night. This is our generation and the people to whom we will be speaking. So let us see how to do it.

Part Two

Harmless as a Dove

14

Submarines and Their Destroyers

'Everyone speaks well of the bridge that carries him over,' says an ancient proverb. New Age enthusiasts may speak favourably of the gospel when we have built communication bridges into their world. Without bridges, there will be no understanding of the gospel story. To paraphrase the teaching of the apostle Paul, 'How can they put their faith in Someone whom they misunderstand? And how will they understand without communication?' (Rom. 10:14). Yet even between two old friends communication is not always easy; a married couple celebrating their fortieth anniversary can still have misunderstandings. Is it surprising, then, to expect poor communication to occur between two persons who may not really know each other or who may feel suspicious, even hostile, towards one another?

Building communication bridges is not about reciting the right texts or applying the appropriate formula. Neither is it about learning a bag of tricks or compromising one's beliefs or engaging in a contest of wills. These and other ploys place strains on any existing bridges and may shatter attempts at building new ones. They can generate bitter feelings or animosity that can last for years. This is particularly true when a contest of wills leaves both parties more deeply entrenched in their positions.

Communication bridges are built as a result of forming relationships with people. Some Christians find it difficult to accept this in the context of the New Age. Yet relationships, and as a result effective communication, can be established with New Age seekers without feeling that we have to capitulate to false views or forbidden practices. Such relationships are possible through 'principled conversation'. That is, we will not compromise our convictions, but neither will we force them on someone else. We will not parrot Bible verses, but neither will we downplay the truth.

Most Christians know how irritating it can be when the Jehovah's Witnesses come a-knockin'. It is easy to sense that they do not really want to get to know you. They are usually more interested in reciting certain texts or the party line or whatever strategy they happen to be using in the area that day. Sometimes they want to recite to you whether you want to hear it or not! No one likes to be treated like this.

So we are not talking about gimmicks or formulae or proof texts or even programmes *per se*. We are talking about and to people. Principled conversation will help us to remain morally   responsible   while   developing relationships with New Age people. Our Lord was like this, surrounding Himself with sinners without Himself falling into sin. Our principled conversation, too, will help us to be 'in' but not 'of' the (New Age) world. So, how can we do this?

Submarines and Warships

Have you ever watched an old World War Two film in which Navy warships are searching for enemy submarines? What happens when a submarine spots these warships, either visually or on radar? Panic strikes. Sailors scurry to their posts, klaxon horns blare ominously, the clamour inside the submarine becomes interminable, and over the intercom the voice of command cries, 'Dive, dive!' While this is happening, the battleships may be blasting away with their big guns from a great distance in an effort to stick a few holes in the submarine before it escapes under water. Figuratively speaking, not a few New Age people react like this whenever they see Christians approaching. We look like enemy warships with guns a-blazin', and they cannot move fast enough to get out of the way.

It is not uncommon for a Christian to lose the New Age person below the surface of communication. You are talking to the person and suddenly the horizon is empty! I do not mean that the person has physically disappeared, but that you have lost contact with him intellectually. The person had been buoyant, i.e. listening, conversation had been proceeding smoothly, but then you said or did something, probably unwittingly, that sent the wrong signal to the New Ager's 'radar'. Suddenly he sees you as dangerous and dives below the surface of communication. You have now lost the person intellectually. He is now insulated from what you are saying. He is no longer really listening. Soon he may be leagues away from hearing what you are saying. What we need to do, then, is to learn how to keep these 'submarines' floating.

As we learn how to keep people listening to us, I hope it will be entertaining as well as enlightening to look at the 'Submarine Communications Model'. Illustration 1 (see page 192) shows how we may appear to New Age people, and of course the question is then one of how to avoid appearing so menacing. If we look more inviting perhaps we will be able to prevent the radar from sounding, 'Dive, dive!' The 'Submarine Communications Model' offers ideas whereby we can create conditions that will help us not to appear so threatening. It is about building strong and effective communication bridges into the New Age world. It draws from the biblical model of 'wisdom' (see Chapters 12 and 13) in the context of principled conversation. Its primary aims are to help us change the way we appear and so send better signals in an effort to keep the listener on the surface of communication.

We will begin by looking at eight characteristics that send the wrong signals. But let me make three quick points about them. First, you may not find that all of these characteristics subvert your communication, though you will probably find, as I did, several relevant ones. Let these challenge you to transform your life therein. Second, this is not an in-depth look into these areas: it is intended to stir up our thinking, in the hope that readers will peruse some library or other books on topics they find relevant. Third, the chapter break in the middle of these eight subdivisions is merely a practical device to help us through this section. So, let's now look at these 'alarming' signals.

1. *Failing to relate to persons*. Given certain problems or conditions it can be tempting to forget that people are people. When you think about it, this is probably at the heart of all failed communication. People need respect and recognition. They need to be able to trust. They probably have different backgrounds and viewpoints from ours, and so they may easily misunderstand and get frustrated, angry or offended. In other words, as people they are prone to human reactions. They are not mere things or computers or abstract entities from 'the other side'. Neither are they mere objects upon which we 'do' evangelisation, as if they are a kind of project we are working on. Nor are they viewpoints, positions or ideas. They are persons.

This may seem too obvious to need mentioning. But as it is people Christ saves, along the way we cannot forget that our relationships with New Agers are relationships with people, which places us in the realm of the complex, of the unpredictable, of strong emotions and of likes and dislikes. It may not be as easy as we think, therefore, to show respect and recognition or for trust to develop. Let's think about these three qualities for a moment.

Concerning trust: if we want New Age people to trust Christ as Saviour, we need to ask what hindrances we may be placing in the way of that. Are we making it difficult for them to trust us as the messengers of Christ? Such an incongruity is disgraceful. Why should they trust Christ if they cannot trust us? How will trust develop if in our conversations we are continually *attacking* that which gives the

I'd get out of the way of this battleship, wouldn't you?

person's life meaning, value, integrity and significance, i.e. their wisdom, which provides them with a sense of coherence, purpose and security in their beliefs and actions? Now I do not mean that New Age beliefs do not need to be discussed, and often critically. We will go on to that. Here we are talking about developing trust, and it is hard to see how that will occur if our guns are *continually* ablaze against that which gives our audience meaning and purpose. When I was a teenager, we had a saying if we wanted to argue to prove who was right: 'Jump on my chest, we'll see who's best!' However, this was said with levity and between close friends, not in a budding relationship.

There may be some pride in our hearts if we find ourselves resorting to confrontation all the time. We may be building up self by tearing the other person down in our minds. Let us be alert to the possibility. And let us not assume that we Christians 'have got it all together'. In our building of communication bridges God will be helping us to grow as Christians, in patience, compassion, caring, insight and so on. In other words, everyone benefits from a relationship of trust.

Concerning respect: New Agers have a value as people so high that Jesus Christ died for them. We think highly of silver and gold— temporal inanimate objects. Surely we ought to treasure those for whom our Lord died. Respect is about courtesy and appreciation. It looks past the spiritual baggage and discovers the person behind it.

Sometimes we fail at respect because we rarely give the other person opportunities to say anything. We may be too busy doing all the talking. If so, we are not listening and the conversation is strictly one-way. This attitude may betray that we do not think the New Ager has anything important to say. What happens, then, is that we give out too much information at once. Overloading circuits blows fuses, and communication breaks down as a result. Being short and sweet in conversation, however, and using discretion, helps build respect.

Concerning recognition: a person's value is worth recognising. New Age people are not total idiots. Sin aside, they are people with strengths, insight and normal ways of living. We should recognise and affirm, rather than ignore and downplay, that which is of value in them.

Recognition comes when reassurance is given in an area where the person is obviously right. New Age people have some things going for them, and if you take time to affirm what these are, this brings recognition. Christians often have difficulty offering recognition to New Age seekers. So when recognition begins to take place it can be a powerful means of building a communication bridge.

2. *Identifying with a caricature.* It is not uncommon for our caricature of New Age people to prevent us from relating to them as persons, and *vice versa.* New Age adherents may perceive Christians as behind-the-times Bible thumpers who are narrow-minded, unintelligent, superstitious or a host of other discrediting adjectives. But let's talk about our caricature of them. Effective communication is not made of the stuff of political cartoons or of *Spitting Image.*

Caricatures are often created by labels, and labels can be handy excuses for remaining

intellectually sloppy or lazy. Christians
frequently say, 'Oh, that's "New Age" ', but they
would find it difficult to describe what 'New Age'
is. Using it makes them appear informed, but it
may be a label without content.

Labels can also be depersonalising. I once
read about a psychologist—he must have been
quite honest—who told of how he did a Ph.D. in
Advanced Labelling (Clinical Psychology). He
said that before university he might have
categorised someone's thinking as 'weird' or
'screwy', but after university he would have said
'neurotic' or 'psychotic'! He concluded that such
words might sound more scientific but are no
less alienating and depersonalising. It is not
that labels are necessarily wrong. It is a matter
of usage: tools for thinking or devices for
depersonalising?

Caricatures, too, are often about expectations. We frequently alter our behaviour on
the basis of our expectations. If we have expectations based upon a caricature we shall
probably be responding to a caricature rather
than to a person. We may even be acting in
Christian caricature ourselves, which will
probably heighten the tension of the
conversation because it will affect the behaviour
of the other person towards us.

There is no such thing as caricature-to-
caricature communication. Here, then, our task
is twofold: to dispel any Christian caricature
that may exist in the minds of New Age people,
and to get rid of any caricatures of New Agers
which we may have in our minds. So it is a
two-way street, but I am afraid the onus is on us
to start down the road first.

The words 'Christian' and 'Christianity' are

bad labels these days in much of the media. We
must learn how to get round this. In the 1970s
and early 1980s it was different. Then it was
fairly trendy to be into Christianity. Charles
Colson, for example, had no problems
popularising his testimony book, even though it
was titled *Born Again*. And this was the period
when even American presidents, beginning with
Jimmy Carter in 1976, came out of the closet
about being 'born again'. Things are the other
way round now, which poses a whole new set of
problems.

Christianity is about following Jesus, and
He is still calling people to follow Him. But He
uses His Christian messengers to do this. The
trouble today is that Christianity looks so weird
to most non-Christian spiritual seekers that
they are saying (to adapt Nathanael's words,
when he was called by Andrew to follow Jesus),
'Christianity! Can any good thing come from
there?' (John 1:46).

There is a kind of vague 'background
Christianity' in Western culture now; it is a
distortion, but that is all people know about it.
It is a kind of rumour, and it has changed the
true character of Christianity into a caricature.
Most people, therefore, haven't a clue as to what
true Christianity, with its love and teaching and
Saviour, really is. No wonder there is little or no
interest in what the Church stands for. In
dispelling the caricatures, you will be perceived
as you really are, and Christianity will be
perceived as it really is.

Sometimes you will have to be fairly
creative to get around the Christian caricatures.
During one seminar I was doing on the New Age,
a Christian asked me what he could say to his

friend who was an astrologer. When I asked if the person would come to the meeting the next day so that I could speak to him, I was told no, because the astrologer always refused to attend Christian gatherings. I then asked if he would mind speaking to me by phone. The next day I was told that he would talk to me by phone, and later I had a long conversation with him that way. This was much more profitable than me trying to relate information second-hand. Another time, a YWAM friend of mine and I met some members of a band in a pub, to talk to them about Jesus, because they would not come on our turf. So you may have to be creative.

In order to have communication, both persons must be getting through to each other; they are not engaged in communication if they are speaking to each other's caricature.

3. *Sounding like the demanding boss.* If you want to get off on the wrong foot with New Age seekers, this is the perfect way, as I have discovered. It took me a long time to stop sinking submarines this way.

The Christian sounding like the demanding boss easily threatens the listener who then dives below the surface of communication. Here is the judge, the dogmatist or professor, looking down his nose from behind the podium, lecturing and so creating distance between himself and his audience. The demanding boss is full of 'do not's', 'no's', 'must not's', 'ought not's' and suchlike. He lays down rules and laws. He is generally hypercritical and negative. He points the finger, often with a horrified look, and says, 'You must put a stop to that!' His attitude is that such-and-such is 'nonsense', 'stupid', 'ridiculous'. A New Ager

would never know that a Christian is someone
with Good News when he is being overwhelmed
with so much bad news. On the lips of the
demanding boss, there is no gracious speech
seasoned with salt. The demanding boss often
produces a false, heartless submission within
the listener and walks away feeling mollified.
Or, conversely, he may have promoted further
defensiveness to Christianity, or even rebellion.

To the New Age person, the demanding
Christian boss may remind him of a parent who
used to criticise, lecture or talk down to him
when he was a child. Such a Christian is
stirring up bad memories.

New Ager: I've been taking yoga classes
for three months.
Christian: Oh no! That's not a good
idea. Don't you know where that stuff
comes from? It's . . .

Or:

New Ager: I'm learning about channelling.
Christian: But that's dangerous. It's
forbidden by the Bible. You're not
supposed to contact demons. That's . . .

The problem here is that the New Age
person, now an adult, is hearing, 'Go and cut
the grass,' or, 'Go and tidy up your room,' or,
'Get back to bed.' To this he is thinking, 'Now
look here. You can't tell me what to do!' Such a
person had enough criticism and parental
lecturing as a child. We do not want to set
ourselves up in that role.

When there are responses like the above,

the Christian is mistaken if he thinks the New Age person is listening. Rather, it appears as if the Christian is blasting away, so the New Age person is going to dive a safe distance away from such fire power. Now a Christian may not even see himself this way. He may in all sincerity be doing his level best. Nevertheless, the net result is the raising of a communication barrier or the shutting down of lines of communication that may already have been established. The other person perceives an attack and is sure to get out of the way. He thinks: 'Here it comes again. Another lecture about what I ought not to be doing. He's going to correct me like my father did. He's going to force me into something, like my demanding boss.'

Some people have had so many terrible experiences with demanding Christian bosses that I wonder if they think there is any other kind of living epistle. These people are already well-submerged at the start of any conversation with Christians. Having been offended or wounded, they are going to make certain they are well-insulated and protected in any Christian context. The thing to do, of course, would be to work to refloat these people, to raise them back onto the surface of communication. Unfortunately, what generally occurs is shown in Illustration 2 on page 200.

'The submarine has been located underwater. Can't use the big guns now, but man the battle stations and drop the depth charges.'

I have yet to discern why some Christians think this is a way to refloat submarines. If you discover a New Age seeker below the surface of communication, or if one is about to dive, work

Depth-charge bombs destroying a
submarine under water: an odd way to try
to refloat it!

to correct the situation. Even if it means taking a moment to apologise for upsetting the person, conversational equilibrium must be restored, or you may as well pack up and go home. I was once invited by two friends to speak privately to a medium and the woman to whom he was a mentor. After the five of us had had a fairly reasonable and productive conversation for about an hour, one of my friends accidentally—yet wrongly—called the medium's character into question in a very sensitive area. Though my friend apologised immediately for his *faux pas*, I am not sure that the medium, or the woman, was ever fully with us afterwards on the surface of communication.

Better still, rather than making it necessary to have to restore communication, try to get off on the right foot and remain there. Be harmless as a dove. This means having adult-to-adult communication. This engages both parties in a mature and objective appraisal of *whatever* subject is being considered. Here are two examples:

New Ager: I've been taking yoga classes for three months.

Christian: That's interesting. I know a person who took yoga, but she's not doing it any more. How much time each week do you spend on it? Do you think it's helping you?

New Ager: It's much more than just exercising. There's a lot of meaning in the positions and some of them are pretty strange. I spend a couple of hours a week at it and still find some of the positions difficult to get into. I don't know if it's really helping me or not.

Christian: I've never had an interest in it myself. What got you interested?

Or:

New Ager: I'm trying to progress spiritually as much as I can, so I'm getting into channelling.

Christian: I recently heard someone talking about that. Doesn't it put you in contact with spirit beings?

New Ager: That's right.

Christian: What does that involve? I've never talked to anyone who was actually doing it.

These are adult-to-adult exchanges and communication is taking place. And believe me, when it is, the New Age person thinks: 'This is different. Here is a Christian who is willing to talk to me. He is not lecturing me. He is giving me space to say what I think and feel. I think I will listen to him.' The effect? A communication bridge is being built.

Coercion is not communication. People do not like it, and it can produce undesirable results even if the person knows that what he is hearing is right. People may even reject what they know is true if they think they are being coerced into following it.

I was once in a small group-counselling context once a week for three months. It was led by a wise Christian psychiatrist, and I am thankful that it was. One afternoon a situation arose in which a rather demanding-boss type of person in the group said that he had something important to say to me. Mike, the psychiatrist, being considerate of my thin skin, asked me if I was willing to listen to what this person had to say. I agreed to listen, and I must admit that what came forth, though aggressively given, was accurate. You could have heard a pin drop afterwards when Mike said, 'Charles, you know that what [he] said is true, don't you?'

I said I did, and then Mike continued, 'But what [he] doesn't understand is that you're not going to receive it, are you?'

I replied that I was not.

To which Mike said, 'Would you be willing to explain to [him] why you won't receive it from him?'

To which I burst out, 'Because I don't like being forced. [He] rubs me the wrong way. [He's] being demanding. I have never like being forced, and if I think I'm being forced I will usually refuse to co-operate.'

This was quite an eye-opener for the brother, and probably the rest of the group as well! It did not cross his mind that to me he sounded like the demanding boss or the lecturing parent, and he was astounded to discover that he could share a valid insight and have it rejected because of the way it was delivered even when the listener knew it was true. But there you have it.[1]

So try to be conversational. Think about how you talk to your spouse or a friend concerning a film or a restaurant you would like to go to. Think about how you would discuss getting a pay rise from your employer, or the way in which you would agree with a stranger for the price of a house. You won't get very far by dictating your demands to your boss or the home owner!

4. *Expressing inappropriate emotions.*
Emotions and feelings play a big role in
communication. This means that some
communication headaches are not relieved
merely by understanding a person's thinking.
Getting to know a person's beliefs, assumptions
and viewpoints is to become acquainted merely
with ideas. But people are emotional as well as
thinking beings.

As both parties bring a mix of emotions to
the relationship, emotions which can help or
hinder communication, they will need to
examine how they feel towards each other. So,
how do you feel about New Age people? The
answer can sometimes be discovered by
examining what you think about the New Age.
Thinking often influences feelings, which shows
the relevance of our earlier consideration of
caricatures and labels. Some Christians exhibit
an *un*healthy fear.   Some are nervous,
suspicious, upset, worried or angry. Others are
confident and relaxed. The models for thinking
about the New Age that we discussed during the
'Inter-Mission' may generate certain of these
feelings, and you may want to peruse that
section again if you are wondering about yours.

A suspicious or fearful Christian may trigger
an angry response from the New Age seeker,
who, thinking he is under attack, may become
defensive and stop listening. He may even
respond with inappropriate emotions of his own.
Your tone of voice is important here. If your
voice sounds like rifle shots firing at a target,
how do you think the listener will react? But if
you have control over the tone of your voice you
are probably in control of your emotions. The

best tone is perhaps the one in which it is evident that you are teachable, for it sends the signal of a willingness to be corrected if wrong.

Some people do not think that feelings, emotions or tone of voice matter. A teacher, for example, may say, 'I'm only interested in my students learning the subject. I don't care what they feel.' I must have had an Algebra Two teacher who had this attitude. After several weeks of trying to tell her that I was really struggling with the subject, she remained unconcerned with what I felt, and I dropped the class.

Emotions can speak even louder than words at times. They can communicate a great deal, especially in forming first impressions. With highly-strung people, feelings or *the way* one communicates may be more important initially than spoken words. Should emotions start to run high, step back. Find ways to defuse. Perhaps it would be best to make your feelings known before emotions run high. Being honest about your feelings with the other person (yourself too) can help maintain a conversation's equilibrium. Talking to the other person about your feelings is all right. It does not hurt to say, 'You know, I get the feeling that we are misunderstanding each other. Do you feel this way?' Or, 'I'm sorry for getting upset. I suppose I'm a bit uptight and nervous.' It will feel good to the person who hears you say this. Verbal conflicts that seem irredeemable can be cleared up through the sharing of feelings.

You may find that in some situations the other person will feel free to pour out his feelings after you have expressed yours appropriately. If so, let him. Try not to react. It may be the first time that he has ever felt free to vent his frustrations—perhaps about Christianity—to a Christian. Try to hold your emotions in check and really listen. His feelings may be real barriers to the gospel, and if he can get these out of the way, he may then open up to listen to a Christian. His complaints may even be on target. If so, it is foolish to gainsay or downplay them, which will only make matters worse. Recognition is the key here. Humbly acknowledge any validity in the person's observations, and if possible seek to bring redemptive change to the complaints (more on this later in Part Two). An unwillingness to agree with someone who is obviously right is a sure-fire way to lose the person below the surface of communication, but recognition helps establish trust and keeps the person floating.

Inappropriate emotions may also prevent us from gaining the grace of empathy. It is difficult to see how we can be empowered by empathy when fear, suspicion, anxiety or anger have taken possession of us. Empathy feels a sensitivity towards people that helps us tune into them more fully, rather than the partial focus that comes from zeroing in only on 'the facts'. We may find ourselves conversing with people whose New Ageism becomes a peripheral matter because they are hurting deeply. These people will need empathy much more than a *tête-à-tête* over 'isms'. When we approach our Lord when we are hurting, we know that He has felt what we are feeling and that He will care for us. Will a hurting New Age seeker feel our empathy when he approaches us? If the situation requires empathy more than facts shared coldly and objectively, which of these two kinds of communication will be more valuable for helping the other person feel understood? The day one of my brothers died unexpectedly, an aunt kept whispering in my ear, 'Praise the Lord, Charles. Praise the Lord. He's with Jesus. He's with Jesus.' It was not the words but the fact that she had her arms around me and was grieving: *that* communicated.

As the saying goes, empathy walks in the other person's shoes. If the listener thinks, 'I'm still not sure what he is trying to say, but I can tell by his feelings that he is trying to understand and help me . . . ', then your emotional sensitivity is building a communication bridge, over which you may get a hearing, later, for 'the facts'.

Empathy is most likely to be expressed when we have experienced something similar to that of the other person—the death of a loved one, divorce, separation, childlessness, abusive parent, deceased parents, chronic unemployment, disease, car accident, property loss, time spent in prison, rehabilitation, counselling and so on. Yet empathy can be developed apart from shared experiences through our imitation of God in Christ. In the father-heart of God and in His Son, empathy finds its highest expression. God is 'the Father of compassion and the God of all comfort' (2 Cor. 1:3). The writer of Hebrews states that in Jesus Christ we have a high priest who is sympathetic with our weaknesses (4:15) because He has been made like us in every way (2:16–17). This is the God who, when He became incarnate in Jesus Christ, entered our 'frame of reference' to share in our pitiful condition. The grace of empathy awaits to be gained by those who will be imitators of this.

15

Setting Off the Alarm

This chapter concludes the section on eight characteristics of conversation that are likely to drive the New Age person below the surface of communication. In the previous chapter we considered 'failing to relate to persons', 'identifying with a caricature', 'sounding like the demanding boss' and 'expressing inappropriate emotions'.

   5. *Corking our ears.* Sometimes we are not really listening. This frustrates the person who is speaking. Think of the times you have noticed that someone was not really listening to you. All of us have been exasperated by those conversations in which we are hoping to be understood but the 'listener' is using his mind elsewhere in the universe rather than in the discussion at hand. Being off in another world is a kind of insult and disrespect. It is a disinterested silence; the person is aloof, perhaps wishing he were somewhere else, or bored, or thinking how he will spend the next pay cheque. A form of non-listening that I find annoying is when it occurs to me that the other person has made up his mind that he already knows what I am going to say (maybe he's right!), and while I am talking he is arranging his *a priori* response. Instead of really listening to what I am saying, he can't wait to talk.

Let us be wise so as not to fall into such offensive demeanours. A good listener listens actively. He pays attention. He remembers what he has heard, e.g. the other person's name, whether she is working or unemployed, married or single, children, what areas of New Ageism interest her and so forth. How embarrassing to be arranging another meeting and have to stop to say, 'What did you say your name was?' Surely the person must be wondering what else you were not listening to. James 1:19 says that 'Everyone should be quick to listen, slow to speak.' We each have two ears but only one mouth. Perhaps this is God's way of indicating that we should listen twice as much as we speak.

Listening will help you get a feel for *the other person's* emotions and an understanding of *her* perceptions. What you are hearing might be distorted or muffled by some wrong inner associations (caricatures?) that you have about the New Age, which you may have brought into the conversation. If this is the case, you are not really hearing the person; you are hearing what your inner associations set you up to hear. Try to suspend wrong inner associations and focus on what she is actually saying. This may be difficult if you are fearful or suspicious. If you are confident and relaxed, you could gently interrupt with, 'Is this what you mean . . . ?', or, 'I'm not sure I understand . . . '. Her answer to responses like these could help reveal if you have any wrong inner associations.

The Christian who is listening is discerning. If he is unsure about what is being said, he asks for clarification. The Christian who is listening is therefore learning. The person will respect your gentle questions. She will realise that you are not trying to score points, respond mechanically or recite. She will see that you are trying to understand *her*. (For Christians who do not as yet have a knowledge of the New Age, and so shy away from it for fear of getting in over their heads, finding some New Agers to listen to may easily make up for that. It could be a great crash course!)

Note, too, that understanding is not agreeing. Once the person has indicated that we have understood her, we are then free to disagree gently. We do not even have to like what we are hearing. What is important is that we hear what is being said, and that we do not let inappropriate emotions hinder any response we may choose to make. Without understanding, how are we going to persuade someone in a direction other than the way she has been going? Without understanding what the person's direction is, how shall we convince a seeker of another way? Understanding is a prerequisite to persuasion, and listening is a great qualifier.

Listening actively will also help us discern the person's attitude towards Christianity *without having to ask*. Perhaps there is no problem, but if there is, a chip on the shoulder of a New Age person, a bad attitude, a negative experience, a misunderstanding or bitter feelings could easily contribute to failed communication. Listening will help us discern attitudes without having to embarrass the person about them. We can then work redemptively to get these hindrances out of the way and so establish a relationship.

In *Life Together*, Dietrich Bonhoeffer wrote,

'One who cannot listen long and patiently will presently be talking beside the point and never really be speaking to others, albeit he is not conscious of it.' And we may have to listen for a long time indeed. Even if you are well versed in the subject, your first few times in the presence of New Agers does not automatically guarantee that you will have something to contribute. The 'ministry of listening', then, may be the best service you can render by way of contribution.

Of course, the ideal is that New Age people will also listen to us. I was talking with John Stott once about this, and he called the idea 'reciprocal listening', saying that both parties grow from the conversation. I like that. Both persons further their understanding, both gain. Again, we come to this thing as disciples, that is, as learners. We will also gain insight from the Holy Spirit, who will be speaking to us about the person. After all, He is listening!

There are times, however, when no matter how hard you try, you may not be able to listen because the New Ager is playing a 'mind game' with you or arguing. This once happened to me at the Platt Christian Fellowship in Putney, London. I was doing a public meeting on the New Age, and after the meeting ended I tried to have a conversation with a woman who was deeply involved in *A Course in Miracles*. She began the conversation by asking me what I thought was wrong with it. I took her question to mean that she would be interested in my answer, but just as I began to reply she cut me off sharply. I tried again, and she cut me off again. This occurred many times in the space of a few minutes. She never let me get more than a sentence or two into my response. It was plain rudeness, and I broke off the 'conversation' because she did not really want to know what I thought. It was most likely a game to her, to see if she could rattle me.

6. *Underrating irrationality and passivity.* A Christian's inability to work around these two intellectual/spiritual dynamics can easily hinder communication. These dynamics were the topics of Chapters 5 and 6, where we saw that New Age adherents take on board passivity of mind through meditation, and that the irrational offers them a way of transcending the rational in their efforts at spiritual evolution, enlightenment and mystical experience. During the communication process, both passivity and irrationality are very touchy radar-sensors within the New Ager. Both dynamics must be kept in mind when we are speaking to New Age enthusiasts. During a conversation, passivity is touchy to aggressive Christian witnessing and the irrational is hypersensitive to rational and reasonable spiritual answers. We want to be careful that we do not send wrong signals to either of these dynamics and so lose the person, whose radar may be saying 'Danger, danger! Close the hatches. Guard all entrances. Dive! Dive!'

Because passivity and irrationality act as radar against a biblical Christian witness, it is essential that we learn how to outwit them. One thing can be quickly said about this: it does not involve *us* in becoming passive and irrational! In the following chapters some solutions to this problem will be offered.

7. *Ignoring New Age beliefs and practices.* By this point in the book it will be obvious that

communication entails some knowledge of a person's beliefs and practices, so I do not want to be repetitive. Several ideas about the necessity of research, however, are worth spending a few minutes on here.

Some Christians find themselves outfoxed in conversation simply because they refuse to admit that they are in over their heads. It is not wrong, necessarily, to find ourselves in this situation; yet because it embarrasses us we have a tendency to try to save face rather than ask for help. A New Age adherent is probably well-informed about certain subjects, about which a Christian may know little or nothing. Yet the Christian may try to appear as if he is well-informed. Worse still, he may think that his scanty knowledge about the subject is enough to justify himself as well-informed. The New Ager, however, spots such pretence a mile off. (Recall the times you have seen the holes in someone's position.) Christians who put up false fronts do not earn the right to be heard. They remind me of a gaggle of thirteen-year-olds who traipse out of the school library as if they are the repository of all knowledge and are now set to take on their teachers.

Rather than foolishly putting up a front, a mature response would be, 'I'm not too familiar with that, could you say more about it?' or, 'That's a new one to me, what is it?' Sincere vulnerability such as this is often missing from our relationships. We have not been taught how to be honest about our ignorance. Yet for those who desire to be as harmless as doves in communication, it is a characteristic worth cultivating.

I think it would be helpful, by way of

example, to cite a specific area (it's a big one, and controversial) in which Christian conversation with New Agers often goes haywire precisely because of the above tendency. And along the way we'll try to take hold of some principles to help us respond more appropriately. I have in mind holistic health care, or alternative and complementary medicine.

We may not like the case put so plainly, but we Christians have a tendency towards pride in the area of holism. We read one or two Christian books on the subject, if that, and suddenly think this qualifies us to instruct holistic health-care professionals. Now I am certainly aware of the specious rationales, the groundless testimonies, the preposterous hyperbolising and even the dangerous occult entanglements one finds in holism. However, I am also aware of Christians who are only superficially informed about holism and yet have decided that they know it all. We must be wise enough to see the whole picture and humble enough to recognise any strengths in holism. For example, it calls our attention to the need to develop a health-care system that includes body, mind and spirit. And there is also the need to sort out any scientific–medical validity holism has apart from New Age philosophy and spirituality.

Let's get down to some details. Take crystals as a case in point. There are valid and false uses of crystals. A false use of crystals would be that which assigns a mystical or spiritual meaning to them in which someone then places his trust. In biblical language, this makes an idol out of a created thing; it exchanges the truth of God for a lie, as one worships and serves the created thing rather than the Creator (Rom.1:25). The ultimate horror is that if the idolatry is not repented of, at some point demonic bondage can result. (This is something we may want to learn how to communicate to New Age enthusiasts.)

Here is how I have come to understand this, and you may want to be thinking of a way to put it in your own words, in order to be able to express it to New Age seekers. Throughout the first chapter of Genesis it says that the things God created were 'good'. Whether animal, vegetable or mineral; whether trees, birds or fish; whether sun, moon or stars: it was all *good*.[1] This means there is nothing intrinsically evil about leaves or rocks or birds and bees. To this, the Christian will readily agree. Yet let's get more specific. What if the leaves are herbs and the rocks crystals? Is there anything intrinsically evil about them? No, God created them 'good'. It is in their misuse, by giving them mystical meanings, that the use of crystals goes haywire.

Another example is the palm of the hand. I rather like the palm of my hand. It is a good thing. I wash with it, shake hands with it, steer my car with it. It is used in hugging my wife, in holding a knife and fork so that I can eat, and in receiving an honorarium! But when the palm reader comes along and convinces me that there is a spiritual meaning to my palm, that by it I can read my future, the good thing turns sour, and I would be heading for idolatry if I believed it. So, too, with the moon and the stars. God created them and they are good. Astronomy is the science in which they can be studied. But when I was an astrologer I made idolatry of the stars and the planets and offered people their 'hidden meanings'.

Jesus said that when we know the truth it shall make us free. This truth about created things is very freeing indeed. It means that my wife can hang Swarovski crystal from the kitchen window so that we can see the colourful rainbow designs made by the morning sun shining through them. This is a valid, or natural, use of crystals, and there is nothing wrong with it. Crystals were used in early radio sets, and they are occasionally in use today in chemistry, electronics, photography and biophysics. Such uses are natural and proper. It is another story entirely when people use or wear crystals because they believe in their supposed mystical meanings.

So, too, with herbs. The herbalist who works strictly within a natural use of herbs in a medically valid way is on the right track. Yet in much of what goes under names like homeopathy, macrobiotics or Bach flower remedies there exist mystical and spiritual meanings, interpretations and uses. A 'natural' practitioner who believed this would put himself in jeopardy through his idolatrous misuse of the good things of God's good creation.

The rainbow is another case in point. I have met Christians who seem scared to death of rainbow symbols, often after reading Cumbey's best-seller *Hidden Dangers of the Rainbow*. Yet there is nothing wrong with a rainbow; it is a beautiful and good phenomenon that God has created, and it carries with it a covenant promise from God (Gen. 9:8–17). Where this goes wrong is when the New Age world appropriates the rainbow and gives it a mystical or occult meaning. Christians ought to be speaking into this unfortunate situation to recover its goodness. As someone aptly said to me, 'God holds the copyright on the rainbow.' Yes, and on all the other things He created as well.

The above merely highlights areas where we may have put up false fronts. As Christians, we need to do much more thinking and research. Sorting through medical and scientific writings, as well as the Bible and relevant Christian material, will help us to build strong and effective communication bridges. We will not have to try to save face, and it will give us topics for conversation that New Age people never thought of. We need to answer questions such as: what else in the Bible is relevant to this? Is there any scientific medical validity and natural use of acupuncture, acupressure, shiatsu, reflexology, iridology or other complementary medicines? As to the latter, at the time of this writing and after not a little research (I am not through yet), I have my doubts. And because the jury is still out, at least in my mind, I am not a believer in them. And until, or if, I am ever at peace with any possible validity that may be discovered in any of these practices, I will stay away from their use if they are ever recommended to me as treatments.

The importance of research is therefore unquestionable. It is even commanded in the Bible. Consider these two overlooked passages from Deuteronomy:

> If you hear it said about one of the towns the LORD your God is giving you to live in that wicked men have arisen among you

and have led the people of their town astray, saying, 'Let us go and worship other gods' (gods you have not known), then you must inquire, probe and investigate it thoroughly. And if it is true and it has been proved . . . , (13:12–14).

If a man or a woman living among you in one of the towns the LORD gives you is found doing evil in the eyes of the LORD your God in violation of his covenant, and contrary to my command has worshipped other gods, bowing down to them or to the sun or the moon or the stars of the sky, and this has been brought to your attention, then you must investigate it thoroughly. If it is true and it has been proved . . . (17:2–4).

In other words, if we hear that any sort of counterfeit spirituality has appeared in our towns *or* within the covenant community itself (note the slight but significant variation in contexts), we are not to run around spreading rumours, because they may be untrue. Quality research is to be done to sort fact from fiction, and then to refute the rumours and deal with the facts.

There is an idea floating around in some Christian circles that 'outside research' is unnecessary and that the only requirement for an effective witness is a knowledge of the Bible. To support this, the story is told of bank personnel in the United States who attend a two-week course to learn how to spot counterfeit money. These bank personnel do not receive the kind of instruction one might suppose. They never study any counterfeits. They concentrate on the features of 'real' money. There are too many ways to counterfeit, so the theory is that by becoming skilled in the genuine article they will then be able to recognise any counterfeit that passes through their hands.

I like this as an illustration of how we ought to be getting to know our Lord and the Bible, so that we become spiritually discerning (1 Cor. 2:14–15; Heb. 5:11–14). But this is only half the picture if what we seek to do is communicate what we know to New Age people. Because they do not believe in the authority of the Bible, we will need to have facts from other sources that will be authoritative for them. When they are beginning to trust us, then we can try to move them along to discover the authority of the Bible. So, for instance, we may want to discuss with them the difference between a natural and a spiritual use of herbs or crystals or planets. Or, we could honestly admit that wholistic health care is very biblical, and enter into a discussion about how the Bible emphasises the whole person: body, mind and spirit.

Notice, however, how I spell wholistic when I am talking about the biblical picture. It has been a long-standing contention of mine that we Christians ought to place the letter 'w' to the word and try to recover the good from what has become questionable or wrong. 'Wholistic' would give us a label by which to mark off biblical from non-biblical 'body, mind, spirit' models. It would give us a way to communicate biblical models of health care that emphasise the importance of the whole human being and the interrelationships of its 'parts'. It could give us the freedom to have a wholistic view of health that did not have to be informed by New Age wisdom.

If this could be achieved in the power of the Holy Spirit it would make holism look rather bland by comparison. Then we would have something to communicate! And I think New Age enthusiasts would listen. As it stands now, we have precious little to offer by way of a wholistic biblical alternative.

Another tendency in Christian circles is to overlook research because everything will get changed through intercession or praise marches for Jesus. Now we may not be thinking this consciously, but the attitude may lurk in our presuppositions. In saying this, I am not suggesting that we stop doing such activities. I am asking us to be careful that the activities do not become convenient excuses for not doing research.

If you feel called only to prayer and never to communication, this may be enough for you. But for the vast majority of Christians, research is essential. What tends to happen is that in our excitement about doing 'spiritual warfare', through intercession and praise marches, research comes to be seen as a kind of secondary spiritual activity. So we neglect it. It pales in our minds by comparison with the really exciting stuff of 'spiritual warfare'. And, yet, research is not secondary. It is to a certain extent the second rail of track along which the engine of spiritual warfare runs. This may give us an idea as to why Moses was so keen on research, as we saw in the above passages. Research can give our prayers direction, and prayer can make our research effective when we communicate it. Both ought to run side-by-side to guide the engine of spiritual warfare.

Research is not just about spending long hours in university libraries. Research can be as simple as writing a letter of inquiry, making a phone call or taking a small portable tape recorder and going to interview someone. You meet some interesting people, and you can get to the heart of matters quickly. Research can be enjoyable, gratifying and even entertaining at times. It can be as easy as talking to a reference librarian and then digging around in a few books, magazines or journals for an hour. It never ceases to amaze me what this can produce. Lack of simple research in Jesus' day kept people ignorant of life-saving facts. In John 7:41–42, people are arguing that Jesus came from Galilee and therefore could not be the Christ, who they knew would come from Bethlehem, Judaea. A short conversation with his mother, however, would have cleared this up. So let us be wise as serpents here.

Research, therefore, is essential. It gives a means by which to communicate more effectively. And sometimes during research we discover the falsity of our own assumptions or conclusions.

8. *Failing to separate people from their beliefs.* This eighth characteristic brings us full circle to the first: failing to relate to persons. It is about that common Christian assertion: Jesus loves the sinner but hates the sin. In this and the previous chapter we have concentrated on people; yet still we may so dramatise and hammer away at New Age beliefs and practices that we pound the person to pieces in the process.

It is chilling to find this spirit and tone even

in Christian material and books on occasion. And some of the authors must be feeling their own blows, for they insert the odd sentence or two that says, 'We don't have anything against these people personally. We love them. We're just standing up for the truth.' Yet truth spoken without true love is like trying to coax someone into open heart surgery without the provision of an anaesthetic. We cannot slip a fuzzy sentence about love into material which has the effect of shrapnel exploding all over the New Ager and think that we have done what love requires.

On the other hand, to love people as distinct from their beliefs is not the same thing as divorcing them from what they believe. As we saw during the 'Inter-Mission', people are so 'mixed up' and as one with their beliefs and assumptions that they are held accountable for them. So it gets a bit tricky, but as we have the precedent for it in the gospel itself—Christ dying for the person and not the lie—it is possible.

An idea that has helped me make a proper distinction between people and their beliefs, and so speak right to them, has been to recognise the difference between my roles as an evangelist and as a defender of the faith. Dean Halverson's research brought this to light for me, and it has helped me to be much more at ease in my conversations. The idea is that the defender of the faith, or apologist, will want to make as wide as possible the gulf of dissimilarities between New Ageism and Christianity, while the evangelist will wisely seek common ground between the potential convert and God in order to create a dialogue to close the gap between the two. Halverson cites the theologian Chadwick, who aptly states:

> Paul's genius as an [evangelist] is his astonishing ability to reduce to a vanishing point the gulf between himself and his [potential] converts . . . to 'gain' them for the Christian gospel . . . The [evangelist] must minimise the gap between himself and his potential converts. Very different is the defender of orthodoxy; he must make as wide as possible the distance between authentic Christianity and deviationist sects against whose teaching the door must be closed with all firmness.[2]

Now we know that Paul certainly knew how to defend the faith. Yet he also knew how and when to slip into the other, evangelistic, role. Like the writer of Ecclesiastes, Paul understood that there was a time for everything, a season for every activity—a time to plant and build (relationships), a time to uproot and tear down (false teaching). Prophets, too, fill both roles. Jeremiah, for example, was not only commanded to uproot and tear down but to build and to plant (Jer. 1:10). When trying to 'gain' converts for Christ, we must be harmless as doves here.

We see this closing of the gap between Paul and potential converts as he padded around Athens, a beautiful city known as the cradle of democracy. Yet it was also a city of gross idolatries, everywhere entrenched, from the meat markets to the ivory towers (Acts 17:16–34). It seems that Paul's appreciation of the city's aesthetics and democratic uniqueness

paled in comparison with his grief over a city
'full of idols', which 'greatly distressed' him. Yet
though he was deeply grieved and perhaps
offended by what he saw, he refused to 'jump on
their chests to see who was best'. Sorrow over
their idolatries fuelled his passion for the
Athenians as persons, many of whom were
spiritual seekers, as implied in Luke's reporting
of their time in Athens. Paul saw and met with
people who were 'very religious'. Others were
'devout persons', i.e. God-fearers. There were
also some serious-minded philosophers and
moralists, as well as the body of men called the
Areopagus, who met with Paul on Mars Hill.

When Paul spoke to this human mosaic he
worked diligently *to close the gap* between his
listeners and the gospel. He did this by
choosing ideas from sources that would place
them on common ground with him. For
example, Paul spoke of their shared interest in
the Creation and in the infinity and all-
sufficiency of the Divine Being. He quoted the
poets Epimenides and Aratus, not to flaunt his
insider knowledge of the Greek poets but
because his audience was familiar with them,
and the verses gave him some common ground
to 'close the gap' between them and God. By
mentioning that 'in him we live and move and
have our being' (Epimenides) and 'for we are
indeed his offspring' (Aratus), Paul was in
essence saying, 'I agree with part of your
concept of the Divine Being.' He was not using
his heavy guns on them trying to blow their
idolatries out of the water. Rather, he set aside
his work as an apologist, here, and worked as
an evangelist, which entailed closing the gap
between his listeners and the gospel, that they

might be saved. He set aside attacking their idolatrous beliefs and spoke about what they had going for themselves as human beings. He concentrated on *the people*. He wanted to present them with the message of repentance and resurrection, and to accomplish this he took their minds off false beliefs and concentrated on the real thing.

And wonder of wonders, Paul got their attention even more deeply by using one of their very idols as a springboard for closing the gap! It has been said that the Greeks had the idol to the 'unknown god' (v. 23) in case they had overlooked placating a god in their polytheism. When Paul comes along and says, 'I'm going to tell you who this is', he is in a sense redeeming the thing, and they're deeply interested because it is something for which they already hold an appreciation.

Paul really knew how to capture the imaginations of his listeners. We, too, will learn how to do this as we continue to move through Part Two. In the meantime, remind yourself of Illustrations 1 and 2, in order to recall how we may look to New Age seekers. Then look at Illustration 3 on page 227 to see how we could appear less threatening and much more friendly. If we transformed ourselves into a luxury cruise liner, we would be sending better signals to the submarine's radar. The 'sailors' might even wonder about our destination and contact us to find out where we are going. They might even come on board to go with us. Wouldn't that be a change!

Well, we have made a start. Just before we move on, ask yourself a few questions: do I really have a love for New Age *people*? Why am I

Non-threatening luxury liner: the transformed look

speaking to them? Is it because I have a passion to see them 'gained' for Christ, or merely to prove I am right? Do I care for them, or am I building myself up by tearing them down? How do I really sound? When we are evangelising, we do not want to sound like adversaries but reconcilers.

Be dead honest in answering these questions. If you are unsure, ask a couple of trusted friends to give you some feedback. You see, we like to pride ourselves that we have the fruit of the Spirit. Maybe we do. But I wonder if this fruit is as prominent as it could be in the practical matters of patience, kindness, gentleness, peace, love and self-control in our relationships and conversations with non-Christian spiritual seekers.

16

Out of the Question

There is a national crisis. Journalists, reporters, presenters, television and media people are facing leading politicians with cameras, microphones and notebooks. The public is poised, listening. What will be said? Well, there is one thing that you will rarely hear from the news people at such times. They will not make straightforward statements or assertions about the crisis. They will ask questions, because their job is to inquire. And sometimes they ask very loaded and cleverly worded questions.

Questions call for a response; they constrain the one questioned to answer. A news person who went around pronouncing his conclusions to politicians, saying for example, 'If you hadn't done that, we wouldn't be in this mess,' would soon be out of a job. At the very least, he would not have the ear of any more politicians. But the news person who asks questions will draw the politician into the conversation and the topic. In other words, he helps the politician, who may be in a tight spot, to remain floating on the surface of communication. This principle holds true in most cases: out of the question comes a communication bridge.

If we, too, learn to ask appropriate

questions of New Age people we will draw them into conversation. Even if you do not like me, if I ask you a series of questions—such as: Why are you reading this book? Are you getting anything out of it? How did you hear about it?—each question requires you to think with me and so evokes a response from you. Questions, therefore, attract one's attention and keep one participating in conversation. They help the listener to feel that he is on an equal footing with the speaker, and they help the speaker to present himself as an interested listener. They help change subjects, should the conversation become too intense. They also free the speaker from sounding like the demanding boss or lecturing parent.

'The question' is an effective tool for outwitting the intellectual/spiritual dynamic of passivity (see Chapter 6). We have a lot of truth we want to communicate, but there is a problem. Probably ninety-five per cent of the time when we receive information in Christian contexts (Sunday church services, seminars, reading books and so on), truth is delivered to us in declarative form—a take-it-or-leave-it situation—and this has conditioned us to hammer truth out in the same manner. Now we have already discussed the folly of demanding-boss type messages (Chapter 14). Yet even simple declaratory statements can offend New Age passivity and so shut down listening. This is especially true with New Age meditators, who have been transformed in varying degrees by passivity of mind. Questions will help us outwit passivity so that we will not drive the person below the surface of communication. Facts and truth coming in the shape of questions seem less threatening. When in the presence of New Age people, therefore, we may want to deliver the truth not so much in declarative statements as in the form of questions.

The Bible itself uses many questions. In fact, after the Fall of man, God's first approach to Adam was with a question, for a question can help people deal with painful choices. When Job's counsellors had exhausted their formal theological *statements*, by way of trying to help Job see the light, God deluges him with questions, for questions can open people up to new and different possibilities. Our Lord, too, used questioning to lead seekers into the light, for questions can take a relationship deeper. All of this was done to get at the truth. As blasting away usually generates more heat than light, it might not be a bad idea, therefore, to cultivate 'questioning' as a means of leading people into the truth.

For example, you may find yourself talking to a friend, neighbour or workmate who mentions her growing interest in a New Age subject, let us say reincarnation. Remember, she is taking a risk by opening up to you. She may be sharing something about which she is embarrassed. A few sensitive questions from you will show respect, establish trust and draw her into a conversation in which the error of reincarnation can be dealt with.

You could say, 'I've heard about reincarnation. Where does that belief come from? I wonder how many people actually believe in it. What do you really think about it? Is there any actual proof for it? Where did you hear about it?'

The idea, of course, is not to string a litany of questions together and ask them all at once. Rather, ask one or two and then listen attentively to the answers. You may then want to make a comment or ask one or two more questions. After the give-and-take of ideas and the exchange of information, the other person should be floating on the surface of communication. Your use of questions and the fact that you are listening should not have alarmed any possible passivity of mind.

If the person is 'floating' you now have several options. You may want to end the conversation, or set a time to discuss it later. You may want to change the subject. Or if the person is still interested, you could continue the conversation.

Let us consider the latter option. You could try bringing the conversation around to the Bible, still using questions of course. You could say, 'This is all very fascinating. I've never thought about some of these things. But it's interesting what the Bible says about reincarnation.' Though you have not asked a specific question, you have created the kind of interest that a question does. By concluding with 'it's interesting what the Bible says . . . ', you are probably going to stir enough interest for the person to ask you a question, such as, 'What does the Bible say about reincarnation?' If the person asks *you* a question she is usually ready to listen to you.

Let's go a step further—again, using questions, but now leading into an opportunity to express a biblical view. For example, concerning reincarnation, the Bible does not state anywhere that 'reincarnation is false'. In fact, it never uses the word 'reincarnation'. That reincarnation *is* false, however, is implied by biblical wisdom as a whole and also by the truth of resurrection and individual verses like Ecclesiastes 9:6 and Hebrews 9:27. But it may be inappropriate to haul out your Bible (it may seem like a confrontation), even if she asks what the Bible says. That's no problem. If the person asks, I usually take the 'indirect approach' to the Bible, which allows the truth to be told without scaring her off with the actual Bible.

For example, I would probably respond to her question simply by saying that the Bible does not actually use the word reincarnation. Then in an unhurried manner, I might go on to say that the Bible does give an overall way of looking at 'the next life', but that that precludes a reincarnational view. Then I would pause to give her time to absorb this new information.

You have worked to keep her buoyant on the surface of communication, and she has now given you the green light to bring the Bible into the conversation. This may be the first time, at least in a long time, that she will be listening to the Bible. So you are beginning to move from the use of questions into the area of persuasion, and you will want to be sensitive here. You are offering food for thought, not preaching. This is why I frequently opt for the indirect approach to the Bible, offering the biblical position in my own words rather than quickly lugging out the Book and pointing to verses. Then I will take a step back (in my mind) and ask myself, 'Now what is reincarnation (or whatever happens to be the subject) concerned with?' Well, it is about 'the next life'. I will then think about what the Bible has to say about the next life,

and carefully try to express that in my own
words, keeping it chatty and informal. By this
means I hope to raise the person's level of
interest in what the Bible has to say.

So let's say that she has absorbed what I
have said, taken an interest in it, and asks to
hear more. Here is a progression of thought
that I find it helpful to express at this point:

It is interesting that there seem to be only
three views of what happens after death.
One view is that of complete extinction,
that after death there is nothing else.
You're gone. *Finis*. You are nothing more
than a zero with the rim knocked off. Yet
not too many people hold this view. It's a
bit too pessimistic for optimistic-minded
Westerners.

This leaves them with the two other
choices. One is the reincarnational view,
which is becoming increasingly popular.
As you probably know, if there is any one
universal New Age belief, this is it. It gives
people the hope of a better future after
death, and that many times over.

The third view is the resurrectional
view—a person lives but once and at the
end of his life he comes before the God
who made him, to be judged by Him. This
is the teaching of the Bible, of Jesus, of
the apostles and of the Christian Church.
It is not a popular view, probably because
people realise the moral constraints it
places on them, and we live in a time
when most people are not much interested
in following the moral blueprint of the
Bible. I think this may explain why

reincarnation is becoming increasingly popular. Since the view of complete extinction is too hopeless and the resurrectional view is too morally challenging for most people, they are left with the reincarnational view of the next life. But this is not what the Bible teaches.

Now you do not want to parrot this. You will want to put it in your own words and in a way suited to your personality. As you are bringing your comments to a close, you will want to be ready to pause and give the listener the opportunity to respond. Try to be attentive and discerning. Have you lost the person at some point, or is she still with you in the conversation, floating on the surface of communication? Has she received some truthful food for thought? If so, you have got there through the use of 'the question'. You have been a successful interviewer!

I cannot predict what will be said next. You will have to work with whatever response follows. As you do, try to continue getting at the truth through questions or gentle, respectful comments that create the same kind of interest as questions do.

Let us say that the person says, 'I've never thought about it like that. I'll give it some thought.' If you have had a background like mine, you could round off the conversation with a bit of personal testimony. For example:

Christian: I can relate to what you're saying. Did you know that I once believed in reincarnation for several years?'

New Ager: I think you told me that.

Christian: I even believed in it for the first few months I was a Christian.

New Ager: Really?

Christian: It's true. Then I came across a couple of verses in the Bible that convinced me reincarnation wasn't the way. We could take a look at them later if you'd like. But it wasn't only that that made sense to me.

New Ager: What else happened?

Christian: Well, it's curious actually. It's obvious that the reincarnational and resurrectional views cannot both be true. One cancels out the other. So it occurred to me that even if it were possible for both to be true, I would be foolish to choose reincarnation instead of resurrection.

New Ager: Why is that?

Christian: Well, why mess around with many lifetimes, especially when you can never be sure whether you will be suffering or happy? Why bother with all that when there is a shortcut with guaranteed results in Jesus?

New Ager: Hmm . . . I see what you mean.

Now, of course I have created an ideal exchange here. Yet as we become adept at communicating the truth through the use of questions, conversations like the above will occur.

Another tip: try not to ask the kind of question that evokes only a 'Yes' or 'No' answer. There is, of course, a time for 'right-wrong' kinds of questions, but here you are trying to ask questions that stimulate fresh thinking and create new windows of perspective for people. 'Yes' or 'No' questions merely ask people to affirm their foregone conclusions. This is why I suggested questions such as: Are you enjoying yoga? What are you getting out of channelling? What kinds of spiritual things are especially interesting to you these days? How did you get interested in that?

Open-ended questions like these generate fresh thinking in the New Age person. Just because someone is interested in New Age thinking does not mean that he agrees with all of it. By asking open-ended questions and by listening to the answers, you can discover what someone really thinks about it and how deeply involved he is. This, of course, is going to influence how you move the conversation along. For example, if you presume the person is a serious New Ager but he is only casually interested, then you are going to be miscommunicating.

But what if the person becomes argumentative, perhaps when you appeal to the Bible as the authority on reincarnation? She may have objected, saying that the early Church fathers removed all references about reincarnation from the Bible. She may have said that John the Baptist was a reincarnation of Elijah. She may have said that Jesus was so enlightened that He did not have to reincarnate. It is all right if you do not know how to respond to such New Age ideas. Remember, you are not trying to save face but to keep the person floating. Be honest. Be vulnerable. Simply mention that these ideas are unfamiliar to you, and then *ask* the person some questions yourself such as: Where did you

hear these things? Can I have a look at those
books you mentioned?   You could also offer to
find out what other books have to say, and then
ask her if she would like to meet with you to discuss it further. (See the recommended reading
list for Christian books on reincarnation.)

Of course there is the entire galaxy of New
Age subjects for topics of conversation. I have
just given you some of my reincarnation
homework to get you thinking, but I am not
going to do all of your homework for you! You
must make your own decisions as to what areas
to study and discuss. These may be based on
the frequency with which you encounter the
same subjects, or what the most popular New
Age beliefs and practices are. And the beauty of
it is that by using questions you do not have to
become an expert on a particular subject in
order to be an effective communicator. You
merely have to know how to ask good questions.
In listening to the answers you will learn
quickly. As you are asking questions and
listening to answers, you will begin to discern
pockets of ideas about which you can ask
further questions.

In conclusion I want to say that with
practice you will get used to recognising the
times when you are losing the person below the
surface of communication. It is essential to be
alert to the undulations. If the person is diving,
try to work to correct the situation. Retract or
modify what you said. Apologise. Ask the person what he is feeling. Communicate your feelings. Use humour, especially at your own
expense. Suggest another talk later. Change
the subject. Bring the conversation to a close.
Do whatever it honestly takes to keep the person

floating. You are building a communication bridge and you do not want to place any unnecessary strain on it now; it is going to hold enough strain later.

Be especially sensitive if the person is signalling that he has had enough for the time being. He may not want to hear any more, and he may not want to upset you by saying so, in which case he will be sending out hints. Do not coerce. Let the person back off. You are speaking to someone in an 'unreached people group', which means that even small amounts of new information can be overwhelming to him. The information may seem insufficient, minor or ordinary to you, for you are conversant with it. But to someone in another world it may speak volumes. Whenever you sense that the person wants to bring a conversation to a close, let enough be enough.

After all, the Submarine Model, as you can guess, certainly is not about flooding the person with information!

Perhaps the best policy would be for us to discontinue the conversation before the New Ager becomes inundated with new information. It is all right to leave people hanging. This was one of our Lord's methods. It almost guarantees that the listener will want to hear more later. It takes a certain discipline and humility of mind not to rush ahead. If you take a moment to turn several pages back to the conversation on reincarnation, you will find that I had the Christian put the brakes on his questions and comments at places where he could have progressed to the next point. These pauses and silences were for the purpose of permitting the New Ager time to think. This is one of the initial goals when building a communication bridge, but it does not take long to develop a feel for this.

Perhaps this chapter has stirred up some questions in you. Good!

Signs of Truth

We noted in Chapter 8 that deceptions and lies have a power to fascinate, allure and even to solicit obedience because they are distortions of truth. Of course, the human heart is already deceitful (Jer. 17:9), but that only makes it easier for these devilries to lead people astray.

People get excited about New Age wisdom, therefore, because some of its beliefs deal with 'lost truths' about life. Thus it is scratching people where they itch, temporarily at least, but it is not ultimately satisfying because it deals with the 'lost truths' in a distorted manner. I have found it quite effective to help New Age people to 'undistort' the truth, so to speak, about various matters.

An obvious example is 'spirituality'. Before New Ageism arose in the West, most Westerners were usually closed to discussion about God, Jesus, the soul, the supernatural and similar topics. 'There are two things we don't talk about around here: politics and religion.' How often I heard that as a child. During those years, Christians had to spend time prying people open to talk about the spiritual dimension of life. But we have a head start now. Tens of millions of Westerners are now open to spiritual matters. This gives us an excellent opportunity to build communication bridges because it *is true* that there is a spiritual dimension to life. Thus one of the strengths of New Age wisdom is that it is awakening increasing numbers of people to 'spirituality'. As Christian communicators we can come alongside New Age people and say, 'That's right, there is a spiritual dimension to life,' and then work to 'undistort' what New Age wisdom teaches about 'spirituality'.

Spirituality, therefore, is what I call a 'sign of truth' (perhaps we could call it a 'point of light') in New Age wisdom. People see it, and it is one of the drawing cards. The effective communicator will recognise truth wherever it is found. Jesus Himself at times acknowledged truth when He discovered it outside the 'covenant community'. His conversation with the Roman centurion in Matthew 8:5–13 is a case in point. Jesus affirms the centurion's insights about 'faith'. The effective communicator will learn to do the same thing in his or her relationships with New Agers, who will listen more closely because of it.

The purpose of this chapter is to point out several common 'signs of truth' and to offer suggestions for making the crooked straight. We will have our listeners' attention because these signs of truth, or points of light, already interest them. What we want to do is come alongside these 'submarines' and use the Submarine Communications Model (it will be expanded here) to communicate the 'true truth' of the matter.

• God. New Age wisdom posits a wide variety of God-concepts, with distortions ranging from pantheism to gnosticism. If you find that a New Age seeker is willing to talk about 'God' try to use questions as a way of expressing biblical truth about God. Helpful questions are: What do you believe about God? Where does your understanding come from? Have you ever thought about what the Bible says about the nature of God? What are the differences between God as impersonal Energy and as a personal Being?

You will remember that one of the benefits of the Submarine Model is that you do not have to be an expert to be an effective communicator. Asking questions lets you discover where you may be lacking, and it shows how you may want to respond.

If the person remains open, you will want to work carefully to make the crooked straight. If you have been respectfully listening to the New Ager's view of 'God', there should be no reason why he or she will not want to listen to your view. You may want to offer the idea that God is personal in nature, or trinitarian, or creative, or that He is Truth as well as Love. You could then springboard off these ideas to suggest that we, as human beings, have characteristics such as personality, love, forgiveness and a capacity for truth because we are made in the image of this God.

One idea I like to develop is to help the person understand that the word 'God' is a most ambiguous word and can mean virtually anything or everything until one defines what one means by it. Never take for granted that you know what someone means by 'God', or that he knows what he means by it, or that he knows what you mean by it. Both of you have got to put some clothing on the word and give it an image. Then you can start to make some sense

to each other, otherwise the word 'God' in the
conversation is ambiguous, and neither of you
are really communicating. Helping the person
to give some meaning to his view of 'God' can be
a great clarifier for him. He may decide that he
does not like holding to a thoroughly impersonal
view of God, and you may be the first person to
bring this to light.

Remember, too, to let yourself be
vulnerable. Forget about trying to save face if
you find yourself 'in over your head'. You are in
the realms of theology and philosophy here, and
it is all right to admit your limitations. There
are many other signs of truth ready for
discussion.

• Jesus Christ. The historical Jesus is
another sign of truth within New Age wisdom.
One of the common distortions, here, is when
New Age wisdom makes Jesus a 'cosmic Christ'.
This is what occurs when Eastern religious
thinking informs a person's view of Jesus
Christ; the historical *man* Jesus is held to be
separate and inconsequential to the enlightened
office of 'christ' that came upon Him and
subsequently departed from Him immediately
before He died. *The Aquarian Gospel of Jesus
Christ, The Unknown Life of Christ,* and *The Lost
Years of Jesus* are three popular books that distort the person of Jesus Christ along these lines.

This distortion in particular undermines
the gospel story at the fact and meaning of the
resurrection. Josh McDowell's *Evidence that
Demands a Verdict* is a good book to refer to on
this vital point. This topic can get historically
technical, and you may want to let some
Christian books do your talking for you. You

could say, 'I know of two books which show that
the evidence for Jesus ever having been in India
is highly questionable and probably false. I was
wondering if you would like to read them?'[1]
Even if the person refuses, you have planted a
seed of doubt about the New Age view of Jesus,
and this may be enough for the time being. But
let us say that the person wants to see the
books. If so, I suggest that you purchase one or
both of them as a gift. Offer to do that, but try
to get a firm commitment from the person that
he will actually read the books. This is how I
usually go about it. I will spend money to get
Christian books into the hands of New Age
seekers, but in turn they must be willing to read
them. If the person is merely trying to be polite
and accept a gift that he has no intention of
reading, then I do not need to spend my time
and money on it. One way you can almost
guarantee, before you buy the book, that the
person will read it, is to arrange a time to
discuss it after he has read it.

Another suggestion is to ask the person to
think about what he *personally* believes about
Jesus Christ. Many people will respond by
saying that He was a great teacher or a prophet.

Christian: So, then, you believe what
Jesus taught?

New Ager: Sure.

Christian: Why, then, don't you believe
that Jesus rose from the dead, or that He
is the only way to the Father, or that He is
God incarnate?

New Ager: I'm not sure I follow you.
Where does that come from?

Christian: These are some of the things

that Jesus taught about Himself in the Gospels. And there's no point in saying that Jesus was a great teacher if we are not willing to accept what He taught about Himself, especially His claims to be God and the Saviour of the world. Jesus has not left any opening for us to believe that He was just another great human teacher. As C. S. Lewis has said, 'He did not intend to.'

Another way to provide food for thought here, is to offer the three possible explanations for Jesus' claims. Either Jesus deliberately misrepresented His identity, or He was sincere but deluded, or He was sincere and correct. As someone has said, He was either liar, lunatic or Lord. And now with the New Age view of Jesus as an avatar we have a fourth option. One must make a choice, and we can offer the possibilities to the New Age person.[2]   The idea, here, is to highlight the option that Jesus Christ is Lord, God in the flesh, Saviour and Redeemer. The person may not yet believe it, but in expressing the truth about Jesus Christ you are helping to 'undistort' the matter. You are giving the person something to think about.

• The Fall. Even though New Age wisdom offers people a supposed godhood status and an unlimited potential to create their own realities, it would not get much of a hearing if it refused to admit that something is preventing this from happening. That is, something is very wrong with life, with the world and with us. And of course people know that something is wrong. The issue then becomes: what 'wisdom' are you going to use to explain the 'wrongness'—theft, murder, poverty, injustice, heartache, alienation, suffering, sickness and all the rest? This brings us to the distorted sign of the Fall of Man within the New Age world.

If you ask New Age people what is wrong, they will give any of a number of answers: bad karma from past lives; the failure to integrate the 'dark half' of self into the personality; nothing is really evil or wrong, that is just the way one perceives it. As you are listening to what he thinks is wrong with life, the goal afterwards is to try to coax him around to offer him biblical ideas on the subject.

There is an important point to keep in mind here. I am thankful to the late Dr Francis Schaeffer who pointed this out years ago in his books. There is not much point in talking about what is wrong, i.e. the Fall of Man, if people have little or no belief in Creation. This will be true for most New Age adherents. Schaeffer's advice was to discuss the Creation story first. The Fall of Man, sin, its attendant miseries and death make sense only against the backdrop of the Creation story. By talking to the person first about Creation you have produced a context in which the Fall of Man now makes sense. It may not as yet be believed, but at least the New Ager will have to admit that it makes sense against the backdrop of a pristine creation.

When talking about Creation, it would be important to say that God desires people to have a loving relationship with Him. Historically, 'something' happened to interfere with that, but God had planned the way back should it happen. People can once again have friendship with God just as Adam and Eve did before the Fall.

Notice how the previous paragraph is worded. It is put in such a way as to arouse the listener's curiosity so that he will ask us *what* happened to interfere with that relationship and *what* is the way back into it.[3] In the context of Creation, a discussion about sin and redemption will not seem so out of place to the listener.

Some Christians may think, 'These suggestions are just so much dilly-dallying. Let's get straight to the heart of the matter, man!' However, these suggestions are far from a waste of time. We Christians already have an imagination in which the gospel story makes sense. Not so New Age enthusiasts. What often happens is that we Christians tend to take it for granted that everyone has an imagination in which the gospel makes sense. As a result, we live with a kind of unspoken conclusion that non-Christians understand the gospel but they just do not care about it and are rejecting it, knowing full well what they are doing. Yet many New Agers are not accepting the gospel's offer simply because they do not understand it. They live with an imagination in which the gospel does not make sense. It cannot make sense in the context of New Age wisdom. Our task as Christian communicators is to help their imaginations through a process of transformation wherein the gospel will begin to make some sense to these people. We can accomplish this by creating new 'windows of perspective' in the person's imagination. This is one of the reasons why Jesus used parables, stories and questions. The ideas that constitute the Submarine Communications Model are similar.

New windows of perspective are created in

the person's imagination as we carefully express
the ideas and truths of biblical wisdom. This is
a significant task because slowly but surely it
gives the person an imagination in which the
gospel will one day make sense to him. And like
all windows, they function two ways. They allow
a person to look out and they permit light to
enter in. By sharing biblical insights about God,
Jesus Christ, spirituality and other 'signs of
truth', as well as topics that will be brought up
in the following chapters, we are helping New
Age seekers to see life through new (biblical)
categories of thought.

However, the light of God also shines *into*
the person's imagination through these new
windows. This is exciting to me because the
light of Christ can then enter into the person's
shadowy world, and the coat no longer has to
look like an intruder! Things can be understood
for what they really are. The person may not as
yet believe, but as the bits and pieces of biblical
wisdom begin to fit together in his mind you are
helping him to make a decision to believe. *Then*
doors will be opened for gaining these spiritual
seekers for Christ.

This is the process, and let us not be put off
by it, ashamed, impatient or think that it is a
waste of time. It is not a sub-spiritual task. It
is vital if we hope to 'gain' people for Jesus. If
we work diligently and faithfully here in the
power of the Holy Spirit, we will hear our Lord's,
'Well done.' New Age people need a sound basis
on which to place their faith in Jesus Christ.
Without this there will be false births or poorly
conceived births that lead to backsliding
because they did not understand what they were
doing. Therefore, we want to introduce New

Agers to ideas in which the gospel will one day make sense to them.

• Redemption. Just as New Age wisdom offers reasons for what is wrong with life, it offers hopes for a solution, e.g. enlightenment, higher or expanded consciousness, the round of rebirths, spiritual evolution, asceticism and others. If these come up for discussion, the sign of redemption is nearby.

When you are identifying the person's hope, remember that the word 'redemption' carries with it ideas which the New Age seeker will not understand. Try painting some new windows of perspective by talking about it in terms of being rescued, freed or ransomed, which will help 'undistort' the matter.[4]

We could also help the person come to some understanding about the nature of the various New Age solutions to what is wrong with life. As a general rule New Age wisdom offers either a metaphysical or an epistemological hope of a solution. From the metaphysical point of view I am too small, too little, too finite in comparison to 'God', and the solution is sought in mystical, or spiritual, experiences, by which it is said I can increase my spirit in bigness and so discover my godhoodness. This is why the intuitive, the irrational and the supernatural play an important part in New Age wisdom. From the epistemological viewpoint, I simply do not know enough, spiritually speaking. I am in ignorance about 'God' and my nature as part of 'God', and the solution lies in studying the ancient wisdoms, esoteric religious and occult knowledge, or by meditating upon Eastern religious thought. In this way I can accumulate a wealth of hidden knowledge that will 'save' me. The true solution, however, is not found in a long course of metaphysical shots in the spirit or in becoming wiser than Solomon.

Much can be honestly discussed about our littleness before God and our pint-sized knowledge of Him. But this is not what separates us from God, and therefore the hope of a solution is not found in knowledge or experience. It is found in a relationship, because our problem is a *moral* one. There is nothing wrong, necessarily, with being 'spiritually little' or lacking in knowledge, but there is something unavoidably wrong when we are moral rebels in the universe. It is not increased spiritual size or enlightenment that we need. We need to regain our personal *relationship* with God, which was broken off by our moral failure.

Again, in the conversation you may only be trying to make some distinctions between the nature of various solutions offered to the human problem. For the time being, it may be enough to leave the person thinking that the real solution is not metaphysical or epistemological but moral and relational. We need to get back in orbit around our Maker.[5]

• The Supernatural. A discussion with New Age people about the sign of the supernatural can become highly charged. Be as harmless as a dove here. If you think that the person feels threatened, try to restore conversational equilibrium.

In the New Age world there are many explanations about the nature of the supernatural realm and its attendant beings.

As you are talking to New Age people you will hear about ascended masters, entities, channelled energies, spirit guides, UFOs, Higher Self, the Force and so on. One suggestion is to ask the New Ager why he believes what these spirit beings say. After all, there is no way to give a 'spirit guide' a lie detector test. Maybe it is lying when it says that it is a 35,000-year-old warrior spirit from Atlantis (J. Z. Knight's 'Ramtha'), or a highly evolved being from the seventh dimension (Penny Torres' 'Mafu').

It may be helpful if the New Ager could see that ultimately he has only the spirit being's word on the matter. Could it not be lying? If the New Ager does not think that the spirit beings are lying, ask him why not. Suggest that he ought at least to allow for the possibility that the 'entities' are not telling the truth. Maybe the 'guides' are a Trojan Horse at the gates?

Related to this is the issue of faith, and this too may be something that New Age people have never thought about. Now I do not mean the Christian faith here but the principle of faith in general. There is a tendency in the New Age world to accept declarations from spirit beings about God, Jesus, karma, reincarnation, spiritual evolution, and so on as if they are statements of scientific fact. This is because much New Age literature purports to document scientific evidence to back up its metaphysical and epistemological claims. The literature thus capitalises on the almost unquestionable authority and drawing power that science has today over the minds of Westerners. If something can be made to seem scientific, we are convinced. The problem is that most New Age claims must be taken by faith, faith apart from any real proofs of science.

For example, in states of deep hypno-therapy people have reported events that are interpreted as 'past-life recall' experiences. These anecdotes have piled up over the years and are now considered by many to be *proofs* that we have lived before. The effective comm-unicator will want to point out that there are other significant interpretations for the experiences that are being labelled 'past-life' or 'reincarnational'. The experiences themselves, whatever they are, may at times be real enough, but are they necessarily 'reincarnational'? If a person chooses to believe that the experiences indicate 'reincarnation', he may never have thought that the grounds for this are not scientific but religious faith assumptions.

Not too long ago the British magazine *She* ran a major article on reincarnation. It began by saying, 'Many scientists are finding that children often provide the best reincarnation case histories.'[6] (Notice the many hidden assumptions in that statement alone.) The article then trots out three modern incidents of children claiming to have had past lives. It is not that these children have not had some sort of mental or mystical experences; it is that their betters interpret them as 'reincarnational'.

We can offer New Age seekers two suggestions here. One would be the other ways to interpret such experiences, such as buried memories of events in *this* life suddenly surfacing; people wanting to feel special; adults recalling incidents from historical novels they have read but forgotten until hypnotised; even self-deception or hallucinations. All of which, and more, have been documented as the more reliable interpretations. The other suggestion, which is perhaps valid more often than we care to admit, is that reincarnational experiences in deep hypnosis may be generated by demonic powers.

The author of the article concludes, 'A few years ago I was definitely among those who maintained that a serious belief in reincarnation was simply nonsense or superstition. But looking at the latest evidence, it does not seem so likely any more.'[7] By her use of the word 'evidence' she assumes it to be that which proves the fact of reincarnation, and this is the misunderstanding. What the 'evidence' actually proves is that some people are having strange mental, spiritual or supernatural experiences. That is the only thing it actually proves. But then people want to know what these experiences mean. The question then becomes, by what 'wisdom' are you going to interpret these experiences? If it is a New Age wisdom, there will probably be a reincarnational meaning assigned to the experience, but this meaning is based on a faith assumption that the Eastern religious view of the after-life is the correct one. We will want to point out that the experience itself does not prove the reincarnational meaning to be true. All the experience 'proves' is that you had an experience. There are other ways to interpret the experience, and those meanings, if believed, will be based on faith assumptions, in most cases.

Now this 'faith principle' ought to be brought up in many New Age contexts. The Christian communicator will want to help the person to see that much of what he or she believes is based not so much on scientific evidence as on a leap of faith.   Many New Age people have never considered this to be true, or its ramifications.

A final point, if you will allow me the image, is that you could bring the conversation around to the greatest 'spirit guide', the *Holy* Spirit. How about asking the New Ager why he wants to fool around with an innumerable multitude of 'lesser entities' when he can have a relationship with the Holy Spirit, who is one of a kind? Why not suggest to the person that he can have the Holy Spirit as his own personal Counsellor today, and that you will help him discover how this is possible? Of course, this will mean that first he bows the knee before God and receives Jesus Christ as Lord. But that is what you are there for. You never know what might happen.

• A 'New Age'. I feel a sense of loss that in the sixteen years that I have been a Christian I cannot recall hearing a message preached in the Church about the new age to come (though I did hear an indirect message on this topic *once*). Has this been your experience? Sometimes when I am on the road I ask audiences for a show of hands here, 'How many of you have ever heard Christian preaching or teaching on the new age that the Bible speaks of?' To this, only one or two persons may raise their hands. Nevertheless, the sign of the true new age to come is another muddied point of light that people find in New Age wisdom.

The Bible is not silent about a coming new age; it even speaks of 'coming *ages*' (Eph. 2:7). It speaks of a time and a place where 'There will be no more death or mourning or crying or pain, for the old order of things has passed away'

(Rev. 21:4). Old order? Hmmm! It speaks of a time when 'The wolf and the lamb will feed together, and the lion will eat straw like the ox' (Isa. 65:25), and

> The leopard will lie down with the goat, the calf and the lion . . . , and a little child will lead them. The cow will feed with the bear, their young will lie down together . . . The infant will play near the hole of the cobra, and the young child put his hand into the viper's nest. They will neither harm nor destroy . . . (Isa. 11:6–9).

That is a new age indeed! It is about the kingdom 'of the rock cut out of a mountain, but not by human hands', the kingdom of 'the God of heaven' that He Himself will set up and 'that will never be destroyed nor left to another people' (Dan. 2:44–45). And the Church is a kind of first fruits of this coming new age, wherein is 'righteousness, peace and joy in the Holy Spirit' (Rom. 14:17).

The city of this new age 'does not need the sun or the moon to shine on it, for the glory of God gives it light, and the Lamb is its lamp' (Rev. 21:23). Its river is 'the water of life, as clear as crystal, flowing from the throne of God and of the Lamb down the middle of the great street of the city', and on each side stands 'the tree of life, bearing crops of fruit every month . . . and leaves . . . for the healing of the nations' and 'no longer will there be any curse' (Rev. 22:1–3). New Age? Certainly.

This true new age makes the dawning new 'Age of Aquarius' pale by comparison. In fact, there is no comparison, only contrast.

Astrology's mythology about the 'Age of Aquarius' states that the earth is leaving the 'Age of Pisces' (said to be the last two thousand years, the passing Christian era) and entering into two thousand years of peace and harmony, the 'Age of Aquarius'. This Aquarian mythology has been touted in various forms by 'New Age' people since the late 1800s. It is just getting more publicity in the media these days.

You may want to point out in your conversations that the evidence seems to be *against* any possibility of Aquarian peace and harmony dawning on the earth. Instead there has been an increase in wars, border disputes, starvation, environmental catastrophes, urban suffering, broken homes, crime, poverty, epidemics and suchlike. Despite the fall of the Berlin Wall and the collapse of Communism, at the time I am writing this the US Army has a list of more than forty trouble spots in the world. If we are looking forward to two thousand years of peace and harmony on the planet, and if the past hundred years are indicative of what is to come, it does not look too hopeful.

You may want to ask the person, 'Why are you opting for only two thousand years of peace? Isn't that a bit short-sighted? And besides, what is going to happen afterwards?' Hopefully, the question will trigger the response, 'What do you mean by that?'—to which you could carefully mention that you are opting for an *everlasting* life of peace and harmony. If the person shows further interest, you will have created a new window of perspective.

These are just some of the 'signs of truth' or 'points of light' that one finds within the New Age world. These are its strengths, so to speak, its drawing cards. It will only take a few conversations with New Age seekers before you discover possibilities of Christian witness in these and other areas. When you discern a 'sign of truth' in the conversation, you can either ignore or affirm it. By ignoring it you may well lose the person, but if you affirm it you have the opportunity to capture his imagination and open his mind to what you have to say.

18

Areas of Agreement

Despite the extent to which the Christian view differs from that of New Age people, there is nevertheless territory that they share, common ground. After all, both groups are human and so share mutual concerns and interests. This will occasionally land both parties on what I call 'areas of agreement'. And as with our use of questions and our discussions about the 'signs of truth', areas of agreement, or common ground, provide contexts for building communication bridges. In fact, areas of agreement are perfect for establishing relationships, which we have already noted are essential for ongoing effective communication.

Jesus, for example, knew the background of the 'woman at the well' (John 4), and He had important things to say to her. He found some common ground between them—water—to say it. Consider also the prophet Nathan's 'common-ground language' with David, when he was sent by God to rebuke David for committing adultery and murder. Nathan was in the presence of the king of Israel, who could have had him executed because of what he was about to say, for showing the king his sin. But Nathan's story about the evil done to the poor man's little ewe lamb, which was like a daughter to him, struck a deep chord in David's heart (1 Sam. 12). Nathan's story was a work of art that invited David into the picture. David really related to this, and it then produced what it was sent to accomplish: the king's repentance.

'Areas of agreement' are also superb for helping to dispel the notion of Christian irrelevancy, to erase caricatures, to create new windows of perspective and to establish trustworthiness. Here are several 'areas of agreement' worth reflecting upon.

Global Issues

No one any longer doubts our need to be aware of global problems. Though domestic, regional and national concerns remain priorities, no one with a radio, television or newspaper can doubt that global ills demand urgent political and economic action as well. Our Christian thinkers are going to have to become 'systems thinkers' in a biblical sense, using the wisdom of the Bible to help all of us to think and offer solutions for global ills. Global issues give us quite a large 'area of agreement' with New Age people. Because this is such a large area, I am only going to take up one subject here, to show how we could 'close the gap' between New Age people and the gospel.

The media hype surrounding Earth Days, World Healing Days and harmonic convergences has given many people a global perspective. Since the mid-1980s, principally, large numbers of people have been gathering at selected locations around the world at the same time to think, meditate and visualise world peace and planetary healing. The figures for the numbers in attendance are generally highly inflated, but on the whole the popularity of these 'planetary activation' events is increasing. Participants are in part motivated by friendliness, goodwill and the issues by which they hope to ensure that there is a planet here in the future for their children to enjoy.

'Unity of thought' seems to be their key as they assemble as many like-minded people as possible for a 'global mind-link', to meditate on understanding and trust internationally and on the healing of all global ills, be they economic, political, environmental or whatever.

Organisers know it will be a long, arduous task but are not deterred. To contextualise their ideas they use terms such as: global village, global consciousness, planethood, Gaia, Earthmind and global interfaith peace strategies. They write books, hold symposiums and enter politics. They believe the strength of their movement is founded in everyone's desire for world peace and planetary healing. 'We are world citizens,' they say, 'our thoughts and actions affect each other, so let's all get together and "think peace" instead of war, "think healing" instead of dis-ease.'

The rallying point seems to be the 'planetary activation' events. As far as I have been able to discover, the first of these to be held on a large scale was the World Peace Meditation Day on 31 December, 1986. A very highly publicised 'harmonic convergence' was then held on 16–17 August, 1987. Then came Earth Link Day, February, 1988, and then a massive Earth Day celebration on 20 April, 1990, in memory of the first Earth Day in 1970, which was a sort of turning point, environmentally, for many Westerners. There have been regional events as well, such as Star Link (1988), Crystal Light Link (April, 1989), and Time Warp (November, 1989). Both the regional and global mind-links are considered to have 'thought' both the planet and humanity into varying stages of universal Oneness, planetary healing, brotherhood, love and so on, or at least to have had a transforming effect that ushered people into new levels of consciousness.

Then on 11 January, 1991, came a fairly high-profile planetary activation called 'Opening the Doorway of the 11:11'. This one was held at selected locations worldwide, but it was centred at the Great Pyramids of Egypt and on the South Island of New Zealand. And on 8 June, 1992, there was Earth Chant Day, which was held to coincide with the United Nations Conference on the Environment and Development that took place in Rio de Janeiro.

So the word is getting out. If we all assemble to think, meditate, visualise and chant with one mind we can tap into the universal Oneness of all things to release peace, healing and transformation to ourselves and our world. The idea is that the people participating in these mind-links are 'resonating together' with the universal Oneness of all things in an effort to draw the rest of humanity into it. Many participants believe that they are communicating telepathically or psychically with the universal consciousness and its highly evolved spirit beings, who will help us in solving global ills if only we will co-operate.

Global mind-links seem to have taken a cue from the Maharishi (Mahesh Yogi) who for years, long before the popularity of harmonic convergences, had been telling his TMers that they could lessen poverty and crime and reduce accidents and hospital admissions in their locales by gathering regularly to practise transcendental meditation (TM) in small groups. The Maharishi is now more scientific about it than ever before. He claims (even running expensive two-page advertisements in major newspapers) that it only takes the square root of one per cent of the population of a country practising the 'Maharishi Technology of the Unified Field' (an exponential kind of TM), to transform national consciousness, produce greater health, enliven student awareness and (note this) give nations victory *before* war by 'creating an invincible armour of coherence and radiating an influence of friendliness and harmony that prevents the birth of an enemy'![1]

It may be a different beat, but it is not a different drummer. It's the same old story with a new set of words. The Maharishi's goal for his TMers agrees like soup with water with the purpose of harmonic convergences.

Certainly we can agree with non-Christian desires for global ills to be resolved. But the Christian knows that harmonic convergences, world healing days and 'thinking peace and wholeness' will never solve the fundamental problems. You may be able to talk to New Age seekers about the radical difference between a harmonic convergence and united Christian prayer.

I once attended a festival and heard a Jesuit priest speak on the topic of praying about global problems. By the time he had finished speaking to us, I was unsure if he really knew what Christian prayer was. His idea was a sort of New Age version of prayer. To pray for world peace, he told us to visualise the United Nations building in New York City, then visualise the people inside it changing. To heal the ozone, we were to visualise its holes being healed. And so on. I regret that at the time I did not know what to say. Today I would question him about why he did not tell us to pray that God would bring repentance and grace to the hearts of the people who contribute to the ongoing problems of global ills. You may want to try to bring a conversation around to this.

Ecology

Ecological concerns and the environment are high-priority items in the New Age world. We may not be able to agree with a New Age analysis or solution for nuclear waste disposal, the ozone layer, the diminishing tropical rainforests, industrial pollution and so on, but certainly we can agree that there are real and weighty problems in need of attention. These could provide common ground for building relationships.

For example, when speaking to a 'Green' New Ager (not all 'Greens' are New Age), you may find that he has some good points to make, or, conversely, you may find that he draws from the viewpoint of 'Deep Ecology'[2] for his analysis and solution. It is not possible for the Christian to say Amen to Deep Ecology because its religious and spiritual mantle is pantheistic monism, which is a kind of eco-mysticism. Still, you could have agreeable discussions around any good points the person is making, such as the menace of industrial pollution or radioactive waste.

Conversation can begin with questions such as: What do you think about the deforestation of Brazil and the Philippines? What can be done to prevent a nuclear reactor disaster? What do you know about the Green political movement? How can we be better stewards of the planet?

Remember, when you are listening to the replies, you want to be conscious of your limitations and keep your responses to areas that you feel confident with. Remember, too, that you may have to listen a long time, to earn the right to be heard. When listening to a reply with which you disagree, the temptation is to jump right in with, 'Yes, but . . . '. Yet if this is a new and growing relationship, I would suggest holding off on discussions about areas of *disagreement*. Of course, if the person is enthusiastically floating on the surface of communication, you may want to try out your disagreements; but not dogmatically, I think, with this particular issue. Who actually has the right answers for our ecological dilemmas anyway?

If you should find yourself becoming dogmatic, turn off your demanding-boss persona and restore conversational equilibrium. There is a lot to be said for the calming word 'perhaps'. 'Perhaps I ought to take a look at that more thoroughly.' 'Perhaps I had it wrong.' 'Perhaps that's a better way to look at it.' For the sake of communication bridges, this may be the best approach at times. Later the conversation can be moved to biblical ideas about ecology and earth stewardship. 'Perhaps there's a better way to look at it. Could I tell you about it?'

I was weak in this area until I began to understand that the gospel of Jesus Christ, and the Bible, have a redemptive message for the ecological dimension of life. The Old Testament in particular has much to teach us here.

As part of your research, you might attend a meeting of the Green movement or the Green Party, or read through some 'Green' literature. Some Christians in England are working *as Christians* within the Green Party, partly because they feel it gives them a better outlet than the other political parties in which to discharge their burden for the environment, and partly because they do not want to see the Green Party overwhelmed with New Age thinking.

I have talked with Christians who have a hard time appreciating what their brothers and sisters in Christ are doing in the Green Party. There is a widespread rumour that Green politics is completely off-limits to Christians because it is seen as entirely New Age. In other words, they see much too much that is non-Christian and unbiblical about it. Yet ask yourself if this is not also true of all the other political parties. If it is, why do we hear no hue and cry from Christians that we ought not to get involved in those? I think we are guilty of a double standard here. When we are talking about the Green Party, we are talking about the dimension of life called politics, not the Church of Satan. Surely there is no doubt in anyone's mind any more that God has called some Christians into politics. If we are going to apply a 'taboo' to one political party, we have to apply it to them all, or our duplicity will be obvious to all.

Let us therefore use all available resources, 'Green' Christian politicians included, in our efforts to have something intelligently biblical to say to New Age environmentalists.

Health Consciousness

An increasing number of people are becoming health conscious. They can no longer ignore the large body of medical evidence that an improper diet, for example, can cause a great deal of ill health, and they are now interested in what constitutes sound nutrition and a diet balanced for their individual needs. Some are changing their eating habits to help alleviate allergies, arthritis or migraines. Others are interested in the role of vitamins and minerals and the balance of fats, carbohydrates and protein. It is no longer unknown that foods brimming with saturated fats increase the potential for heart and circulation disorders, that caffeine can cause headaches, that excess weight can shorten life expectancy and that a diet high in refined sugar can produce a host of ills. As a result, freshly cooked foods are more frequently served, low-calorie diets abound, junk foods are eaten less and people are happier and finding themselves with more stamina and energy.

Certainly there is much here that we can agree with. Yet what is happening is that many people now let New Age wisdom inform these areas of health consciousness. That is to say, the cosmopolitan spirituality of the New Age is taking them far beyond any natural or physical interpretation of health concerns. New Age wisdom contains many spiritually false beliefs about health concerns, and this is leading well-meaning people out onto dangerously thin ice. People are going on spiritual cleansing diets, extensive spiritual fasts and relying on unusual substances in the place of basic foods. Others are trusting in mystical-minded herbalists, turning to Zen macrobiotic diets or becoming vegetarian to pay off their bad karma.

One line of reasoning that we could take would be to help New Age people see the difference between natural and spiritual, or religious, uses of health-care procedures, so creating a new window of perspective for them. Many of these people have moved into a religious meaning for health care without being fully aware of what has happened. Take macrobiotics as an example.

I have talked to several people who were either on or had been on a macrobiotic diet because they thought it was strictly something natural. They were quite surprised to discover that macrobiotics is much more than a diet. In their definitive text *Macrobiotic Diet*, Michio and Aveline Kushi (perhaps the leading Western purveyors of macrobiotics) write that 'Macrobiotics is not simply or mainly a diet. Macrobiotics means the universal way of life . . . with which we will maintain our health, freedom and happiness.'[3] Strong claims for a few choice carrots and turnips! Yet the Kushis are even more forthright: 'Macrobiotics includes a dietary approach but its purpose is to ensure the survival of the human race and its further evolution on this planet.'[4]

One senses a kind of 'divinity through eating' metaphysic at the back of this. Years ago, Michio Kushi was a political science student in Japan. There he met George Ohsawa who was a teacher of Zen Macrobiotics. Ohsawa challenged Kushi with a theory about applying dietary principles to solving the problem of world peace. Kushi says that he then stopped studying political science and took up Zen Macrobiotics. Afterwards he lopped off the word 'Zen' and brought it to the United States.

If one is going to use macrobiotics it is not possible to separate the nonbiblical religious philosophy from the way the vegetables are prepared, for instance. The idea is that carrots, turnips, lettuce, tomatoes, potatoes and suchlike resonate with certain subtle universal life-energies, with which they are 'one'. We, too, it is said, are 'one' with the universal life-energies. The vegetables must then be cut and prepared in exactly the right way in order to release these life-energies into the person, that all might be One. Amusing? Don't forget about the foolishness of two different wisdoms.

Now it has been argued that we are just talking about vegetables. Yes, but it also involves the mystical 'energy-meaning' that has been assigned to them. If a person is going to eat macrobiotically it is not possible to separate this religious philosophy from the diet. If the person so eating thinks he has, then why is he still bothered with cutting the vegetables only in a certain way? The religious philosophy teaches that this is done in order to release the universal life-energies of the vegetable(s) properly. We may be able to help the person see the difference between a natural and a mystical use of vegetables.

Another case in point is one's reasons for being a vegetarian. It was for Eastern religious reasons that I became a vegetarian during the latter years when I was a New Ager. This was a logical outcome of trying to live consistently with New Age wisdom. I reached a depth of involvement where I encountered teaching which said that to eat animals produces bad karma. This belief is found in Hinduism, and it is appealing because one can accrue good karma by not eating meat. Since I have never been much of a compromiser with whatever I choose to believe, I had a long heart-to-heart talk with myself and decided to stop eating meat.

As into a pool of cold water, I eased slowly. For a year I did not eat red meat, and then I encountered teaching which said that I would accrue even more good karma if I stopped eating poultry and fish as well. I took that next step 'up the ladder of spiritual evolution'. Now I was a 'lacto-vegetarian'. Really on my way!

Several months before my conversion to Christ I had soldiered on to the next phase to become a 'strict vegetarian', one who eats only nuts, grains, fruits and vegetables. Funnily enough, you find yourself buying much less variety but spending three to four times longer in the grocery store shopping for food. I vividly recall the scene: a tall, thin young man with a Fu Manchu moustache, tight bell-bottoms and long brown hair hanging straight down to the middle of his back; he is standing virtually motionless in every grocery aisle scrutinising the labels of cans and packages to ensure that what he buys is not 'contaminated' by any kind of animal products. It takes a long time to shop that way! The Eastern religious motivation for vegetarianism had me in its grip, so much so that I remained a vegetarian for several months after my conversion to Christ, though I had gone back to eating all foods except red meat.

It was my uncle Louis who helped me sort it out, and he did it during a long-distance phone call to me in which he asked a lot of good questions. 'Have you ever thought that you could start eating meat again?' he asked. After we had chatted about this for a few minutes, he then asked me if I was familiar with the story in Genesis 9, when God talked to Noah after he left the Ark to begin his life again. I said that I was not familiar with it, and then Louis suggested that I might want to read it sometime. 'God had changed things around,' Louis said. 'He permitted Noah and his family to eat meat.'

This got my attention because for years it had been drilled into my head that 'God' was severely displeased with meat-eaters because He was 'one' with animals. My uncle said that this was a common misunderstanding, and that Jesus Himself had to clear it up once when He was talking to the Pharisees. That was news to me too, so Louis suggested that we get out our Bibles and read a couple of passages. I returned to the phone with my Bible and we read Matthew 15:11: 'What goes into a man's mouth does not make him "unclean", but what comes out of his mouth, that makes him "unclean".' We also read 1 Timothy 4:4: 'For everything God created is good, and nothing is to be rejected if it is received with thanksgiving, because it is consecrated by the word of God and prayer.'

I certainly hung up the phone that day with a new window of perspective. Books on vegetarianism had put a fear on me that if I ever ate meat again I would probably become ill, as well as spiritually inferior. Yet after several days of mulling it over, I decided to put Jesus' words to the test. I was not up to cooking meat at home, so I drove to a favourite restaurant. With some trepidation I ordered and ate a really great-tasting beefburger and then waited anxiously for some kind of negative physical or spiritual reaction. None came. And at the restaurant I even bumped into an old friend whom I had not seen in years, and when she asked me what I had been doing lately I talked to her about my recent conversion to Christ. You just never know.

Being able to eat meat again brought much greater freedom into my life. I do not attribute this freedom so much to the actual eating of meat again as I do to no longer being bound to a false religious belief. I had made an idolatry out of vegetarianism; now I was free of that. I do see that people can be vegetarian for strictly natural or medical reasons, and that would be all right. But I have felt such great freedom in this area now that I have not had any desire to return to even a natural kind of vegetarianism.

The above are but a few areas where Christians may find common ground with New Age people on health issues. If none of these are of interest, you will not have to fish around long to discover other 'agreeable' health-care topics for conversation.

Oneness

This large patch of territory also has some shared ground with the Christian. Let us review for a moment. In Part One, we noted that irrational mystical experiences may produce altered states of consciousness that the New Ager thinks are his discovery of the 'oneness' of all things. He makes this assumption because New Age wisdom instructs him that this is what such experiences mean. It teaches that the things of creation are not really individual separate entities but part of an undifferentiated whole. This fascinates many people today who are tired of the great influence of Cartesian science—which pulls life apart to analyse it, and then pulls the analysed bits apart even further. Life becomes fragmentised. We see ourselves as drops separate from the ocean rather than drops *in* the ocean. This three-hundred-year-old habit we have of breaking things up into pieces is said to have led to the fragmentation and alienation that is so much a part of our lives today. It is said to have resulted from overemphasis on Cartesian rationalism. According to New Age wisdom, this has blinded us to an intuitive awareness of the oneness, or wholeness, of all things. The New Age solution, therefore, is to adopt some kind of monistic (oneness) view of life.

Christians would agree that we have indeed lost the forest for the trees. We would also agree that there is a certain interconnectedness and interdependence within the 'things' of the creation. After all, all things are dependent upon God for their existence, and without Him would become nonexistent. Yet it is a little more subtle than that, for the objects of creation, though distinct from each other, share things in common. Take, for example, minerals and leather-bound Bibles. Any 'interconnectedness' there? Let's see.

Minerals are found in soil, which, through the natural 'building blocks' that God has established, the grass 'takes up' into itself so that it may grow. Grass, therefore, is dependent upon soil that is dependent upon minerals, which means that grass, too, is dependent upon minerals for its existence. Then along comes a lumbering, four-footed beast munching grass. The cow's existence is therefore dependent on the grass, which is connected to the soil, which is connected to the minerals. Here, then, is a biblical understanding of the interconnectedness and interdependence of all things. Yet the process goes further. Both the butcher and the leather-binder are dependent upon the cow, and you could be dependent upon both—that is, if you want roast beef on the table on Sunday, after you have read your leather-bound Bible in the morning.

There is therefore a real sense of interdependence among the 'things' of creation, of which the above is barely an inkling. One place where New Age wisdom goes wrong is when it takes this to extremes, either to blur or to eliminate *the distinctions between things* that God has made. The distinctions are not illusory but real. There is therefore both interdependence *and* distinction. But this is not ultimately the case in New Age wisdom.

We can agree that there is a wholeness to life and offer a new window of perspective on it. We must try to help the person get a feeling for the masterly 'substructure' of God's creation. And try to be patient when you come across some of the more eccentric extremes of monism, in which thoughts and actions here on earth are said to influence things even in the farthest reaches of the universe. Personally, I do not believe it. Somehow I find it difficult to believe that I influence the gravity of Alpha Centauri when I tip the dust and fluff off my kitchen floor into the bin.

Shared Sufferings

Grief, tragedy, despair; has any one of us not been touched by them? Divorce, a runaway teenager, a suicide in the family, a friend struck down with a terminal illness; these and a host of other misfortunes may provide common ground for relationship building between Christians and New Agers. Suffering is universal, and it is not unusual to find that disease, adversity or an unexpected loss got someone interested in spiritual concerns. The Christian who finds a parallel in his or her life can speak with empathy here and so build a communication bridge.

This 'area of agreement' is also perfect for Christians who feel they may get 'in over their heads' discussing New Age wisdom. Instead, you could talk about your shared sufferings. For example, in asking a question such as, 'What got you interested in astrology?', you may discover that the person had gone through a divorce and afterwards turned to astrology to find a 'compatible' mate. Now you may be divorced, and perhaps remarried. The temptation here is to push the conversation quickly into the area of the dangers of astrology. Why not set that aside temporarily, show a bit of vulnerability, and say, 'I'm sorry to hear that you went through a divorce. Isn't it awful? When I went through mine it was as if my whole reality had been torn apart.'

> New Ager: It was terrible. When did you go through yours?
> Christian: Almost nine years ago.
> New Ager: I just went through mine last year.
> Christian: It took me a couple of years to really feel as if I was whole again.

Here is adult-to-adult conversation and a relationship is building. All spiritual baggage has been set aside for the time being. With conversation on shared ground, you may find that the person wants to know how you got through your tragedy, e.g. the depression that accompanies divorce. You are moving into the realm of personal testimony here, and it can be quite effective because most New Age enthusiasts are open to personal testimony. They may not believe too much about what you say, but I have never heard a New Ager attempt to argue away a Christian's experience. Yet this is not to say that your testimony is non-influential; it may be very penetrating indeed, though the person may not admit it at first.

If someone is willing to listen, you may want to explain that it was through prayer, grace and Christian fellowship that you were able to cope with the depression. Remember, the New Age seeker probably does not understand prayer or grace, and you are offering him bits of biblical wisdom in an effort to give him some imagination in which he will one day understand these things.

You may be a Christian who first seriously considered the claims of Christ, or came back to Him after backsliding, because of a personal crisis. If you find a parallel with a New Age seeker, you may want to explain that you found what you most needed in Jesus Christ. Again, your testimony can be influential.

You might discover that the person became interested in channelling after a loved one's death. He may explain that he wanted to find some evidence for the soul's existence after death, so he visited a medium, hoping to contact the deceased. This eventually led him into spirit channelling. Instead of jumping right into the dangers of this, you may want to ask if he has found the assurance and comfort he sought through mediums and spirit channellers. If you have had a loved one die, you may want to express how you received assurance and comfort from God. You may even be able to bring a biblical viewpoint of death and the after-life into the conversation.

These and other 'shared sufferings' can be instrumental in bringing comfort into a New Age person's life. They help the relationship develop apart from shared interests in spiritual matters. They help establish common ground with people who suffer and grapple with what it is like to be human.

A brief summary of the principles behind 'areas of agreement' would look something like this: discover places of common ground and begin there; then try to build upon the commonality. As you are doing that, notice the areas where you deviate. Then try to move the conversation along to explain why you believe differently. (Do not forget the submarine's sensitive radar.) If the person remains interested, offer to share further, and then try to arrange times together again.[5]

19

On Being Human

We have noted several times that in New Age wisdom a human being is not seen in strictly materialistic or naturalistic terms, that is, as a biological machine or closed system without any reference to things spiritual or transcendent. The ageing behavourial and deterministic models for 'being human' are seen as old paradigms, and new models that incorporate the spiritual and the transcendent have taken their place in the New Age world. To date, these new models are framed within various attempts to say what it means to be 'body, mind and spirit' from a New Age perspective.

In an effort to give us another powerful area for building relationships and conversing with New Age people, I would like us to explore this from the point of view of 'being human'. I think that New Age enthusiasts are realising their uniqueness or specialness as human beings. Ultimately, this means they are sensing that they are made in the image of God—for it is this that makes us unique. The problem is that they are coming up with the wrong reasons for what they are sensing. Certainly we cannot take issue with the fact that we are unique; as someone has said, we are the 'crown of creation'. We can agree with New Age seekers about this. But we can take issue with the New Age world's

explanations for human uniqueness, for when
its wisdom addresses this significant question,
'all day long they twist [distort] my words' (Ps.
56:5). Most often, New Age wisdom answers the
question of human uniqueness with some
variation of pantheism.[1] And one no longer
need be a philosopher to understand pantheistic
models for what it means to be human, for they
are being made comprehensible and palatable to
the man in the street.

Shirley MacLaine's New Age autobiographies are an example. She and her editors
have found ways to describe and popularise
pantheism. Take just one scene from *Dancing in
the Light*, in which MacLaine is in a trance-state,
talking, so she says, to the 'spirit guide' that she
calls 'Higher Self':

'Then what is the difference between you
and God?' I asked.
'None,' it said. 'I am God, because all
energy is plugged into the same source.
We are each aspects of that source. We
are all part of God. We are all individ-
ualised reflections of the God source. God
is us and we are God.'
[Later in the same dialogue, Higher Self
says,] 'You will each have to deal with your
own inner selves . . . in relation to
knowing that you are God. However, the
discrepancy comes in your not
understanding that every other person is
God also.'
'But down here we believe that people
are people, and God is God, as though we
are separate from God. I mean, almost
everybody believes that.'

'Precisely what is causing the problem,' said H.S. 'You will continue to be separate from each other until you understand that each of you *is* [her emphasis] the God source. Which is another way of saying that you are One. You are having problems with this because your spiritual development is not advanced enough. You each need to become masters of your own souls, which is to say, the realisation of yourselves as God.'[2]

Here is pantheism in pop language, and one can see that if this were true it certainly would be the reason why we are unique. Yet even at this point in her spiritual search (the book was first published in 1985), MacLaine is unsure about accepting pantheism. However, by the end of the book, lest any of her readers remain in doubt as to her 'conversion' to pantheism, MacLaine leaves us with these closing words:

For me to deny the Divine Force now would be tantamount to denying that I exist.

I *know* that I exist, therefore I am.

I *know* that the God-source exists. Therefore *IT IS*.

Since I am part of that force, then *I AM* that *I AM*.[3]

[Her emphases and capital letters]

Though we may find it shocking that MacLaine has used God's words about Himself to Moses—see the burning bush incident, Exodus 3:13–14—we cannot let the fact that we are 'greatly distressed' at the idolatry prevent us from remaining calm and using Submarine Model ideas to speak into this situation. It will probably be fairly easy to bring this topic into a conversation. You could begin by saying that you agree that we are unique, but that there are other ways to account for it.

To offer the biblical alternative, try using the definitive word 'person'. Suggest to the *person* that we are unique not because we are God but because we are persons, created in the image of a personal God (Gen. 1:27). Remember, at this point, that you are trying to create new windows of perspective. Try not to worry if the seeker does not believe what you are saying yet, as you are trying to impart information that he can carry with him and think about.

You may want to capitalise on the person's bewilderment by saying, 'I know this is different from what many people think, and I had difficulty understanding it for a while. I still don't fully understand it, because it is quite a mystery. But I have picked up a few clues about it from the book of Genesis.' If the person remains interested, you may be able to communicate, for example, that it seemed to take three 'ingredients' for God to make a 'person'. One was a physical body formed from the dust into which, two, the breath of life was breathed (Gen. 2:7), and that made Man, three, a living soul, a person.

This biblical idea could be brought into the conversation without hauling out a Bible, and it would give you a context in which to discuss the fixed differences between this and pantheistic models of human uniqueness. You should be careful to say that though the Creation story accounts for human uniqueness it does not support the notion that Man is God. There are certain absolute differences between Man and God. 'Man (is) a limited physical creature . . . totally dependent upon God not only for the origin of his existence, but also for its continuation. Nevertheless, though unlike God in certain important ways, Man (is) like God because Man (is) a person.'[4]

Our being personal, like God, marks us off in certain unalterable ways from other kinds of life. I am so tired of hearing that Man is an animal, however highly evolved. *He is human*. Being made in God's image distinguishes him from the animal kingdom. Dogs may 'hear' commands and 'speak' by barking, but *we* hear and speak not just sounds but language. *We* have not mere instinct but capacities for compassion and understanding. *We* have a mind for thinking and reasoning. *We* have faculties for memory, aesthetic appreciation, moral decision-making and repentance. These and other unique features are intrinsic to our being human. They are what it means to be 'like God' (Gen. 1:26), and they make *us* special— persons—indeed. Pantheism, however, is not content with the uniqueness of being *like* God. It brings its disciples up the mountain by another way, through a secret passage, whereby they think they are God. We can help the seeker make the crooked straight here.

Yet the conversation would be truncated if left at the point of our uniqueness. Our uniqueness is not the whole story, for we live this side of the Garden incident and our uniqueness is now painfully marred. It will be important, therefore, that in our conversations we distinguish between what was sacrificed in the Fall of Man and what was retained of human uniqueness. Again, we are trying to create new windows of perspective. It may be helpful to:

> Distinguish between man as the image of God *before* the Fall and man as the image of God *after* the Fall. Those faculties which are peculiarly human, which designate us as persons—love, morality, reationality, creativity—indicate that we continue to be the image of God after the Fall . . . Since the Fall . . . these faculties . . . have been defective . . . We no longer reflect God's perfect moral character. Though perfect at the beginning, humanity is no longer so. As we pollute our physical environment, so we pollute our moral environment. We pollute because we ourselves are polluted: 'For from within, out of the heart of man, come evil thoughts, fornication, theft, murder, adultery, coveting, wickedness, deceit, licentiousness, envy, slander, pride, foolishness. All these evil things come from within' (Mk. 7:21–23 RSV). In this respect we are unlike God.[5]

It strikes me as amazing that our being in the image of God was not lost in the Fall. Thus, even very idolatrous persons may still sense their uniqueness. Dr Francis Schaeffer used the apt metaphor 'glorious ruin' to describe our current situation. He used the discovery of an old, soiled and deteriorating painting as a starting point. No one was quite certain just who the artist had been, but all were agreed it was done by a genuine master, someone who knew how to use his superb gifts. The decomposition was taken to the proper expert who lifted the stains, unsullied the canvas, examined distinctive brush strokes, analysed the style, discovered the time period and so on. After his careful scrutiny, he was able to declare who the artist was beyond any doubt, even though the work was now in ruins. So, too, when we help people see through sin and fallenness, the great Artist of the human being is revealed. Yes, we are in a state of ruin, but our uniqueness can be traced back to the former glory given us by God.

We have not lost what it means to be persons. This is why we can still approach one another as persons and why we can have relationships with anyone, including the Person of God.

When I was a child we used to play a game called 'Pretend'. You could play a very instructive adult game of Pretend with New Age seekers:

New Ager: I'm not sure I can believe all this stuff about being in the image of God. It doesn't make sense.

Christian: I'm not asking you to believe it until you are convinced. But what if we were to pretend for a moment that it was true? Could you think of any evidence of God's image in yourself or someone else?

New Ager: What do you mean?

Christian: Well, based on some of the things we've been discussing, does any of it make sense? Does it seem to fit our human situation?

New Ager: I'm still not sure what you mean.

Christian: For instance, if God is an impersonal energy, as you say, I have always found that that assumption about God's nature makes it impossible for me to see how I can have personality. I mean, you cannot get personality out of impersonality. You can't squeeze blood out of a rock.

New Ager: In that case I guess it does make sense that from a personal God you could easily get personality.

Christian: That's it. And what else?

Again, this is adult-to-adult conversation. You are showing respect and recognition. You are working to keep the *person* floating on the surface of communication, to dispel his Christian caricature and to create new windows of perspective. This is communication.

In closing this chapter, I would like to say something about the Bible's view of pantheistic beliefs. God Himself seems to take them quite seriously. If the New Age follower is interested in hearing what the Bible says about them, here are my suggestions.

In Isaiah 46:1–2, the prophet disclosed the futility of two Babylonian gods, Bel (sometimes called Bel-Marduk)[6] and Nebo. These were important deities and Nebo was Bel's son, a god of learning and *wisdom*. With stinging wit, Isaiah contrasts the false father–son gods with the true and living God. The former have no life but are heavy loads that must be borne about by beasts of burden. Because of their stone nature, they are wearisome for people who are already tired and burdened and who will be brought even lower by the heavy weight of Bel and Nebo. Later in the same chapter God the Lord is then revealed as life-giver, sustainer, load-bearer and Saviour.

In the next chapter, however, Isaiah becomes specific as to the teaching of Nebo, Babylon's god of *wisdom*. In many ways, Isaiah 47 makes a useful study because it describes a virtual Babylonian counterpart which is like the cosmopolitan spirituality of New Age wisdom in many ways. Here we will only cite its pantheistic element.

One of Isaiah's descriptions of Babylonian wisdom is that it is a 'wanton creature' lounging in its security and saying to itself, 'I am, and there is none besides me' (47:8). (MacLaine appears to be echoing this 'I am'.) Then after prophesying the great disaster that shall come upon it because of its wickedness, Isaiah says 'Your wisdom and knowledge mislead you when you say to yourself, "I am, and there is none besides me" ' (47:9–10).

Seen in the light of biblical wisdom, the linchpin of Babylonian wisdom seems to have been its pantheistic element, the result of Nebo, its god. But notice it is a wisdom that, like the New Age, misleads. There have been wisdoms like this ever since Eve accepted hers from the serpent: 'When the woman saw that the fruit of the tree was . . . desirable for gaining wisdom . . . ' (Gen. 3:6). Wisdom like this is under God's judgement because, among other things, it falsifies the uniqueness of what it means to be human. It drove a man and a woman from the presence of God in the beginning, and it has been the driving force of many cultures ever since. Again, the New Age is not really new. It is 'error' (Isa. 47:15).

Try to recover what it means to be human for the New Age seeker.

20

Flxybl

NEW YORK (AP)—American management has become burdened by imprecise and almost senseless words that disguise sloppy thinking, a professor says, and he blames the academic community for it. He cites such words as mission, vision, empowerment, stress, benchmarking, strategic, consumer confidence, self-esteem, career limiting, bottom line and more, and states that they can mean almost anything or nothing. The erosion of meanings has been under way for several decades . . . [1]

Thus began a newspaper article about the confusion of language in the business world. Change the jargon words and this could have been describing the state of language in the New Age world, which Catherine Bennet of *The Times* aptly described: 'the language buckles, meanings bend—and even then there are no words adequate to express concepts . . . '.[2] In describing and defining 'what is', New Age nomenclature takes great liberty with language and those who have not yet met its obscurity and ambiguity are in for a real eye-opener.

Renaming the Game

Amazing examples of what I call 'changing the nouns of the game' can be found throughout the New Age world, as it *renames* the basic elements, ideas and practices of the old occult, mysticism and paganism. Renaming the game seems to be intentional and done without qualm. For a New Age activist, Dick Sutphen is exceptionally transparent:

> One of the biggest advantages we have as New Agers is, once the occult, metaphysical and New Age terminology is removed, we have concepts and techniques that are very acceptable to the general public. So we change the names and demonstrate the power. In so doing, we open the door to millions who normally would not be receptive.[3]

This presents us with a challenging language barrier, and the advice is being taken by New Agers *en masse*, from the stars to the star-struck. I have already mentioned the book *Spiritual Parenting in the New Age*, in which, perhaps taking a cue from Sutphen, the author boldly tells New Age parents to say 'prayer', not 'magic' or 'spell', say 'ceremony', not 'ritual', and so on. And she calls this the language of diplomacy.[4] The language of diplomacy? To trip up those whom you love? It is more like the language of deceit.

When a leading New Age luminary was asked by a journalist why a spirit would choose to be a Jew slaughtered in the Holocaust, the New Ager seized this opportunity for an abrupt change in terminology. 'Don't call them spirits, call them souls, *souls*—spirits sound oogabooga, occult'.[5,6] In this semantic legerdemain, demons and evil spirits are renamed as 'spirit guides', 'channelled energies', 'ascended masters' and suchlike. Spirit mediums become 'channellers' who 'channel' 'entities', and when they do this it is called 'channelling'. Witchcraft passes as 'Wicca'. Astrology is sometimes called 'Astrograph'. Ancient alchemical and shamanistic practices become 'therapies' within much of Jungian 'depth psychology' and 'transpersonal psychology'. Eastern meditation is rife in classrooms as 'centring', 'stilling', 'grounding', 'going within' and other generic-sounding terms. 'Guided imagery' and 'visualisation' become ersatz terms for occult forms of meditation in which schoolchildren can be taught to contact 'imaginary helpers', 'guides', or 'wise persons', which can be appellations for demonic spirits. (I do not say that visualisation and guided imagery are necessarily demonic, but in the sewers of the New Age world they are, no matter how dressed up in the 'language of diplomacy'.)

When the US Navy offered Eastern meditation it was called 'human resource management training'. I have seen Hatha yoga offered as 'stress relaxation therapy'. Zen macrobiotics is now merely macrobiotics, losing its Eastern religious connotation but not its connection. A methodology for so-called psychic healing, very much like what I was taught as a New Ager in the early 1970s, passes as 'Therapeutic Touch'. It was developed by Dolores Krieger, R.N., Ph.D. It is a kind of New Age equivalent to the Christian 'laying on of hands', and she teaches it widely to Western health-care professionals. I once saw Therapeutic Touch billed as 'the actualisation of potential for therapeutic field integration'. I wonder if Krieger has met the Maharishi somewhere on the occult map. His TM has recently been advertised as the 'Maharishi Technology of the Unified Field'.

I have already mentioned the precedent that Carl Jung set for this New Age newspeak (Chapter 10), but the precedent dates even further back. When the eighteenth-century medical community began to take an interest in seventeenth-century 'mesmerism' they changed the name to 'hypnotism'. And in the late nineteenth, early twentieth centuries the SPR (Society for Psychical Research), snubbed and ridiculed by the materialistic scientific community, hammered out new terms for the old occult in order to bypass the word-barrier of terms such as 'seance', 'medium', 'spirit contact' and other occult-sounding phenomenon. In this way the SPR got 'offensive language' out of the way and so slipped occult phenomenon into the scientific community for study under terms such as 'ESP', 'paranormal', 'parapsychology', 'telekenesis', 'PSI phenomenon', 'clairvoyance' and more.[7] But as Jung himself freely admitted, changing the name of the game in no way changes the nature of the game. The Christian communicator will want to bring this point home to his listeners.

Language is about the words we use to describe and define 'things'. It ought to be a vehicle that conveys coherency and consistency between what we are describing and what it actually is. As our choice of words ought to convey as closely as possible the nature of a thing, the importance of right language goes without saying. This is why 'naming' in Hebrew implies an understanding of the things being named. In the first two chapters of Genesis, for example, the language used shows accuracy between word and object. We see this, too, in the often overlooked Genesis 2:19, where Adam names the animals. He was ever so accurate.

I have said that language 'ought to' reflect the things named because we live in a fallen world in which entropy touches even our ability to 'name' things. If we do not struggle against this downward linguistic spiral, little by little our language reflects less and less accurately 'what is'. If this is not checked redemptively, eventually all reality becomes more and more subjective until it all becomes an illusion (at least in language). Yet long before the finale, the ability to really communicate diminishes greatly. Put a whole world together in which this erosion of language is predominant and you speed up the process. I think this is an accurate picture of what is occurring in the New Age community.

But there is also this to consider. According to the Bible, a corporate confusion of language is a judgement of God upon communities or nations whose idolatries reach very dangerous levels. The Tower of Babel story is an example. A large pagan community had migrated a long way from the mountains to the plains. While in the mountains they met with their gods in the high places, which is often a prerequisite of pagan worship. Now they were settled in the plains, hundreds of miles from the heights. To worship their gods properly—that is, according to their tradition—they had to build a tower 'that reaches to the heavens'. The tower was raised, in a sense, by the 'collective unconscious' of a community that needed access to its gods in the heights. This in turn would serve a secondary purpose: keeping order. The priests could maintain the community's security and allegiance to certain established religious principles through 'tower worship'. Therefore, they would not be scattered over the face of the earth. But when the community's idolatry reached a certain pitch, God judged them at the heart of what held them together: language, which broke down and became a divisive rather than a unifying dynamic (Gen. 11:1–9) and they were scattered.

'Language' therefore is an important area in which we will have to work redemptively when speaking to New Age people. We will want to offer solutions to the problem of 'changing the nouns of the game'.

Redefining Biblical Language

Another sizeable language barrier, besides renaming the game, is the New Age penchant for *redefining* biblical terminology, and even doctrine, to conform to New Age wisdom. Never presume that New Age adherents mean what the Bible means by its terms. When New Age wisdom informs biblical terminology, there will be radical redefinitions and subsequent communication headaches. Those who are unaware of this will assume that both parties were in agreement on certain points because biblical terms were used during the conversation. Both parties, however, may have been miles apart in meaning.

Here is a striking example. In *A Course in Miracles*, the language of the Bible is used throughout to convey New Age ideas (wisdom). (*Course* is now one of the most widespread books of 'spirit-channelled material' in the New Age world.) *Course* implies that 'the true author is Jesus Christ speaking in the first person. As the work progresses, however, it radically redefines the person of Christ, the meaning of the atonement and the concept of revelation. None of these redefinitions is in line with the scriptural teachings of Jesus.'[8]

Course redefines much more. We will look quickly at one area: forgiveness. Throughout *Course*, forgiveness is said to be a key for the healing of relationships. So far so good. Yet after the reader's attention has been caught, the distortion begins. According to *Course*, forgiveness is not about pardoning sin or offence because there really are no such things; they are merely illusions. Forgiveness, therefore, is merely about a change of perception. I only perceived that you sinned against me. *Course* teaches that it was not really sin because sin does not really exist. I only perceived that what you did was sin because of the prevailing Christian ethos in the West. I therefore merely need to change my perception of what you did to me. You really did not do anything to me. This is forgiveness. 'What you thought your brother did to you has not occurred. [Forgiveness] does not pardon sins . . . It sees there was not sin.'[9] 'Sin is the home of all illusions [and stands] for things imagined . . . '.[10]

If this is true, then God Himself has been pretty foolish, for we did not really sin against

Him. Instead of sending His Son to die for our
sins, He merely ought to have changed His
perspective of what we did! *Course*, of course, is
wrong, and in making such wild claims has
declared open warfare upon biblical truth.

We must be alert. We can have a failure of
communication even though both 'people
groups' are using the same language, English.
Remember, two different wisdoms are using
English and there is a failure to communicate
because each wisdom uses the language in a
radically different sense. '[When] we talk the
same language but we do not understand each
other, this must mean that there is a difference
of thought behind the same words—what St
Paul would call a different wisdom, a different
way of making sense of the creation.'[11]   We
discussed this at some length during the
'Inter-Mission', where we noted that very real
communication barriers are created whenever
two different wisdoms use the same language.
St Paul, in 1 Corinthians 1 and 2, spoke of the
foolishness that exists between different
wisdoms. We also noted that 'foolishness'
(between two different wisdoms) is the bridge
that must be crossed before effective
communication occurs. We will discuss this
further in a moment, but first a look at a third
language barrier.

Christianese

In the arena of language, we are not only up
against a renaming of the old occult, paganism
and mysticism and a redefining of biblical
terminology. Renaming and redefining things

are problematic areas *within the New Age world* itself that we must overcome. Another handicap to communication exists within the Christian community, and that is the mischievousness of Christian jargon, buzz words and clichés. When we use them in our conversations with New Agers, misunderstandings are commonplace.

There is the story of the concerned mother who came upon her dejected five-year-old late one afternoon:

'What's wrong, David? How come you're not outside playing?'

'My teacher called me names today,' little David replied sulkily.

'Oh, I don't think Mrs Green would really do that, do you?'

'Yes she did. She called me a scurvy elephant.'

'Well, you're certainly not a scurvy elephant are you? Now you run along and play and I'll call you when it's time to eat.'

'This calls for a quick word with Mrs Green tomorrow morning,' thought David's mother, 'when I drop him off at school.'

'A scurvy elephant?' said Mrs Green with surprise. 'No, no. David was getting a little out of hand yesterday and I told him not to be such a *disturbing element*.'

I am afraid that this is an apt analogy for us. We may be saying something that is clear to us, but it is picked up differently inside the 'submarine'. In general, New Age people will mishear words such as 'born again', 'saved', 'Gospel', 'converted', 'minister', 'share', 'fellowship', 'Lord', 'God', 'Jesus' and many others. Nor will they understand our frequently used phrases such as: 'Jesus died for you', 'give your life to Jesus', 'the blood of the Lamb', 'confess your sins and repent', 'are you saved?' and so on. Words and phrases that fairly gush out of our mouths are by and large not communicating to New Age seekers. This is *our* problem. It is like speaking without thinking. Someone has called it the Christian mouth on automatic pilot.

I have to laugh when I look back to when we long-haired, bell-bottomed hippies spoke the jargon of the Aquarian counterculture in the 1960s and early 1970s. We thought that we were pretty 'hot stuff' and that we had all the right answers. The more zealous among us thought that all we had to do was 'shoot off our mouths' for all the 'outsiders' to see the sense of it and quickly become Aquarians. It was a long time before I realised why we alienated more people than we 'converted'. The longer one remained in the counterculture, the more one's vocabulary shrank. I am not joking when I say that some people ended up with a vocabulary of only one or two hundred jargon words, which only the 'elect' understood.

No wonder our parents, neighbours, teachers, employers, fellow employees, the parents of our boyfriends and girlfriends, acquaintances and others remained outside the Age of Aquarius. They could not understand a thing we said. We understood it; it was in the music we listened to, the books we read, the films we watched and the people with whom we associated. And we assumed, falsely, that outsiders would understand. What a joke! We thought we had the Answer to life, but the only clear message we gave was that we had no answer at all. Our language crippled our message. It was the dilemma of Scotty Briggs in the extreme.

Non-Christians are tone-deaf, so to speak, to Christianese, and we must take great pains to see to it that we are understood.

Words for the Wise and Harmless

So: how can we get around these three language barriers? Let us start with renaming the game. Using the ideas of the Submarine Model, try to call attention to the original language. If the person is into astrology, tarot, spirit mediumship, channelling and suchlike, you could try to paint a window of perspective that would show the adherent the potential for demonic contact. If you have a history like mine, personal testimony could be brought into the conversation as evidence. You could express how it took Jesus Christ to free you from demonic influences that you once thought were benign.

Probably, the New Age seeker will dismiss this and say that it has got nothing to do with the devil. Remember not to sound like the demanding boss. For the moment you are merely trying to create some new windows of perspective and keep the person floating on the surface of communication. You could at least cast doubt upon what he believes. Simply ask the person if he can *prove* that demonic supernatural influences cannot ever be associated with astrology, or channelling. Or, ask how he can be so sure that the Bible is wrong about this. Even if you do not see any immediate fruit for your labours here, you are nevertheless redeeming the language by introducing into the conversation terminology that is more accurate and consistent with the nature of the thing being discussed.

In the second area, the New Age's redefinition of biblical terminology, the best idea is simply to ask the person what he or she means by words such as: 'God', 'Jesus', 'spirit', 'forgiveness', 'love', 'transformation', 'spiritual', 'prayer', 'the holy', 'the sacred' and so on. Give the person plenty of space to say what he means. You may find that he is not too sure himself. After you have listened, try to offer biblical meanings.

And may I emphasise something here. I mentioned in an earlier chapter that some Christians seem scared to death of rainbow symbols. So, too, there are Christians who are paralysed when it comes to using words like 'transformation', 'transcendent', 'paradigm', 'global village', 'holistic', 'green', 'interdependence', 'oneness', and even 'psychology', as well as many others. This is because some Christian schools of thought imply that such words are strictly taboo, as if they were evil in themselves. As a result, Christians who use these words are thought to be closet New Agers.

However, cursing aside, we are not to be afraid of language; we are to be those (of all people) who redeem language. There is nothing wrong with the terminology. The fault lies in the wisdom that informs the terminology. The terminology, therefore, can be informed by biblical wisdom. This is hardly inconsequential. It gives us a means to redeem language. Therefore, 'Let your conversation be always full of grace', that is, redemptive, 'seasoned with salt', that is, tasty, 'that you may know how to answer everyone' (Col. 4:6), including New Age seekers.

So our battle is on two fronts here. One, solving the riddle of renaming the nouns of the game and, two, recovering the meaning of biblical terminology. Each front engages us in the redemption of language.

This still leaves us with the problem of Christianese. Are we speaking so as to be understood or merely setting our mouths on automatic pilot? The very least we can do is help our listeners *try* to understand our biblical terminology when we use it. It is all right to stop and ask the other person if she has understood. She may say that she has. If so, do not take that for granted. Carefully ask if she could paraphrase what you said, so that you can ensure she really has understood a particular term. When you are sure that you have been understood, then continue the conversation.

Yet there is another means that would be good for us to adopt. Besides being careful and clear in our use of biblical terminology, we could try to bring fresh ideas about the gospel into our conversations. New ways of expressing the old gospel can be devised using the thought-forms of today's New Age imagination. This will take some forethought and reflection, but the effort will be well worth it.

When I say 'new' ways I am absolutely not talking about a *new* gospel, a gospel other than that of Jesus Christ. By 'new' I do not mean 'original' in the sense that it has not been around before. 'New' here is about that which is

fresh to one's experience and relevant.
Something like this is behind one of Jesus'
rather curious statements. It is found in
Matthew 13:51–52, in a passage about communication, understanding, Bible teachers and
the kingdom of heaven.

'Have you understood all these things?'
Jesus asked.
'Yes,' they replied.
He said to them, 'Therefore every teacher
of the law who has been instructed about
the kingdom of heaven is like the owner of
a house who brings out of his storeroom
new treasures as well as old.'

The word 'new' here is not about what has
not existed before. It is close to our English
word 'freshness'. Those who are instructed in
the kingdom of heaven bring out something
other than stale bread and stagnant water.
They bring out something other than jargon. As
the Amplified Bible puts it, they bring forth
'the fresh [as well as] the familiar'. As
communicators, they offer to their listeners that
which is satisfying and alive with meaning. It
may be familiar to us but it has to be fresh to
them.
If any reader is wondering just how
important this is, ask yourself this. You are
sitting in church on a Sunday morning when the
preacher says, 'Turn in your Bibles to John
3:16.' Or perhaps it is Romans 12:1–2, or 1
Corinthians 12—14. Insert any passage that
you have heard preached on so many times
that, well, let us be honest, you are tired of
hearing it. And you are tired of hearing it

because it has become a cliché to you, passages so overworked that they are consequently without appeal. Wouldn't you like something other than shop-worn preaching? Wouldn't you like something fresh, the same glorious truths preached from unfamiliar passages? I think we would all like this. We want something fresh and alive, and so do our listeners. We want to turn them on, not off.

I tried to do this in chapters 12 to 14 of *What Your Horoscope Doesn't Tell You*. While writing the book, I put myself opposite myself on the other side of my typewriter and said, 'What would have made sense to me if I had heard the gospel story during my years in the New Age world?' I then tried to put fresh meaning to biblical truth by using some New Age concepts such as spirituality, life after death, metaphysical power and wisdom. This approach has really spoken to some quite dedicated New Age followers.

There are many precedents for this in the Bible. One need only read our Lord's parables to see that He showed a mastery of the thinking of His day and how to use its images and language to communicate. The early apostles and evangelists also faced this problem of how to catch the imaginations of people of different wisdoms. John and Paul in particular show great skill in putting the gospel in the language of their day, and they felt quite free to do this.

John's use of the word *logos* is instructive here. If the early Greeks were known for anything, it was for their search for the ultimate reason or meaning for life, what we would call God. They were part of a tradition that looked for a *single* principle that was comprehensive enough to explain *all* of life, and they felt that this single principle was operating through the mind. Thus for them, the one explanation for the universe and all of life became Reason or, more correctly, Reason that found expression. Their word for this was *logos*, which was commonly used in the religious and philosophical discussions of the day; it was made especially popular by the Alexandrian Jewish philosopher Philo, at the time of Christ. *Logos*, therefore, was chiefly used by the Greeks to signify that which was behind all of life; also thought of as Abstract Reason or World of Ideas. Thus, surrounded by the great jigsaw puzzle of life, the Greeks hit upon the single principle *logos* to explain it all, to give it meaning and coherence, to rationalise and justify what they did and how they lived.

For this reason, *logos* had a strong association with ideas surrounding the creation and that which sustains it. Thus when John used the term to begin his Gospel (John 1:1–3), the Greeks were immediately with him. It struck a deep chord within them. 'Yes, yes,' they might have said, 'we have no trouble with you calling the *logos* God.' Harmless as a dove, John used the language of the day to capture their imaginations. And they would be pretty much in agreement with John until he disclosed that the true *logos* became flesh and blood (v.14). To that the Greeks would not agree. It was unthinkable to them that their Pure Idea, their *logos*, should become 'contaminated' in the evil material world by incarnation in a human body. Greek wisdom precluded that the *logos* could ever take on flesh and bones. Thus they never conceived of the *logos* as a person but as a kind of thoroughly pure spiritual Idea. But John came along and said, 'Look, you're right up to a point. *Logos* is certainly about the creative activity of God, but this creative activity is not a Spiritual Idea or a Principle. It is a Person. Jesus Christ. God the Son.'

John had found some common ground in the contemporary language of his day and he built a communication bridge with it to show them the distinctly biblical Christian truth about the *logos*. His statement that 'the *logos* became flesh' marks off his use of the term from that of Greek wisdom. This distinction would be crystal clear to John's Greek audience, and it would take a humble Greek to bow the knee and accept it. Yet this is what John was aiming at, and he used the language of his day to do it.

Other examples are found in Paul's use of contemporary language. In a previous chapter, we saw that when the apostle was among educated pagans and philosophers (Acts 17:16–31), he used some of their concepts as a springboard to make the gospel known. Paul clearly understood this secret of communication. When he was amongst uneducated rural folk (Acts 14:8–18), he used little religious terminology, which they would have found difficult to understand. Yet when in a synagogue Paul used the overtly religious 'language of Zion' because that was familiar to his Jewish audiences.

This must be part of what Paul meant when he said, 'I have become all things to all men so that by all possible means I might save some' (1 Cor. 9:22). Even Paul's use of the word 'redemption' was redemptive. 'Redemption' in Paul's writings, such as Ephesians 1:7 or

Colossians 1:13, is a picture taken from the slave market. It was a general practice in the ancient world for a slave to be bought and set free from some evil *by being dedicated to a god.* The person became free by becoming a slave, at least technically, to Zeus, or Ares, or Artemis, or whomever. This was called 'redemption'. The apostle captures the contemporary imagination by his use of the term, but then, like John, Paul shows his audience the distinctly biblical Christian meaning and truth of it. 'If you want true freedom, and not just in a technical sense,' says Paul, 'you want the redemption that has been bought for us by Jesus Christ.'

Let us therefore take a cue from these apostles and from our Lord. 'Our business is to present that which is timeless (the same yesterday, today, and tomorrow) in the particular language of our culture',[12] or of the world into which we are sent with the gospel.

> To conclude—you must translate every bit of your Theology into the vernacular. This is very troublesome and it means you can say very little in half an hour, but it is essential. It is also the greatest service to your own thought . . . Power to translate is the test of having really understood one's own meaning.[13]

21

Effectual Prayer

What soil is to seed-time and harvest, so prayer is to effective communication and evangelisation. Thus we do not minimise the importance of prayer but we pray that the lost might hear and believe. In this chapter I do not want to interfere with the way you pray, by weighing one school of prayer against another. Neither will I offer new prayer models. What I have in mind is to suggest several contexts for prayer that seem particularly effective as regards the kind of spiritual seekers we have in mind in this book.

These contexts can then be taken into whatever kinds of prayer models you use. 'The prayer of a righteous man,' wrote James, 'is powerful and effective.' Christian communication is also made possible by effectual prayer. I find this comforting, for it asks the Holy Spirit to be with us in the communication process.

Prayer Contexts

• Pray for New Age seekers to understand God as Creator and the implications of this. Many, if not most, New Age followers think that God is an impersonal energy, and they have also been steeped since childhood in evolutionary views of the cosmos. The gospel story makes no sense in this milieu. It will take God Himself to help these people understand that He created all things. Once that puzzle piece falls into place, it will help them to understand what has gone wrong with life and why the gospel is the Good News.

• Pray that God will send the Holy Spirit to convict the New Age seeker of his sinfulness. This may seem too obvious to need a mention; yet it is a particularly good prayer in this spiritual environment because New Agers, in general, do not believe that they are morally guilty before a holy God.

It was an increasingly weighty conviction of sin, which, interestingly, seemed to come from out of nowhere and was quite unlooked-for, that started the month-long process which ended in my conversion to Christ. During a long, leisurely drive from Michigan to California (I was alone), I suddenly felt horribly guilty of sin. The weight of this intensified daily and was extremely annoying. Worse still, several days after this had begun, I remembered from my childhood religious training where sinners went! I did not see flames or anything like that, but I was thoroughly convinced that I was a sinner, that hell was real, and that I was on my way there.

Try as I might, I could not shake the conviction of God that I was a sinner. This certainly got my attention, I can tell you. For years I had believed that my 'problem' was my bad karma; sin and its consequent moral guilt were *passé*, illusions of outdated religious traditions. I could save myself by paying off my bad karma with my good karma, through the round of rebirths. Of course, it was a doctrine of self-salvation, but it made sense to me. Now I was under daily anguish and despair over my sinful nature, without any hope of a solution. I *knew* I could not save myself.

Furthermore, this 'attack' upon my wisdom was even more frustrating because I did not know where it came from. I did not know that there was such a Person as the Holy Spirit, whom Jesus had said He would send to convict people of their sins (John 16:8). This was a very trying month for me. I thought I was possibly 'cracking up'. Yet it was necessary. It freed me of false beliefs and awakened long-forgotten memories about the truth of human nature and the eternal state of one's soul. Pray, therefore, that the Holy Spirit would convict New Age enthusiasts of their sin.

• Pray for the power of God to dismantle false intellectual strongholds within the person's wisdom and mind. You may have some clues as to what these are, but God will clearly know what they are and how to discharge them from the person's mind.

This may seem an unusual prayer, yet it was the second phase in the process of my conversion. And effective it was, too! During the more than seven years that I studied occultism, meditation and mysticism, tenets of New Age belief organised themselves powerfully in my thinking to become dominant features of my wisdom. These greatly influenced my behaviour, and part of the process of my conversion had to be to get these out of the way. It happened several days after the conviction of sin had begun, and just as suddenly. My New Age wisdom, neatly arranged on the shelves of my mind, somehow disappeared as an authority (power) over me. It was as if God bulldozed the library of my mind, and it left me scratching around in wide open spaces intellectually. I now had no recourse to previously held beliefs about the big questions. And I was now grappling with the biggest one!

It was not that I had lost my mind (well, maybe I had, in a sense!). I could still *think* about karma, or spiritual evolution, or astrology, or meditation, but they had lost their power of appeal to me, completely. What were previously treasured beliefs were now only words; the power that had informed them and had made them fascinating was no longer there. This convinced me that something was terribly wrong with New Age beliefs. They now seemed a fabrication, without substance. In turn, this forced me—I always tried to be honest with myself—to call into question my years as a New Age follower.

This was an important turning point for me for the following reason. I had grown up in the United States, and one of my chief reasons for entering the New Age world had been a thorough disillusionment with the American Dream. The West did not have the Answer, so I looked East. Yet now the Aquarian Dream had been 'blown out of the water'. Where else was there to look? Whatever meaning and power New Age wisdom had had over me, it had now disappeared. Pray, therefore, for God to disarm New Age followers of the power of false beliefs and intellectual strongholds.

• Pray that the New Age seekers would believe in and accept the reality of a loving and living infinite–*personal* God who longs to forgive them. An impersonal God-force cannot forgive.

The best that can be done with it is to manipulate its spiritual laws or principles, like those of karma and reincarnation, in your favour. The problem is that laws and principles cannot forgive you; only a person can forgive. Now if the forgiving Person happens to be the infinite–personal God, then the potential for life is indeed endless and can begin straightaway. This makes the hope offered by reincarnation look bleak by comparison, bleak in the extreme.

It was the hope of forgiveness that brought to a climax my conversion experience. After weeks of anguish, despair and hopelessness— my sins before me like the Empire State Building, myself a speck on the pavement about to be crushed—I broke down and wept bitterly one evening over my sins. It then occurred to me to ask God, though I did not really know what I was doing, to forgive me. But I did not have a clue as to how to go about that. So while kneeling beside a bed in a small hotel room in Costa Mesa, California, in July 1976, sobbing heavily, my face buried in the duvet, I simply said, 'God, I'm sorry. God, I'm sorry. God, I'm sorry', over and over. For what seemed like the longest time I soaked that bed with my tears. Then slowly, though surely, the knowledge that God had forgiven me washed over me. As someone once described it, it was like finding a sea of liquid love. I *knew* there was a God and that He had forgiven me. I had been forgiven, and the heavenly peace that accompanied it was utterly amazing. Pray, therefore, that New Agers would begin to imagine the possibilities.

• Pray that New Agers would have a change of mind about who Jesus is, that they would see Him as Lord, God the Son, and not as merely another avatar in the constellation of Eastern god–men who are dead, buried and gone. Jesus Christ was dead, buried and resurrected. New Age people must see this.

I will never forget awakening the next morning after the night I have just described. The first question on my mind before I even got out of bed was, 'What in the world happened to me last night?' Immediately a Voice as clear as a bell answered, 'You're working for Jesus Christ now and not Satan. Jesus Christ is now your Lord.' I will always recall the words. A thousand lights suddenly went on inside me, and I was soon to understand that this was the Holy Spirit, leading me and teaching about *Jesus*. Just as I had not known that there was a Holy Spirit who would convict people of their sins, neither did I know that He would instruct Christians about Jesus Christ; but God was greater than my ignorance. And after all, He knows how to care for His new-borns. I was later to read in John's Gospel where Jesus told His disciples, 'When the Counsellor comes, whom I will send to you from the Father . . . he will testify about me' (15:26). There was no longer any doubt in my mind about who Jesus was because the Holy Spirit was indeed testifying to me about His presence, power and person. Pray that New Age followers would begin to see the uniqueness of the Lord Jesus Christ.

• Pray that the person's objections to God would be transformed into calling on Him. I think the devil must work overtime to forestall people from asking for God's help. Something 'unfair' happens, a tragedy strikes or an injustice is felt, and the victim responds, 'Why would a loving God allow that to happen?' Reactions like this are common and they have a cumulative effect on people over the years. Many seeds of doubt are sown and crop up to undermine the goodness of God. People start to question His character and purpose, and as a result, they eat the fruit of a great revulsion to the gospel. It is not uncommon for New Age seekers to hold the gospel at arm's length because of such objections. The Bible, however, indicates that during times of personal tragedy, injustice, grave doubt and suchlike, the humble person seeks God out, whilst the proud inveighs against Him and so meets with resistance, finding little or no comfort. Pray for New Age seekers to open up to God, and to have the humility that brings grace.

• Pray that Jesus would deliver New Age adherents from any possible demonic spirits. I do not want to quibble here over moot questions about demonic possession, oppression, demonisation, deliverance ministries and the like. Rather, because I believe—and rightly so, I think—in the existence of personal devils, demons and evil spirits, and because I understand at first hand their suprahuman power and the bondage into which they can bring people, I conclude that prayer should be made to God requesting Him to deal with *whatever* the situation calls for here. *He* is able.

I experienced 'deliverance' too on the evening of my conversion. As a New Ager I had several 'spirit guides'—I had asked for them, and through meditation and visualisation I had increasing *esprit de corps* with them. It was not until the evening of my conversion that their duplicity was revealed to me by Jesus Christ,

and I saw clearly that they were demonic and
not the helpers and friends the New Age claims
them to be. I cannot take the space here to
relate all that occurred surrounding my
'deliverance' that evening. There was some
struggle, and it was unpleasant to sense, and
even at times to hear, Jesus casting them out.
Yet what stands out most in my mind, and this
too is what New Age people need to see and
experience, is that the mighty power of Christ
made the demonic power seem inconsequential
by comparison. It was perfectly clear to me,
during the process, that they knew who their
Master was and that their power was no match
for His. If you meet a New Age person whom
you believe needs to be 'cleaned up' in this
important area, start praying.

• Pray for discernment to become aware of
occasions when a spirit may be 'sitting in' as an
unwanted third party, influencing a
conversation. This, too, may seem an unusual
prayer, especially for those Western Christians
whose wisdom is still too rationalistic. Yet we
will be talking with people whose wisdom
includes a high degree of the irrational, which
gives the spirit world ample opportunity to
interfere. Whenever this occurs I have found
that effective communication ceases.

Certainly this is a foggy region, and I do not
think that it is even possible to make much of a
map, even by way of outlines, before we face
these curves in the road. Which is why we
should rely deeply upon prayer, discernment
and our Lord's immediate help here. One
marker I do see, however, is that this dynamic
seems dissimilar to the classic sense of
possession in which a demon is deeply

controlling someone's behaviour. Rather, it is a situation in which, without notice, a spirit imposes itself upon a conversation and hinders the communication process.

No one must make a theology out of the following experience, or even think that it is a spiritual law. But as it is not someone else's story, I will risk telling it, trusting that it will shed light on certain curious dynamics that not a few readers may have faced when conversing with New Agers, and who may still be wondering about it.

I met Tom when I was a young Christian and when he was slipping steadily deeper into New Ageism. He was single, in his late twenties and up to his neck in numerology. As our relationship developed, I became even more concerned by discovering his serious interests in meditation and mysticism and that he was under the tutelage of a New Age 'prophetess', whom I eventually met. When Tom told me that he was leaving his job in Michigan to move into a monastery in California, I thought that maybe he had had a secret interest in Christianity which was now beginning to show. But when I asked what kind of monastery, he told me it was a Hindu ashram. (A good illustration of changing the nouns of the game.)

During the months in which I had been building a relationship with Tom, we had established a fair amount of trust and respect for one another. I had worked hard to dispel his caricature of Christians and to keep him floating on the surface of communication. Because of his impending jaunt to the ashram, I felt it was time to have a heart-to-heart talk with him about the dangers of the New Age and the truth of the gospel. I felt that he was 'floating' solidly enough and that I could have this conversation without losing him below the surface. If he was determined to enter an ashram, I was determined he would go there with some new windows of perspective, at least.

We set a day to have lunch at a restaurant near where we worked. The day came, and for the first half-hour our luncheon conversation went smoothly, even though we were not talking merely superficially about the New Age and Christianity. We were listening intently to one another, commenting, and a clear though weighty exchange of ideas was taking place until . . . Subtly (when I look back though, I see it was an unmistakable shift) it became difficult for me to answer Tom's questions in such a way that he was 'taking them on board'. I didn't think I had lost him below the surface; so I did not know what to do. Yet this was only part of the sudden 'new dynamic'. Tom began saying things in a manner that made it extremely difficult for me to make my points. Then, when I knew that a point had got through, instead of his usual habit of mulling it over, he would immediately respond in such a way as to gainsay it. This became very disconcerting because whatever I said next was being answered with powerful (ir)rationalisations that left me befuddled. Soon it was hard to get a word in edgeways, and this was out of character for Tom.

I wondered what was happening, though I do have a confession to make. When the 'atmosphere' began to change, I got the impression that I ought to halt the conversation in order to pray. However, I let the opportunity pass. Rationalisations for not praying controlled my actions. 'It's ridiculous to start praying in a crowded restaurant, too embarrassing.' After I failed to act upon the inner urge, I watched our conversation deteriorate until it was evident to us both that there was nothing else to do except pay the bill and return to work. The thing was, I had not lost Tom below the surface of communication; something else had happened. Some dynamic that I was unfamiliar with had ruined our conversation.

Several months later I happened to be talking to a Christian couple who provided a clue. 'Your conversation with Tom,' they said, 'reached a point where a spirit "surfaced" and you were no longer engaged in conversation with Tom alone. The spirit's presence scrambled the conversation and probably fed Tom all kinds of unusual input to disrupt communication. It was as if you were no longer talking with Tom.' I said that this sounded a bit extreme to me, but they suggested that I think it over and pray about it. They concluded, 'Perhaps now you can see why the Lord wanted you to stop and pray.'

I now think that there is sense in what they said. Tom had indulged in occultic New Age beliefs and practices for a long time, to the point that he had become, to some extent, demonically influenced. When the spirit 'surfaced' to become part of the conversational dynamic, communication became confused, argumentative and at times irrational. I now believe that had I had the nerve to stop and pray I might have received discernment about this, and then in the power of God prayed to bind this spirit from interfering.

Now before we move on, please do not leave this chapter thinking that Strohmer believes or says that every conversation with a New Ager is a talk with a demon. Conversation is often ineffective or breaks down simply due to human denseness, that is to say either party may lack basic communication skills or be ignorant of one another's wisdom. For others, however, a little bell will have rung, as the story illustrates some 'outside interference' they may at times have faced.[1] Through prayer we can become aware of yet another device of our common enemy to frustrate effective Christian communication.

 • Pray about any wounds, bitterness or similar obstacles that the person may have towards Christianity. It is not uncommon that New Age people have had injuries which make them resistant to the gospel, and these may have come from Christian sources. If you discover this, it may be best, for the time being, to make it a matter for prayer rather than trying to help the person sort it out. Or, if the person is ill, or perhaps suffering from an inner wound that is unrelated to being hurt by a Christian, you may want to ask if you could pray for him or her. You never know, this may demonstrate for the person the reality of a personal God who hears and answers our prayers. It could reveal God much more effectively than our words ever could. And if healing occurs, this could give you a context to discuss the differences between answered prayer and New Age explanations for healing.

 • Pray that God will give you the grace to work around the intellectual/spiritual dynamics of irrationality and passivity. We have much more than human resources available to us during our conversations. We have not only God's power but also His wit and wisdom to help us keep the person floating on the surface of communication, even in the face of the irrational and of passivity of mind. Pray for God's grace to help you remain level-headed here.

 • Pray that God would prepare specific groups of people within the New Age world to be saved. Our tendency is to pray for individuals; yet if certain groups of New Age people became Christians it would boost the gospel's impact in that world considerably.

Consider the following. In the nineteenth century, when there was a great disparity between Western Christians and Eastern cultures, Christians often went into these cultures to preach by setting up exploratory mission stations. These missionaries

> acquired a piece of land, often with great difficulty. They built residences suitable for white men. Then they added churches, schools, quarters to house helpers, hospitals, leprosy homes, orphanages and printing establishments. The mission station was usually at the centre of the village or tribe. From it, extensive tours were made into the surrounding country-side. It was the home of the missionary staff and all the activities of the mission took place around the station.[2]

These mission stations remind me of attempts to set up Christian booths at 'Body, Mind, Spirit' festivals, or of sallying forth from our suburban churches to Glastonbury once a year. I am certainly not opposed to this, and it does pluck the odd brand from the fire. But why should we have to settle for that? The

Christians who worked in the mission stations described above will tell you that that kind of missionary approach was never very successful at winning large numbers of people for Christ. It was successful, however, at identifying what 'peoples' were ready to become Christians, and therefore in what directions missionary efforts could usefully be made.

At the time I am writing this, it is my opinion that New Agers as a 'people group' are uninterested in becoming Christians, but how about if we could begin identifying groups within the New Age world which show some deepening interest? If we knew which groups, we could go to *them*. It has been theorised by more then one missionary leader that this was how the apostle Paul went into various Gentile populations to win converts. We know that he had the leading of the Holy Spirit, but he also had his common sense. He probably identified Gentile families who had some interest in the gospel, and then he went to them. How did he identify them? He could easily have had conversations with his Jewish converts who knew Gentiles. Or, once he gained certain Gentiles for Christ, he could easily have asked them who he might go to next. Such information would have been especially useful if the Gentiles were respected in the community, which might have opened more doors for the apostle.

If we could begin to identify particular groups of New Agers who show some interest, we could at least begin praying for them. This is how the Billy Graham team goes about it. Once they target a certain city for a crusade, they raise up prayer vigils in as many churches as possible in that city a year before the actual crusade. I worked in this context once and it was amazing how powerful the effect was on certain groups when the crusade finally came to town.

Perhaps you have already got one or two lines of communication open with New Agers. What kind of New Age interests do they have? Is there a particular New Age group that they usually associate with? Is this group at all open to your influence as a Christian? If the group is open, pray that God will help you to influence it in the direction of Christianity. If you cannot identify any groups that are open, perhaps you could start a prayer group just to pray for New Age groups.

No doubt you will be able to think of other prayer contexts. Pray in faith, believing. And remember that effective communication is helped along by effectual prayer.

22

Getting Peripheral Vision

It was suggested earlier that we should transform ourselves from battleships into luxury cruise liners, in an effort to appear less threatening and more inviting (see Illustration 3, Chapter 15). I trust that we have made at least some alterations in our appearance by now! The ultimate goal is not merely to keep the 'submarine' floating but to get New Age seekers to come on board with us and head in our direction. Illustration 4 (see page 324) would be the ideal. Yet even if we take the material of the previous chapters to heart and are transformed, there may still be some mischievous presuppositions hidden within our own wisdom that, after all is said and done, hold us back from building relationships with New Agers. I want us to challenge these presuppositions here.

Have you heard the story about the Christian leader and the butterfly? One sunny afternoon, a Christian leader (I have forgotten his name; let us call him Don) went fishing. With his legs dangling in the cool water as he sat on the dock, his fishing pole resting at his side, Don spied a new butterfly struggling to get out of a cocoon. He watched for some time, never having seen anything like it. But then he felt sorry for the poor butterfly because it was

Former New Age seekers come on board with us

having such a hard time getting out of the cocoon. Don, then, took out his penknife to help the little guy out. He made a narrow slit in the cocoon and out fell the butterfly— grotesquely deformed, especially its wings. It could not fly and now would never be able to fly. 'That's just like you, Don,' the Lord said to him suddenly. 'You cut my people out of their struggles and think you are doing them a favour, but they are walking around half-transformed instead.'

We, too, must finish our God-ordained struggles in order to be thoroughly transformed by His grace. I say this because you may find some of the following subdivisions quite personal and challenging, and so may not want to struggle with them. These subdivisions may indicate areas where your presuppositions are holding you back from interaction with New Age seekers. If so, you will want to struggle with them, by God's grace.

The Fortress Mentality

Jerram Barrs calls it the 'castle mentality', and aptly so, I think.[1] When we get saved, the drawbridge is lowered to us and we are received into the Christian subculture and religious scene as into a castle. Then the drawbridge is raised and we are left to roam around inside this massive religious fortress. Here we learn lifestyles that make it possible to go for long periods of time without having to be around non-Christians. I realise that this is changing, slowly. Some churches are recognising the problem, that they have been isolationist, and they are overhauling their structures to allow themselves to be more involved with non-Christians. Nevertheless, many of us still must admit that we find it puzzling to communicate with non-Christians simply because, in our disassociation from them, we do not know how they think or what their interests are. We have superficial associations with fellow employees, the habitual 'Thank you' to shopkeepers, the occasional 'Hello' when passing a neighbour. But do we have any significant relationships with 'outsiders'? If not, is it any wonder that our attempts at 'outreach'—personal or group—often fail miserably?

Life in the fortress has left us unable to relate to 'outsiders'. As I travel, I find that some churches like to hold 'public meetings' in non-churchy-looking buildings, to create contexts for inviting and reaching non-Christians. So far, so good. Yet with rare exceptions—so far, we are working on it!—as I look around during these so-called public meetings, it is obvious that the audiences are almost entirely Christians. What happened to the point of the meeting? Where are the New Agers? The problem lies in what was done to get them into the building. Posters were tacked up around town, an advertisement was run in a local newspaper, perhaps several radio spots were aired, or maybe leaflets were handed out on the High Street. That is to say, the process of inviting *persons* was largely *im*personal.

Life within the fortress has made it difficult to know what else to do. Sallying forth with 'advertising' becomes our chief activity, and it is nearly pointless for drawing a crowd of non-Christians unless your guest speaker is well known. The solution would be for everyone in a congregation to extend *personal* invitations. Pleasant and appealing invitations are rare, however, because we do not know non-Christians well enough, or if we do we are still inept at extending invitations. Sadly, I have seen entire congregations look at me with a blank stare when I have tried to fire them up to invite New Agers to these public meetings. I know that they would like to know how to be able to do it, but they just do not know how. For too long they have been taught their Christianity from presuppositions that forbid them even to have an imagination for being involved with non-Christians. They have been indoctrinated to believe that spare time ought to be devoted to more religious meetings and activities inside the fortress, where isolationism, and its fruit irrelevancy, become the normal Christian life.

Now we may agree with the problem, but some of us will still have difficulty lowering the drawbridge and getting out to build relationships. For one thing, the fortress mentality has created in us an 'us-them' mentality, that is to say 'an embattled feeling; we feel like a beleaguered minority surrounded by an aggressive culture which is attacking and destroying us.'[2] This has produced in us an *un*healthy attitude and fear of non-Christians, especially New Agers, and it is hard for those who perceive people as enemies to feel free to associate with them. For another thing, for many of us, lowering the drawbridge will mean disentangling ourselves from far too many weekly or monthly religious meetings and activities and then using that free time to initiate relationships with non-Christians. Perhaps I could suggest that we could get involved in so-called secular activities and community programmes, such as PTA, school boards, volunteer work, local election work or involvement in social action projects, where we will meet secular people who are being transformed by the cosmopolitan spirituality of the New Age.

If you think I am being tough on you here, you are right, I am. Contemporary Christianity is seen as irrelevant by and to the New Age world because largely it is. We are seen as being out of touch with reality because to a great extent we are. We have been made into a people, many of whom have a private religion with no public applicability. I have been tough on myself about this. And it is going to take some time before the world sees us differently, even if we all lowered the drawbridge tomorrow. I do not know about you, but it has occurred to me that in my efforts to protect myself inside the walls of the fortress I would have got trampled under foot anyway, for that is the place where salt which has lost its flavour ends up.

That Uninviting Look

Besides being a *Church Without Walls*,[3] we are going to have to become approachable to New Age seekers. Our churches (I do not mean the buildings only) often have fronts that not only fail to attract these people but seem designed to keep them out. Even an interested New Ager may see no way into a congregation. The solution to this, I think, is that we are going to have to be more relaxed and appear slightly frayed at the edges. I have been in several churches where this is being tried and the results are amazing. One particularly striking illustration comes to mind.

The occasion was the Sunday morning when I preached at Fairlight Christian Centre (Tooting, London) on the differences between New Age and Christian spirituality. The meeting hall, which was not churchy-looking, was chock-a-block with people. I am glad it was because the Satanists in the back were hidden from me, and if I had known they were listening I might have become tolerably reticent! As it was, I finished the message and was soon introduced to them, a married couple who were fully open about being Satanists. It would have been impossible to hide it anyway. They were completely dressed in black, decorated with several Satanic-looking tattoos and ornamented with the idiosyncratic jewellery of their beliefs, perhaps purchased at Glastonbury. What was even more instructive, for me, was that they had their three children in tow and the wife was pregnant with a fourth.

Fairlight was having a community lunch in the hall following the service and we asked the family to join us. They said that they should probably get going, but when we continued to extend the invitation they gladly accepted. We ended up talking to them for several hours, and here is a part of their story that really impresses itself on my mind.

Though they lived just down the road, this was their first visit to Fairlight, and they almost stayed away. When we asked why, they said that there was a church across the street from their flat and that its minister had made it impossible for them even to get into the church building. When we asked what had happened, we were told that the minister could not understand them.

'We've been into Satanism for a long time,' they told us. 'And now we have some doubts about it. We decided to check out a Christian church and went across the street. But the minister couldn't handle us. He told us that if we wanted to be in his church we could not wear black or our jewellery. He threatened us with judgement and told us that we were under God's curse. We tried talking to him but it was useless. We got upset and left.'

This heavy-handed approach is not uncommon and certainly puts up an uninviting front to Christianity. Frankly, I was surprised that they then took the risk of approaching Fairlight, and so I asked about this. Earlier that week they had seen a leaflet advertising my Saturday seminar on the New Age at Fairlight. They had called the church on Friday to find out if I was the kind of speaker who would ridicule them. The church secretary told them that she did not know me but, due to my background in the New Age, she felt that I would be understanding and would welcome them to the seminar. The secretary sensitively extended an invitation, but as it turned out they were unable to attend on the Saturday. Yet it was on the strength of that phone call (the *personal* touch) that the family turned up on the Sunday morning. They stayed through the message, through the meal, through, in fact, the entire afternoon. They talked openly and seriously with several of us. I eventually had to leave, but

I found out afterwards that the family stayed around to give the minister a lift home. It seems that the minister needed some work done on his car, and the husband was a mechanic.

The Lord does move in mysterious ways. As far as I know, this couple have not become Christians, but what I do know is that by making themselves approachable, Fairlight built a communication bridge into their needy lives. Certainly, it meant taking a risk and being frayed enough at the edges to put up with some unpleasantness. But, then, the Christian life is not about comfortableness.

Brand Names

There is an important question that needs to be asked when we are moving away from the fortress mentality and into approachable church settings: are we offering people religion or Relationship? Christianity 'hit the world running' with a Person. It turned the world upside down by attracting people to a Life. *Life*, not dogma, philosophy or ritual, was the Good News. People were dead and Life was being offered to them as a gift from God through a relationship with His Son, Jesus Christ,

It happens all too often that Christians stop ministering Life and start serving up brands of religion. Maybe we ought to push the clock back to what it was that made us Christians, and start offering that Life. The problem today is that New Age people look at Christianity and see its religious trappings and paraphernalia. And no wonder; it is so paramount to the outsider, who observes Institution rather than a Life.

Some Christians are thrilled because Jesus has come to 'destroy the works of darkness'. Yet are we big enough to admit that when He comes with such destruction He may also destroy half of what passes for Christian religion? (Several Christian scandals in recent times are cases in point.) We want to be careful about what we are ministering. Is it religion or Relationship? Is it the power of an indestructible life or a form of godliness (2 Tim. 3:5)?

This is not to say that God does not work through denominations and churches, nor to say that we are to sacrifice Christian theology on the altar of mystical existentialism. That is far from the case: we will drift from the faith if we are not anchored to a knowledge of what that faith is. Thus we are admonished to 'examine ourselves to see whether [we] are in the faith' (2 Cor. 13:5). This is not a verse about whether or not we have faith in general. It is about whether or not we are in the Christian faith in particular. How will we answer the question without knowing what the Christian faith teaches about itself? And this we learn from our denominations and churches.

Nevertheless, it is the power of an eternal life, not religiosity, that will capture the New Age imagination. A demonstrated Life in the Spirit will make the power of the New Age world look like a parlour trick. They may be willing to accept the life of the Spirit, but not religious trappings. Christ's life can penetrate their hearts; a crystallised religious system, never.

The AIDs Test

Before we offer people the Supreme Relationship, we may need Attitude Inspection Day. Some of us have derisive attitudes towards New Age people. The mocking, scoffing tone of some of our writers, and even pastors, who snicker at people such as Shirley MacLaine is disgraceful. 'Ha, ha! That scatterbrained redhead with her New Age ideas. She's crazy. What a laugh!' This completely misses the point of people like MacLaine who have a sharp native intelligence and are on a spiritual search.

The Christian publishing industry has allowed books to be written on the New Age that are unchristian in spirit and tone. They demean people, and this communicable disease has infected readers. Such books are generally written from the embattled and defensive position of the fortress and are therefore antagonistic and disrespectful. Rather than offering crackerjack arguments in a spirit of humility, they lambaste New Agers, mete out sensationalistic conclusions and generally misunderstand the paradigm shift occurring today in the West (see 'Inter-Mission'). The problem is that most New Age people would not recognise themselves on the pages of such books. We would not like it if New Age writers demeaned us like this. And if we carry this lack of recognition into our personal conversations, why should a New Age enthusiast listen?

What will our AIDs test reveal? The apostle Peter tells us in what spirit and tone we are to express our findings: give an answer with gentleness and respect (1 Pet. 3:15). If we used this as our criterion, we would probably have to withdraw some Christian books from the shops. The apostle Paul has this way of saying it, 'Let your conversation be *always* full of grace, seasoned with salt, so that you may know how to answer everyone' (Col. 4:6). 'Always', he says, 'always'.

We have indeed created some uproar in the secular community, but that has been largely a result of our mocking and scoffing. Uproars will come, but must they result from our derisive attitudes? Why not create the kind of uproar that comes from persuasive arguments that cannot be gainsaid and are delivered in the spirit of humility? Impossible? It happened in the book of Acts (19:35–40), and when it did God saw to it that even the secular town clerks were on the side of the Christians. They even commanded the crowd to be silent in favour of the Christians. When we have incisive arguments in the right attitude, I look for the 'town clerks' to be on our side too, by God's grace. We shall then get a hearing for the Life we are offering.

Our AIDs test may also reveal intolerance towards New Age people. This may be the result of being offended at people whose values and beliefs are non-Christian. And yet Jesus calls us into contact with these people, which means that we will need some tolerance. Dick Keyes writes:

> Tolerance is living side by side with others who have real and deep differences with us. [It is] living with respect and civility in our personal attitudes as much as possible. Tolerance is not relativism and has no necessary relationship to

relativism. A common confusion today is to think that if you question relativism, you must be intolerant. There are some sad chapters in our own Christian history at this point (as there are in all other world religions and secular ideologies). Christians have sometimes been cruel and arrogant to those who did not agree with them. [Yet] followers of Christ are called to live with faith and patience, love their enemies, seek the welfare of those who would do them evil, and be salt and light in the world. Jesus and the whole New Testament encourages [this]. Tolerance does not demand that we never try to persuade someone of the truth. It does demand that we hold that person in respect in spite of areas of disagreement.[4]

The Complaints Department

The insufficiencies, failures and even the evils done at times by Christians are lamentable, and any number of these might come up as a New Ager's remonstrance against becoming a Christian. It is foolish to whitewash obvious Christian delinquencies. The offences must be squarely faced, honestly admitted and humbly discussed. You may have passed your AIDs test, but nothing can ruin a Christian's attitude quicker than receiving complaints about Christianity from 'outsiders'. However, when we learn how to work in the Complaints Department with humility and grace, we will be able to keep building communication bridges.

A litany of legitimate complaints can come

up—immorality, hypocrisy, our high divorce
rate, greed, irrelevancy and more. Others will
complain of seeing no life in the Church, or of
painful experiences with Christians and
ministers. The point is, we do create offences.
The problem is, these may keep New Age seekers
from Christian fellowship. If we discover that
they are wounded, the wounds have to be
treated with balm. Some people who are now
New Agers have backslidden from the Christian
fold into the New Age world because of being
hurt by Christians. Healing balm is needed
here.

Perhaps the best way to work in the
Complaints Department with humility and grace
is to concede whatever legitimate complaints
come our way. As representatives of the
Church, we can ourselves accept rather than
whitewash complaints on behalf of the
Christians who injured people. It is a kind of
intercession. As representatives of Christianity,
we can apologise to the New Age seeker on
behalf of the system. And if you yourself have
been hurt similarly by a believer, and if you
have been healed, so much the better. It is very
powerful to be able to say, 'I've been hurt like
that too.' The other person is probably
expecting your denial or a cover-up, but when
he hears you owning up to these offences that is
an effective witness.

The power of this kind of intercession came
washing over me one evening when I was
having fellowship with a Franciscan whose
name is Father Duane. This story has deep
roots and is fairly complex, but here is the gist
of it. I was born into the Roman Catholic
tradition, and for various reasons, some

legitimate and some not, I rejected it in my mid-teens. By my late teens I had become rebellious and was getting interested in New Ageism via the 1960s counterculture. During those years I only darkened the door of any church when it was absolutely necessary, such as for the odd wedding or funeral. Also during those years my feelings towards the Catholic Church hardened.

After my conversion to Christ, with the redemptive grace of God now motivating me, I went at intervals to talk to various priests in an effort to get rid of the 'chip on my shoulder' against the Catholic Church. Every one of these attempts failed, and it was difficult not to feel more justified in my negative feelings. I finally gave up the attempt and forgot about it.

Several years passed and I met Father Duane, who lived in a Fransciscan seminary in a suburb north of Detroit, Michigan. I attended a course he was teaching called the 'School of Evangelisation', the object of which was to lead Catholics into a personal relationship with Jesus Christ and then to train them to lead other Catholics to Christ.

Father Duane and I struck up a relationship during those weeks, and one evening after sharing an evening meal together at the seminary, we went back to his rooms to talk and pray. Later that evening the conversation included my grudges against the Catholic Church. How this became a topic, I do not recall; it was not planned. I opened up my feelings to Father Duane. When I realised that I could trust him to listen at a deeper level, I talked more freely about the hurts I had sustained as a sensitive boy in Catholic schools.

Unleashing the repressed anger and bitterness took some time, but Father Duane was a good listener. When I had finished, I was thoroughly surprised, and pleasantly so, at his response. It certainly was in the opposite spirit from what I had got used to hearing.

'Charles,' he said, 'you certainly do have some legitimate complaints about how we brought you up in our schools.'

'I thought that I did,' I said, 'but I was beginning to wonder if maybe it was all my fault. I have tried several times to discuss this with a number of priests but they have never understood me.'

'No,' he said. 'I can see that we have hurt you. We haven't done a very good job for you.'

I could hardly believe my ears.

'More and more,' he continued, 'we are discovering how we went wrong with so many of you young people, how we could have done so much better. As a representative of the Catholic Church I ask if you will forgive us.'

Tears had been filling my eyes, and now the dam burst. Father Duane had been what I had needed all along, a powerful witness of Christ's compassion and love. I had been deeply wounded. Someone within Catholicism had finally understood. In the profound and long silence that followed, Christ was with us, pouring the balm of healing grace into me.

Many New Age people are waiting for Christians to understand their complaints too. When we do this in humility and grace, we are clearing a lot of hurt out of their lives and so helping them to open up to the redemptive message of the gospel.

Be wise, however, when working in the

Complaints Department. You may be able to agree with the person that such-and-such has hurt you too, but if you yourself have not been healed, if you still walk around with 'a chip on your shoulder', I would not suggest trying to offer healing balm. If you still have some unfinished business in that area, you will probably send the wrong signal to the other person.

Personal Inreach

This book is an attempt to equip Christians for outreach into the New Age world in order to bring non-Christian spiritual seekers into a relationship with the Truth Himself. I have had a long time to think about the implications of this, and in particular how it relates to *us*. This book on outreach, therefore, would be incomplete without answering the question: how much are *we* co-operating with the inreach of the Truth into our own lives? How fully are *we* allowing Christ to transform us?

Let us not be too quick in answering. I have known times when I thought that I was fully submitted to Jesus Christ, times when, if asked (and I was asked), I would have said (and did say) that every area of my life was deeply submitted in discipleship to the Lord. Later, when important relationships self-destructed or ungodly habits were not transformed, I would have to admit that I had been holding areas back from the Truth and so from renewal. What I had done was to convince myself through rationalisations that I was fully submitted, which allowed me to keep indulging the flesh. I

wanted so much for 'outsiders' to know the
Truth Himself but my own relationship with the
Truth ran a distant second. The messenger of
Christ was not as radiant with Life as he could
have been.

Now I thank God that we do not have to
become *perfect* before we can be His witnesses,
but how *are* we doing in our relationship with
our Lord? It is not enough to say 'All right' just
because we are not consciously backslidden.
The transforming grace of God is also at work
upon Christians who think everything is all
right. It is a bit more subtle, however, because
it may be dealing with *hidden* deceits, sins and
or even idolatries. These can often be identified
by asking who or what motivates the different
decisions we make every day, every week. Is the
Truth Himself really the ultimate influence for
all of our decisions, or is it possible that other
'agents' hold mastery over what we choose to
do? How about ambition, appearance,
affluence, freedom, happiness, sexuality, money,
irresponsibility, individualism? Certainly it is
not wrong to have ambition or to be happy, but
how about when they begin to dominate our
decision-making processes? We could be
holding back such areas from a deeper
relationship with the Truth.

Related to our relationship with the Truth is
our relationship with others. Because I am a
seminar speaker, it has been pointed out to me
that more than a few Christians spend far too
much time seminar-hopping rather than,
for instance, using that time to work on
deteriorating relationships. They are hoping to
become mini-experts in every conceivable
contemporary issue that comes along, while all

along their important relationships may need urgent attention, and their time should be spent attending to them. This is close to my heart because it has made me wonder about what is motivating some of the people who attend the seminars.

If our relationships with others are suffering, it is a sign that our relationship with the Truth Himself is not what it should be. To compensate, we may make a subtle though profound shift that allows us to heap up masses of head knowledge in an effort to know the truth.

There is, however, a common misunderstanding about what it means to 'know the truth'. We often speak about 'hearing' the truth, 'preaching' the truth, 'teaching' the truth, 'speaking' the truth, 'believing' the truth, and 'understanding' the truth; all of which is about our minds, our mouths and our heads. This idea about the nature of truth is not entirely wrong; it is just not entirely right either. It is much more a product of a Western understanding of 'knowledge' than it is of biblical wisdom. The Western idea is about access to facts, figures, data, statistics, measurements, the opinions of experts, research and so on. As translated in Western Christendom, 'knowing the truth' becomes the serious business of accumulating facts and information about the Bible and Christian doctrine, pursuing word studies, memorising verses and so on. The thing to do, then, is to acquire several translations of the Bible, a Strong's concordance, a good Bible dictionary, one or two commentaries, and possibly an interlinear Greek-English New Testament or analytical

Greek lexicon. In this system for 'knowing the truth' we occupy our time studying these resources, reading Christian books, seminar-hopping and listening to as many tapes and videos as possible.

Again, this is not uncalled-for, but it is only a part of, only makes a contribution to, what the Bible means by 'knowing the truth'. It is not the whole story by a long way, as we will discover precisely by doing a couple of word studies.

In the Bible, 'knowledge' and 'knowing' entail having a personal relationship with what you know; a personal relationship that carries with it moral implications. Therefore, Adam *knew* Eve (and she conceived). According to the Bible, 'knowing' a woman was not merely a matter of having her biography, or information about her looks and character. It meant a relationship that carried with it moral impli-cations. Beginning with that invaluable gem of Scripture, this principle regarding the nature of 'knowledge' and 'knowing' builds line upon line, precept upon precept, to include even our 'knowledge' of *im*personal things. (If this sounds foreign to us, it is because here is a place where our wisdom diverges from biblical wisdom and needs transformation.)

Thus the Bible presents us with some rather strange-sounding (to Western ears) statements about 'truth'. One of these is from Jesus when He said, 'I am the truth' (John 14:6). Think about this. A *Person*, not a stockpile of facts and figures, is the Truth. This is quite different from what we normally think the truth is (see above). Now if this Person is the Truth and if we are created in His image, it implies that people are in some real sense 'lower-case' truth themselves, so to speak. In the wisdom of the Bible, therefore, truth is about people and one Person in particular. And so we have a very peculiar statement to that effect in Ephesians 4:15, 'speaking the truth in love'. But wait a moment, that does not sound so odd. No, because the English translation of the Greek is a bit too Westernised here. A closer rendition would have it, *'being* truth', or *'living* truth', in love. But I am told that even that does not do justice to what Paul meant here.[5] It is literally ' "truthing it" in love'. And that sounds odd! This is also the thought behind passages such as 1 John 1:6, where the Authorised Version (King James), which becomes more literal by default with each passing year, states that when we lie, we 'do not the truth'.

This, then, greatly alters the complexion of what it means to 'know the truth'. It is no longer a head trip. Factual and scientific knowledge, as well as Bible study and suchlike, make a contribution to the picture, but it is not the whole story. 'Knowing the truth' is about people, their characters, their relationships to one another and to one Person in particular.

When we think, then, of the question of our relationship to the truth, the moral implications are quite profound indeed, because we have that inclination towards being lower-case *falsehoods*. This is why the apostle Paul urges us to be 'truthing it', and why the apostle John says that even believers may not 'do' the truth.

The apostle Paul is that fellow who, when writing to the church in Rome, said that truth is held *a priori* by people; thus they either express it or suppress it (see Romans 1 and 2). Evidently, it is possible to be 'truthing it' (in

344 Harmless as a Dove

righteousness) or 'falsing it' (in unrighteousness). This gets so personal that to give even a false impression of one's character can be a lie. So: how is your relationship to the Truth? Seminar-hopping is not enough.

Yes, we need to move out of the fortress and become approachable, offering Relationship—Life—not religion; and when we are doing this we are to watch our attitudes and handle complaints with compassion. But throughout all this we must remain mindful of our own relationship with the Truth.

It is not that God will wait until we are perfect before He will use us to reach New Age people. Rather, it is a matter of being judged by God for using a double standard. When we are working to bring non-Christians into a relationship with the Truth, do we have a stricter set of principles for them than we do for ourselves? Without becoming morbidly self-introspective, take a little time out for self-examination. It has been said that the largest room in the world is the room for improvement.

23

Presenting the Whole Gospel

One question remains to be answered. When New Age people convert and come aboard, in what direction are we taking them? Since it is Life we are offering them, what kind of Life are we leading them into?

Yes, the Life of Christ. But what do we mean by that? Well, it's an everlasting, an eternal life. Yes, but what does this Life influence, what does it affect? Well, it influences us, it changes us. Yes, but is that all? For many Christians, that is all.

In the final analysis, we live a life that extends only so far as we believe the gospel of Jesus Christ reaches, or how much of life it touches. And this is dependent on how far we think the process of salvation and redemption reaches. Answer that, and you will know what kind of Life you are offering new or potential converts. That is to say we will lead people in the direction of a Life only so far as we ourselves have understood its meaning and reach, and have ourselves gone. No more, no less.

How far, then, does the gospel reach? Some people think it is primarily about selling people their 'fire insurance'. I hope that by now most Christians would argue that that is a terribly truncated view of the gospel; that getting 'the soul saved for the day of the Lord' is merely the beginning of Life. It reaches further than that, they would say. We have got to get the new convert up and running. You know, the four points of 'follow-up'. We've got to stress the importance of getting the person praying, reading the Bible, attending church and witnessing. Certainly these are the 'next steps', but are there no others? Is this the extent of the process of salvation and redemption? Is the Life of Christ only about the religious dimension of life?

Of course not, others would say. We have got to do good works, behave ethically in our jobs, be more loving to our families, renew our minds and be sanctified. Others would add that we should do a few acts of charity, or perhaps become part of the worship team or get on the evangelism committee, or become a deacon or elder; maybe even go to Bible school.

In such a view the gospel seems to be stretching far and wide, but when you really look at it, it is still primarily influencing only the religious dimension. It is a Life that has little or nothing to say to industry, economics, art, education, politics, ecology, health care and so on, i.e. the rest of life. I am afraid that this is not the gospel we are called to preach, though it has become the gospel for much of Christendom. This contemporary gospel is shaped by the unbiblical idea that life is divided up into two separate realities: the religious (or spiritual) *vis à vis* the secular (or natural, or material), the latter being that which God is not really interested in.

We must travel quite some distance back in

time to find the source of this. Greek thought
from the time of Socrates, Plato and Aristotle
still carries a lot of weight in the West and in
Christendom today. It was characteristic of
early Greek thought to hold a low opinion of the
material world and the body, which was often
felt to be the greatest handicap to the
attainment of true knowledge, wisdom, goodness
and spirituality. The body held men back, it
was said.

In his dialogues with Socrates, Plato
discusses 'salvation' with his mentor, who
suggested that salvation equates with separating
'soul' from 'body'. To these early Greeks, the
soul was considered immortal and imperishable,
the body mortal, perishable. When death
attacked, the immortal soul was liberated and
released from the perishable body, and this
meant salvation.

Not too long after these three philosophers
themselves had moved on into 'salvation', this
kind of thinking took a turn for the worse within
neo-Platonism and especially within the pagan
gnosticism of the early centuries AD. 'Soul' and
'spirit' were identified as *good* in these
metaphysical systems, and 'matter', including
bodies and the material world *in toto*, was
identified as *evil.* The gnostic, especially, was to
have as little to do with the material world as
possible, because 'matter' was considered
utterly corrupt and bad, a 'lower world'; indeed,
the lowest. Spiritual (non-material) things were
the highest, the purest. The gnostic believed
that he had a divine spark within that had been
corrupted by his life in the material world.
Salvation for him therefore meant raising
himself up through the 'lower worlds' to the

higher spiritual levels, where he would be eventually transformed into a purely spiritual being, uncontaminated by the material world.

The end of this kind of thinking is a thorough-going dualism of soul or spirit over against matter, nature or material things. It is seen as essential to get free and clear of the world, for there is nothing good about it. As Christianity spread throughout the Greek and pagan worlds, it certainly took issue with dualistic views of salvation but was itself not left uninfluenced by them. And their influence is felt even today in Christianity, restricting the reach of the gospel to the religious or spiritual dimensions of life. Within the milieu of dualism, the gospel is not understood as that which reaches into all of life, especially secular life, and we end up preaching a two-dimensional gospel to a three-dimensional world.

Though this is foreign to the Bible, much of Western Christianity today tends to read the Bible through the dualistic lens of 'secular/religious', or 'natural/spiritual', and as a result has evacuated the 'secular' areas of life. We just do not think the gospel has anything redemptive to say—at least more than super-ficially—to economics, politics, art, industry and the like. If we are offering this kind of anaemic Life, we are offering New Age people . . . , well, I am afraid they already see the truth in thinking wholistically, and they will see through any kind of dualistic gospel message.

Now there is a kind of hard dualism and soft dualism afoot within Christiandom. In the former 'saving souls' is the most spiritual thing one can do. Missionaries, pastors and evangelists are the most spiritual believers, and down the hierarchy, slightly, come elders and deacons, and then other church-orientated workers. But everything about the world, its art, its industry, its politics and suchlike is irredeemable. It is in the hands of the devil. So forget it. We should not be concerned about such things because Christians are to 'save souls'.

In the softer Christian dualism it is all right to be engaged in some worldly activities and careers, but you have got to be ever so careful. It is probably not good to be a biologist or a scientist because of evolutionary thinking. Political work and law is looked down upon because of gross corruption. Artist? Forget it. You mass-produce 'Christian' knick-knacks and trinkets instead, and fill the shops with them. It may not be Art, but nobody will notice, and besides, it is making us money; after all, it is hard to get into the right kind of work. The caring professions are all right, if you can get around evolution and holism. But there is no way you should be a psychologist or a psychiatrist because that is the devil's playground. Music? Maybe. But only as long as it is a vehicle for 'saving souls' or includes Christian jargon. You might try the teaching profession, if you can find a way to get past the humanism. And within this softer dualism you would be quite free to start up a 'neutral' business, such as accounting or farming, without fear of wrath.

Dualism in the Church puts a lot of false guilt upon those poor mortals who are in a line of work that is so far down the 'spiritual ladder' as to be considered carnal by the more spiritual.

And our speech is filled with the language of dualism. We talk about our 'ministry' as opposed to our 'secular job', e.g. 'I'm looking forward to the day when I can serve the Lord full time.' This language about spiritual callings and natural vocations betrays the spiritual–secular split in our minds, of which the Bible is ignorant because the gospel reaches into *all* of life.

We have this adage: if Jesus is not Lord of all, then He's not Lord at all. Dualistic thinking tends to make this read: if Jesus is not Lord of all of *my life*. As a result, we live with a private faith in a public life. Thus many Christian businessmen, politicians, captains of industry, office managers, teachers, salespeople, small business owners, lawyers and so on are unaware that the gospel can give distinctively biblical ethics and aesthetics to their lines of work. As a result, there may be markedly little difference between the way they go about their jobs and the way non-Christians do theirs. Often, the only difference is that the Christians are in church on Sunday—hearing messages that are presuppositionally dualistic. They hear messages that touch their personal lives only. So they may no longer cheat on their taxes, they may be more easy-going with their employees, and you may even hear them pray or tell someone at work about Jesus. But let them ask their pastors to preach about how the gospel can influence the arrangement of the secretaries' desks in their office buildings, or the design of their new office buildings, or how it can shape running a political campaign, or the nature of law-making, or the use and effect of advertising, and their ministers will either look at them with a blank stare or think that they are joking or daft.

A Good Creation

What kind of Life are we offering? Examine the kind of life you are living and you will have your answer. Is it a religious life or a whole life? A dualistic or a wholistic gospel? Soul salvation or whole salvation? Whereas dualistic thinking closes Christians up and limits the reach of the gospel, biblical wisdom opens us to a gospel for all of life and culture. This is the gospel of Jesus Christ. This is the gospel we preach.

Throughout Church history, a reacquaintance with the doctrine of creation has always served as a good counterblast to dualistic views of life. Dualism errs chiefly in three directions: wrong ideas about God, the creation and salvation. For example, the gnostics could not see how the creation of the material world could have been done by the Supreme God, who is altogether good. Since their assumption was that matter was evil, they asked how a good God could have created it? To solve their metaphysical dilemma, they believed that matter had been created by a lesser, evil god, who was utterly hostile to the good Supreme God. This belief was widespread in New Testament times, and it left the Christians who imbibed it shut up in an evil body in an evil world, neither of which could be transformed or renewed. People could not wait to leave both.

In no uncertain terms, however, the Bible teaches that God made a 'good' creation (Gen. 1). Yes, the human family has fallen into sin and the creation has not been left untouched by it, but this is a far cry from saying it is all worthless. This is to despise the handiwork of God, who made a *good* creation. It is precisely because the creation is not intrinsically evil that it, like ourselves, can be redeemed, renewed and transformed. And this is not about starting over from nothing, either. Revelation 21:5 does not read, 'Behold I make all new things', but, 'Behold, I make all things new' (AV). A world of difference exists between the two; the latter implying that there is something around to work redemption on.

Therefore when the Bible speaks of a new heaven and a new earth (Isa. 65:17, 66:2; 2 Pet. 3:13; Rev. 22:1), it is portrayed in terms of the old renewed, in that it will one day be without sin's influence, and not in an original kind of newness. The apostle Paul goes into this important point in some depth in Romans 8:19–23:

> The creation waits in eager expectation for the sons of God to be revealed. For the creation was subjected to frustration, not by its own choice, but by the will of the one who subjected it, in hope that the creation itself will be liberated from its bondage to decay and brought into the glorious freedom of the children of God. We know that the whole creation has been groaning as in the pains of childbirth right up to the present time. Not only so, but we ourselves, who have the firstfruits of the Spirit, groan inwardly as we wait eagerly for . . . the redemption of our bodies.

It is not just that *we* wait eagerly for the redemption of our *bodies,* but that 'the *creation* waits in eager expectation' too. Nature/creation shares in that which puts man right: redemption. Whereas by man's sin, nature/creation suffered (was placed in bondage to decay), so by God's grace it shares in that which puts man right: the gospel. This is why the gospel we preach must be the one with a Life that reaches *all* of life with its message of redemption. Thus we preach not merely soul but whole salvation; the provision of grace for the whole of creation. This is the Life we want to be offering New Age seekers. This is the direction we want to lead them, because it will give them grace to be Christians in every area of life.

This is not to say, however, that we do not preach repentance from sin and offer the grace of Christ for personal salvation. The Christian communicator will always want to be ready to tell the New Age person how he can become a Christian. This may seem too obvious to need mentioning, but if we are not used to communicating the way of personal salvation to people, we could find it somewhat difficult when the need arises.

During the first seven or eight years that I was a Christian, every year I led one or two people to the Lord. Then there were a few years in which, for whatever reasons, that did not occur. As a result I became inexperienced at knowing how to lead someone to Christ. The funny thing is, I did not realise that I had lost touch with how to lead someone to the Lord until a 'Philippian jailer' situation actually happened to me. It really caught me off-guard.

I had just finished preaching a message at
Above Bar Church in Southampton. It was not
a message on the New Age; it was not even an
evangelistic message. We did not even have an
'altar call'. I had preached on the grace of God,
the meeting had ended and the crowd was filing
out. After a few people had finished talking to
me, and there was hardly a person left in the
church, I was walking around looking for my
wife so that we could find our lift. Suddenly I
was approached by a shy young French girl of
about nineteen.

'May I speak to you, please?' she said. 'You
are probably wanting to leave but could you
spare me a few minutes?'

'Yes, what can I do for you?' I said. 'What's
your name?'

'My name's Patricia, and I was really
listening to what you were saying tonight. My
life does not seem right. It seems very dirty. I
want to know Jesus, but I don't know what to
do about it. Can you help me?'

You could have bowled me over! At first I
was not sure if I was hearing right, or if she was
faking this, or if perhaps it was not some
distraction sent by our common enemy.

'Sure I can help you,' I blurted, wondering
what on earth I was going to do and say next.
'Perhaps we could take a seat over here, and you
could tell me more about it.'

We sat down and had a heart-to-heart talk.
The first thing I discovered was that she was
absolutely serious about her sinfulness, though
she did not know it was called that. It was
evident that the conviction of the Holy Spirit had
been upon her for some time. But as I was

gently trying to sort this out with her, it hit me that I was not sure how to actually say what had to be said to lead her into a personal relationship with Jesus. It had been so long since I had led someone to the Lord. I had lost touch with how to do it. I was appalled at myself. Of course, I could have mouthed some formula prayer *for* her, but she wanted to meet the Saviour. After a few more minutes of talking with her, I was able to gather my thoughts together and felt confident enough to proceed. I was helped by the fact that out of the corner of my eye I saw my wife and a minister approaching. We waited until they came up to us, and then I mentioned what Patricia was about to do. The four of us then prayed together. Patricia became a Christian and entered into the care of the church.

So you just never know. I suggest that you work out a short one- or two-minute presentation of the gospel and loosely memorise it. In reading through the book of Acts, I have come to the conclusion that this is what the apostles had done. Then whenever they were in situations in which people were morally ready to make a decision for Jesus Christ, they could state the message clearly. And this is what to look for: the person's sincere acknowledgement of his or her moral problem. Into this we can speak about personal salvation in Christ with great confidence.

But there is another reason for having a 'one-minute gospel' presentation at the ready. Many New Agers have never really heard the Good News, or if they have, it has sounded more like bad news because it came to them in a distorted form through some branch of the media. In our 'pre-evangelistic' conversations with New Age people, when all is said and done, and conversation for the time being is coming to a close, and if the person is still floating on the surface of communication, we could ask if he has actually ever heard the gospel. He may say that he has, but we would not want to take that for granted; it may be a distorted version that he has heard. Or he may say that he has not heard it. In either case, we could ask for just 'one more minute' of their time, that day, to share the gospel: redemption from sin.

Try to work out a short presentation of the gospel that you could express at such a time. Put it in your own words, pointing out salient characteristics about the creation, then the fall of man into sin, and how that has affected all of life, and then tell about God's provision for a restored relationship with Him through His Son Jesus Christ. And remember you are not trying to force belief upon the person, but that you are painting for him a new window of perspective, the gospel window of perspective. This would be something that, at the end of your conversation, you could leave with the person, simply saying, 'Think about it.'

I believe it was the Billy Graham Evangelistic Association whose research concluded that it takes six or seven times for the average non-Christian to hear the gospel message before he can make an intelligent decision about it. Is there a greater parting idea that we could leave with our listeners? It could be that in our subsequent conversations with them they will make that decision for Christ.

And once they are 'up and running' in a whole Life, the potential for them is indeed endless. When we present the whole gospel, as applicable to all of life, it will attract spiritual seekers who are already aware that society desperately needs something, just as they do themselves. Think about it.

Epilogue

We have come a long way towards learning what
it takes to be as wise as serpents and as
harmless as doves in communicating with New
Age people. The New Age world has its own
combination-lock of communication problems
that we have worked to decode in this book.
But our mission impossible has just begun, the
ultimate aim being to persuade New Age seekers
to change their minds about God and
themselves, and so to receive saving grace.

The purpose of this book has not been for
readers to learn very much about airtight
techniques and strategies by which to 'reach the
lost'. Rather, we have learned about a life to be
lived in the presence of the lost. We have
discussed at some length what kind of a life it
will take to build relationships; not relationships
in which we are getting involved in
questionable New Age or occult activities, but
relationships in which New Age people are
beginning to take a favourable interest in
Christianity and the gospel. We are not going to
surrender biblical absolutes, become moral
relativists, or take part in ungodly compromise.
As Christians, we have a radical identity with
Jesus Christ, so that we can make a radical
difference. Our lives will witness to both
qualities, as Christ's living epistles.

It was not clever New Age apologists, demolishing biblical wisdom, which drew me into the New Age world. It was, to a large degree, that its teachers and 'witnesses' were warm, sensitive, gentle and considerate of my feelings. They had a certain way with me which was appealing. In this book we have studied ways of making that happen for us, and ultimately for our Lord.

Jesus enjoyed people, and they were sinners. He liked going to where people were. He established rapport. He built relationships. He spent time with people—in the marketplaces, in homes, on street-corners—in order to get to know them, and so that they would get to know Him. None of this displeased the Father. Jesus listened. He was perceptive. He answered. He was the great communicator, and He is our model for that.

If we apply what we have studied (you may want to refer to some chapters or ideas on a regular basis), and now cry out in prayer to God with a desire to reach New Age seekers, He will respond to us. We do not need to be smart. We do not need to be experts. We just need to be loyal. The Master chose twelve 'common labourers' to be with Him. What they would learn when they were with Him would make them His first witnesses. They had little or no formal training. Eleven were loyal, and they were the ones who later turned the world upside down. Still today Jesus looks for loyal disciples, Christians who will be with Him, whom He will transform into effective communicators.

If you are wondering how to begin, start simply, confidently and in the power of the Holy

Spirit. You may want to start by confessing any *un*healthy fears you may have about speaking in the New Age world. Sometimes we have a kind of cringing, cowering withdrawal from New Age people because of their possible occult lifestyles. Yet it is not part of our inheritance in Christ to carry around an *un*healthy fear of things demonic.

Colossians 1:13 (AV) states that through Jesus Christ God has 'delivered us from the powers of darkness' and 'translated us into the kingdom of his dear Son'. This is a powerful image, one with deep theological and practical significance. It testifies to the reality of demonic powers; but more than that it reveals that Christians are set free (delivered) from them. That is to say, Christians live within the confines of God's kingdom, a kingdom in which demonic power has no authority. This is part of our inheritance in Christ, and it means that we are no longer afraid of the powers of darkness. Many Christian lives have been transformed by understanding this.

If you already know this, you may want to proceed by gathering some Christian friends to pray for a plan of action. Perhaps the group could visit the New Agers at a psychic fair, or set up a small booth with Christian literature at a 'Body, Mind, Spirit' festival, or go to a New Age bookshop to talk with the manager or owner. Trust in God and begin something. Do not be afraid to make mistakes, otherwise you may never begin. And do not be embarrassed when you make mistakes, for this is how we learn to do better next time.

Ideally, though, simply try to capitalise on whatever is happening around you, at any given time, to create conditions for Christian sharing that otherwise would never have existed. Jesus did this continually. He was very spontaneous. In reading the Gospels, one does not get the impression that Jesus was programme-orientated. He did not spend His days wondering or worrying about who His 'divine appointments' were going to be. His was an impromptu ministry. He made use of whatever happened to come His way. Without rehearsal, He taught, healed and made His points within the context of whatever people were saying or doing.

New Age people live in a world with a wisdom in which the only ultimate relationship they have is with Self, and their only hope, therefore, is like trying to chase down a desert mirage. As Christians, we are called to build communication bridges that will offer these people the ultimate true relationship as it is known in Jesus Christ, the only true Hope.

Notes

2. *Communication Breakdown*
1. Several of the more influential RE
syllabuses and textbooks that carry New
Age motifs are: *Global Teacher, Global
Learner*, (Pike & Selby); *New Methods in RE*
(Hammond, Hay, et al.); *Better Schools: A
Values Perspective* (Beck); *The New Social
Curriculum* (ed. by DuFour); *Stilling: A
Pathway for Learning in the National
Curriculum* (Beasley).

3. *Meet Success and Failure*
1. The Christian L'Abri Fellowship centres
were founded by the late Dr Francis
Schaeffer and his wife Edith. The centres
are live-in study and work environments
where people can stay for periods of several
days up to an entire term. A large percent-
age of those who come to L'Abri, especially
university-age people, are seeking to
acquire a more relevant Christianity to take
back into their cultures. There are centres
in Europe, England and America, the latter
two addresses being listed here for those
desiring further information. L'Abri
Fellowship, the Manor House, Greatham,
Liss, Hants, GU33 6HF, England. L'Abri
Fellowship, 1465 12th Avenue N.E.,

Rochester, MN, 55906, USA.
2. This myth is exposed as the piece of fiction that it is by two established Christian authors.   See: Groothuis, Douglas, *Revealing the New Age Jesus: Challenges to Orthodox Views of Christ* (Downer's Grove, Ill.: InterVarsity Press, 1990); Rhodes, Ron, *The Counterfeit Christ of the New Age Movement* (Grand Rapids, Mich.: Baker Book House, 1990).

5. The Storm of the Irrational

1. MacLaine, Shirley, *Dancing in the Light* (New York, NY: Bantam Books, 1987), chapters 14 and 15.
2. Chandler, Russell, *Understanding the New Age* (Milton Keynes, Eng.: Nelson Word, 1988), p. 33.
3. Groothuis, Douglas, *Confronting the New Age* (Downer's Grove, Ill.: InterVarsity Press, 1988) p. 111.
4. Kole, André, The Christian Tape Library Inc., 330 N. Range Road, Carmel, Ind., 46032, USA.
5. Kiester and Kiester, 'How to Teach Your Child to Think', *Reader's Digest*, 11 June 1991, p. 141.
6. Naisbutt and Aburdene, *Megatrends 2000* (New York, NY: Morrow, 1990), p. 295.
7. Thompson, Keith, 'Helen Palmer: Setting Standards of the Psychic Frontier', *Common Boundary*, January/February 1989, p. 20.

6. The Calm of Passivity

1. Some forms of Hebrew or Christian meditation would be exceptions to this. They would not engage the person in

emptying the mind of all thoughts but in filling it with a meditation, for example, on God's works (Ps. 77:12; 143:5), or God's law (Ps. 1:2; 119), or God Himself (Ps. 63:6; 104:34). Christian meditation would also engage a person's mind upon the matters of Scripture, preaching, teaching, one's gifts, life or even doctrine, as the apostle Paul exhorts (1 Tim. 4:13–16, AV). What must be stressed is that the common denominator in these non-mystical kinds of meditation is a *filling* of the mind, and it is a filling with what is true, noble, right, pure, lovely, admirable, excellent and praiseworthy. As Paul taught (Phil. 4:8–9), when we think about these things and put them into practice, the God of peace will be with us.

As regards Christianised versions of guided imagery and visualisation, I would say that much of what I have so far encountered is pretty dodgy. I do not practise any kinds of guided imagery and visualisation now. Yet I am strongly in support of the redemption of our imaginations. I am not convinced, however, that this is as easy to accomplish as some Christians seem to think. Of the many, many times the term for 'imagination' is used in the Bible, only once, I believe, is it used in a positive light, and nearly half the time it is used in the context of 'idolatry'. The biblical concept of 'image' gets equally lopsided treatment (see: Alexander, Brooks, 'Visualisation: Mind Power and the Mind's Eye', *Spiritual Counterfeits Project Journal*, 9:3, 1990).

2. Ornstein, Robert E., *The Psychology of Consciousness* (New York, NY: Penguin Books, 1972), p. 136.

7. *The Genesis of Deception*

1. MacLaine, op. cit. pp. 254–55.
2. Monism is a metaphysical system in which all reality, both the material and the spiritual, is conceived of as a unified whole. There are various kinds of monistic systems, and the popular buzz-phrase 'All is One, One is All' sums up the New Age version. In the New Age world there is a strong antipathy towards the strict dualisms of mind over against matter and spirit over against body that are still common in the West today. Monistic oneness gives the New Age follower a way out of these strict dualisms. Now there is some food for thought here, for the Bible itself does not see life in terms of harsh dualisms. It was the early Greek philosophers who gave the West a taste for metaphysical systems framed by strict dualisms, chiefly that of the spiritual over against the material. Yet it was from the time of the philosopher and scientist Descartes (1596–1650) and later Western scientific thought that harsh dualisms were imposed upon Western thought in general. Descartes formulated an almost complete dualism between the physical world and the mind, and later Western scientific thought saw matter as total reality and excluded anything other-worldly from the equation. It is the task of Christian philosophy to respond with the biblical view. There is

indeed a unity of some kind with the universe and all of its phenomena. This unity, however, is not found in the principle of monism, but in the Person of Jesus Christ.

8. Identifying Distortions

1. Biblical critiques of pantheistic monism are presented in several good Christian books. See: Clark and Geisler, *Apologetics in the New Age: A Christian Critique of Pantheism* (Grand Rapids, Mich.: Baker Book House, 1990); Groothuis, Douglas, *Unmasking the New Age* (Downer's Grove, Ill.: InterVarsity, 1986); Mangalwadi, Vishal, *In Search of Self: Beyond the New Age* (London, Eng.: Hodder & Stoughton, 1992); Miller, Elliot, *A Crash Course on the New Age Movement* (Grand Rapids, Mich.: Baker Book House, 1989). Also see Glossary.
2. Cooper, Tim, *Green Christianity* (London, Eng.: Spire, 1990).
3. Peck, John, 'Creation and Purpose', Worldview Series, cassette tape No. 11, (Trinity Arts Group, 14800 Middlebelt Road, Livonia, MI, 48154, USA), 1985.
4. Newbigin, Lesslie, *Foolishness to the Greeks* (London, Eng.: SPCK, 1986), p. 89.

9. Predicting Problems

1. Strohmer, Charles, *What Your Horoscope Doesn't Tell You* (American edition—Wheaton, Ill.: Tyndale House, 1988; British edition—Milton Keynes, Eng.: Nelson Word, 1991), p. 78, British edition.
2. Ibid. See chapters 7 to 9 for a deeper look at how 'self-disclosures' from the spirit

world infiltrate the thinking processes of an occult spokesperson's mind, to feed information to a client.

10. Darkness as Light

1. Quoted in Creager, Ellen, 'New Age Parents Sprinkle Their Spiritualism with Diplomacy', *The Detroit Free Press*, 23 April 1987.

2. Jung, Carl, *Memories, Dreams, Reflections* (New York, NY: Vintage Books, rev. edit., 1965), recorded and edited by Aniela Jaffe, translated from the German by Richard and Clara Winston. Jung wrote this autobiography at the end of his long life, and in it he admits to his earlier encounters with spirit beings called Ka, Salome, Philemon and Elijah. 'Philemon and other figures,' he wrote, 'brought home to me the crucial insight that there are things in the psyche which I do not produce, but which . . . have a life of their own. Philemon represented a force that was not myself . . . I held conversations with him . . . I observed clearly that it was he who taught me . . . .'

   I know of two evangelical critiques of Jung. One I wrote for the *Spiritual Counterfeits Project Journal*, Vol. 9:2. The article is called 'Jung: Man of Mystic Proportions'. It is available by writing to: SCP, PO Box 4308, Berkeley, CA, 94704, USA. The other critique is found in chapter 14 of Leanne Payne's *The Healing Presence* (Westchester, Ill.: Crossway, 1989).

3. Jung, op. cit. pp. 189–91.

4. Ibid. p. 192.

5. Ibid.

6. Ibid. p. 199.
7. Ibid. pp. 194–95.
8. Ibid. p. 349.
9. Ibid. p. 347.
10. Not everything Jung named 'archetype' is demonic. For instance, some were merely universal religious symbols. The reason for introducing the reader to Jung's *demonic* archetypes is to suggest that more may be going on behind the 'seens' of New Age imagery than first meets the eye.

11. Models or Muddles?

1. By way of personal testimony, I would like to say something in defence of the more sensational Christian books on the New Age. After I became a Christian in July, 1976, I looked for Christian books on the New Age to help me. I found none. (Some years later I did discover that Gary North's *None Dare Call It Witchcraft*, now revised and retitled as *Unholy Spirits*—a helpful book—had been around in 1976.) Since I could get no help from books, I sought out ministers to help me. I still feel sorry for them. They did the best they could. But because of the dearth of Christian material on the New Age, they were at as much of a loss as I was. I am grateful, however, that God was present to make up for all our deficiencies. Anyway, I began to pray earnestly that Christian books on the New Age would get published. I prayed about this for several years, a period during which I also talked from my heart to pastors, Christian media-people and others about the growing New Age problem. But there

was a general disinterest and lack of
concern. Most Christian leaders at the
time, in fact, thought that folk like myself
(we were few and far between back then)
were as weird as the New Age we talked
about. We were to be coddled, humoured
and tolerated until the New Age, if ever
there was one, and our zeal had run its
course. It was a rare Christian leader who
noticed the rising temperature of New
Ageism in Western culture in the mid-to-
late 1970s.

My opinion (hindsight being the best
sight, here) is that Christians were asleep to
the problem. Because of that, it took some
sensationalism to 'stab us awake' to the
problem. In my mind, this accounts for the
hue and cry that some Christian books on
the New Age made during the early-to-mid
1980s. Several others have been similar in
spirit and tone since then as well. I believe
God permitted the sensationalism to wake
us up. Now that we are awake, it is time to
move on.

2. A summary of these and other historical
spiritual trends can be found in the
Spiritual Counterfeits Project Journal,
'Empowering the Self: A Look at the Human
Potential Movement', and also the *SCP
Newsletter*, 'Mind Power'.

12. *Wisdom in the Marketplace*
1. Peck, John, *Wisdom in the Marketplace*
(London, Eng.: Greenbelt, 1989), p. 22. I
highly recommend this book. It is about
more than building up ideas and making
them work. It aims to assist Christians in

the personal development of biblical
wisdom which will become instinctive and
govern actions in a spontaneous, godly way.
The book is a great help to Christians who
find themselves ill-prepared for thinking
and acting biblically in so-called secular
life.
2. Ibid.
3. Irving and McCasland, 'Old Truth for a New
   Age', interview with Ron Enroth, *Power for
   Living*, 19 July 1992.

13. Acquiring Wisdom
1. Peck, op. cit. p. 23.
2. From the poem 'Howl', by Allen Ginsberg,
   quoted in Gitlin, Todd, *The Sixties: Years of
   Hope, Days of Rage* (New York, NY: Bantam,
   1987), p. 45. Ginsberg read the poem in
   1955 to a San Francisco audience, in
   answer to the question 'What are you
   rebelling against?'
3. Cooper, op. cit.
4. Ibid. chapter 4.
5. This is a composite statement drawn from
   several leading New Age educators to depict
   their general feeling.

14. Submarines and Their Destroyers
1. This subdivision can be misunderstood. I
   want to emphasise that in calling for a
   'give-and-take' in conversation, I do not
   mean that we compromise the truth or
   become 'soft' about moral absolutes. I am
   not advocating relativism; I am pleading for
   relationships to be established, in the hope
   that people will then want to listen to the
   Bible. Of course people 'ought not' to

practise channelling. Certainly it is 'wrong' to be into astrology. There will be times to say so, to mention the dangers, but not, perhaps, in the early stages of a budding relationship. In the early stages you may want to let your negative feelings about the occult be known *gently*, in a manner that does not alienate you from the person. You do not want to be guilty of dissimulation. But this gentleness is a far cry from the hammering away that some of us do in the early stages, wondering then why we cannot build relationships.

I am not saying you always must take this tack. There are times for plain old confrontation, even in the early stages of a relationship. But if you so proceed, you will have to go cautiously even then. You see, it is unlikely that a New Ager will be gained for Christ during the first conversation. I would think, therefore, that you would want to pave the way, whenever possible, for later conversations, which may occur with Christians other than yourself. You will probably find that it defeats the purpose to play the 'spiritual heavy' early on. An initial conversation is most often an opportunity for attracting the New Age enthusiast to spend further time with you. Principled conversation can help facilitate this. If you are having difficulty with this idea of being 'softer' without being a compromiser, stay tuned. More help is on the way in later chapters.

15. Setting Off the Alarm

1. Here I am leaving aside the entire area of

the creation's subjection to frustration and its bondage to decay, from which it awaits liberation (Rom. 8:20–21). As I understand this, it is not about an intrinsically evil creation that deserves annihilation. Thus it does not militate against what I am saying about God's good creation.

2. Hoyt, Karen & the Spiritual Counterfeits Project, *The New Age Rage* (Old Tappan, NJ: Revell, 1987). See chapter 10, 'Spiritual Autism: Breaking Barriers by Building Bridges', Dean Halverson, p. 211.

17. *Signs of Truth*

1. See Chapter 3, footnote 2; Chapter 8, subdivision on 'Jesus'.

2. Because space does not exist in this book to discuss more thoroughly many such matters that are coming up, readers who are interested further should look at the Recommended Reading list, in which a wealth of information exists. For readers interested in further information about the discussion in question here, see: Buell & Hyder, *Jesus: God, Ghost or Guru* (Zondervan/Probe, 1978); Lewis, C. S., *Mere Christianity* (MacMillan, 1952), Book 2, chapter 3; Lewis, C. S., *God in the Dock* (Eerdmans, 1970), Part 1, chapter 19.

3. Strohmer, *What Your Horoscope . . .*, chapters 12—14, for suggestions about why the spiritual power of the New Age is impotent *vis-à-vis* our moral problem, and why only God's power in Christ returns us to a relationship with God.

4. Ibid., chapter 13, for ideas about presenting 'redemption' to New Agers in a way that

may be more manageable to their imaginations.

5. Ibid.

6. Hodgkinson, Liz, 'You Only Live (at least) Twice', *She* (May, 1989, UK), pp. 84–87.

7. Ibid.

18. *Areas of Agreement*

1. This and other incredible claims appeared in a large and wordy two-page advertisement that the Maharishi ran in the *International Herald Tribune*, 5 April 1990, under the headline 'Unified Field Science and Technology: offers the balance of power in the world to any government'.

2. Cooper, op. cit. chapter 4. Also see: 'Gaia: A Religion of the Earth', *Spiritual Counterfeits Project Journal*, Vol. 16:1, 1991.

3. Kushi, Michio and Aveline, *Macrobiotic Diet*, ed. by Alex Jack (Japan Publications, 1985).

4. Ibid.

5. The two concepts developed in this and the preceding chapter may be new to some readers, who may still wonder, 'How on earth could we ever agree with New Agers about anything? How could they possibly have anything to say to us?' I can understand this because it has been a struggle for me also. But how about this? In Chapters 14 and 15 we looked at a number of problems that can crop up in the way we relate to people. This was where we discussed caricatures, the demanding boss, listening and so on. Was that material helpful to you? If so, you may be surprised to know that some of it came from secular

authors on the subjects of psychology and
communication. I certainly do not endorse
all, or even a lot, of their material, but when
I saw several strengths in it, I recast it in a
Christian context to help us here. So, in a
sense, we learned from several persons who
were not Christians. They helped us with
truths they had discovered.

I mention this as an example of how
Christians can gain from other people, even
New Agers. Interested to know what those
secular books were? Okay, I won't keep
you guessing any longer! See: Berne, Eric,
MD, *Games People Play* (Secaucus, NJ:
Castle Books, 1964); Fisher, Roger, et. al.,
Getting to Yes (New York, NY: Penguin, 2nd
edit., 1991); Harris, Thomas, MD, *I'm
O.K.—You're O.K.*, (New York, NY: Harper &
Row, 1963); Rosenberg, Marshall B., *From
Now On* (St. Louis, Missouri: Community
Psychological Consultants Inc., self-
published, 1977).

19. *On Being Human*
1. For an in-depth look at several pantheistic
   views that are the soil for much of the New
   Age world, see: Clark & Geisler, *Apologetics
   in the New Age* (Grand Rapids, Mich.:
   Baker, 1991).
2. MacLaine, op. cit. pp. 339–41.
3. Ibid. p. 404.
4. Macaulay, Ranald and Barrs, Jerram, *Being
   Human: The Nature of Spiritual Experience*
   (Downers Grove, Ill.: InterVarsity Press,
   1978), p. 13.
5. Ibid. pp. 17–18.
6. Jeremiah 50:2.

20. *Flxybl*

1. 'Imprecise Words, Sloppy Thinking, Poor Management', *The Mountain Press* (Sevierville, TN), 25 September 1991.
2. Bennett, Catherine, 'Shirley Finds Her Spirit Level', *The Times*, 21 October 1987.
3. 'Infiltrating the New Age into Society', *What Is*, Summer 1986, p. 14; quoted in Groothuis, *Confronting the New Age*, p. 142.
4. See Chapter 10, footnote 1.
5. An increasing number of New Agers believe that through so-called 'past-life recall' they now know what 'bad karma' they have accrued to themselves from supposed previous lifetimes. This, they think, helps them understand why they are suffering in their present existences.
6. Bennett, op. cit.
7. Morey, Robert, Dr, *Death and the Afterlife* (Minneapolis, MN: Bethany, 1984). In chapter 6, Morey helpfully documents many instances of occult terminology being changed and the effect of this on Western culture's understanding of the paranormal.
8. Adeney, Frances, 'Revisioning Reality', *Spiritual Counterfeits Project Newsletter*, Vol. 7, No. 2.
9. *A Course in Miracles*, Vol. 2, Workbook for Students (The Foundation for Inner Peace, 1975), p. 391.
10. Ibid. p. 409.
11. Peck, John, Revd, source lost.
12. Lewis, C. S., *God in the Dock*, p. 93.
13. Ibid. p. 98.

21. *Effectual Prayer*
1. See Chapter 9, footnote 2.
2. McGavan, Donald A., *The Bridges of God: a study in the strategy of missions* (World Dominion Press, 1961), p. 45.

22. *Getting Peripheral Vision*
1. Jerram Barrs helped to found the L'Abri Fellowship Centre in Greatham, England, where he was a worker for twenty years. He is now a professor at Covenant Seminary, St Louis, Missouri.
2. Barrs, Jerram, 'Problems and Pathways in Communicating the Gospel in the 90s', L'Abri Cassette No. 2461 (L'Abri Cassettes, PO Box 2035, Michigan City, Ind., 46360, USA).
3. Petersen, Jim, *Church Without Walls* (Colorado Springs, Colo.: Navpress, 1992).
4. Keyes, Dick, 'Pluralism, Relativism and Tolerance', L'Abri Lecture Paper No. 2, L'Abri Fellowship.
5. I am deeply thankful to the Revd John Peck for sacrificing a year of his time to come to the States to teach us at the Trinity House Theatre and Art Group about Christian worldview, and for his ongoing personal correspondence that helps me to 'know the Truth' better.

Glossary

Note: Words in *italics* are also defined elsewhere in the Glossary.

A Course in Miracles: A popular New Age textbook and course that seeks 'to train your mind in a systematic way to a different perception of everyone and everything in the world'. The material is sourced in *spirit mediumship*, or *channelling*. It uses and redefines most cardinal biblical words and doctrines in an antibiblical way.

Age of Aquarius: Astrological lore teaches that the earth's axis slowly revolves through the 12 signs of the zodiac every 25,000 years. The approximately two thousand years that the axis spends travelling through each 'sign' is said to determine at least the general trends on the planet while it is in that 'sign'. These general trends are based on the characteristics of whatever 'sign' the axis is pointing to. Briefly, the earth is now finishing its time in Pisces, which, it is said, gave the earth Christianity. Now we are moving into the sign Aquarius, which promises to bring peace and harmony on the earth for the next two thousand years.

All is One, One is All: A New Age buzz-phrase

for any of several schools of *monism*.

Altered States of Consciousness (ASCs):
States other than normal waking *consciousness*
in which the person becomes open to mystical
experience, the *spirit* realm or *cosmic
consciousness*. ASCs can be entered through
consciousness-manipulating, or consciousness
expanding, techniques such as *TM, meditation,
visualisation* and hypnosis. Within the New Age
world, ASCs are thought to be a great link with
various kinds of healing and *spiritual
evolution*.

Alternative Medicine: A term used almost
interchangeably with *complementary
medicine, holistic health,* holistic medicine, and
holism to describe therapies and healing
practices that fall outside traditional Western,
allopathic, or orthodox, medicine and health
care. The list is long and would include ancient,
folk and pagan practices, such as shamanism
and voodoo, as well as the less offensive
acupuncture and homeopathy. The driving
force of alternative therapies seems to be their
ability to articulate the human being as a single
entity of mind, body and spirit, not only in
relation to the person but to the world. The fuel
for this driving force is various nonbiblical
beliefs about an invisible, *universal life-energy*
that pervades everything and unites us to one
another and the universe. When this *energy* is
unbalanced or blocked within the individual,
disease, disharmony or distress is said to result.
Rebalancing or unblocking the flow of the
'energy' is thought to aid restoration of health.

Spirit contact is not uncommon in some alternative therapies.

Aquarian Dream: See *Age of Aquarius*.

Arcane: That which is known or understood only by a few. Often used of esoteric *occult* knowledge.

Ascended Masters: A term made popular by Madame Blavatsky and her nineteenth-century Theosophical Society to describe the *spirit* beings with whom she was in contact and to whom she unabashedly credits in her many *occult* writings as the source of her knowledge.

Asceticism: In its broadest sense, the practice of self-denial or self-mortification for religious or spiritual reasons. Its aim is usually some form of *spiritual* purification, such as to pay off one's bad *karma,* to please the gods or to attain *enlightenment.*

Astrology: An idolatrous use of the stars and the planets whereby people think to gain information about their lives and futures. Uses a *horoscope* to disclose such information.

Aura: A colourful, invisible 'light' said to envelop the body or *spirit* from which it radiates. This 'light' may be seen, it is said, only by *clairvoyants* and *psychics* so attuned and who may diagnose the person's 'energy body' thereby. Various aura hypotheses of a *spiritual* nature are used by New Age healers in their efforts to cure bodily illness.

Avatar: The appearance of 'The Divine' in human form, often to reveal necessary truths to certain ages. ⎺ Rooted in *Hinduism* and *Buddhism*, in the persons of *Rama, Krishna* and *Buddha.* In some New Age schools of thought, Jesus Christ is considered an avatar for the Christian millennia.

Bhagavad Gita: One of Hinduism's most widely read sacred books and perhaps the most important for understanding Eastern *mysticism.* Contains much commentary, explanation, instruction and doctrine from *Krishna* to his bosom friend Arjuna.   Topics include the fundamental Hindu beliefs about *Self,* renunciation, *karma, yoga,* castes, the soul, nirvana and so on.

Biocentrism: A prevailing view in so-called *Deep Ecology* in which all living organisms—plant, animal, human—have equal intrinsic worth. This reduces the value of 'being human' to that of a Georgia peanut.

Brahma(n):   In *Hinduism,* the all-pervading 'God' or essential divine reality of the universe that is manifest in all that exists.   It provides a seedbed of thought for *pantheism.*

Buddha: Born sometime in the sixth century BC.   He practiced severe *asceticism* and austerity.   Considered an *avatar.*

Buddhism: A religion of eastern and central Asia built on the teaching of *Buddha.*   Several of its basic tenets include the avoidance of extremes, non-violence, friendliness to all, continence, reaching Nirvana (bliss) and escape from the round of rebirths *(reincarnation)*.

Centring: Broadly speaking, this is a term used particularly in classrooms as a substitute for the term *meditation*. *Grounding, stilling* and *going within* are other terms being substituted for 'meditation'. These terms are regularly used in the context of New Age body-work therapies, breathing exercises, relaxation techniques, creativity workshops, *visualisation, yoga* and so on. They are all basically generic-sounding, nonreligious labels for Eastern and mystical meditative techniques.

Channeller: Though some New Agers would argue that there are a few significant differences, this is fundamentally the New Age euphemism for *spirit medium.*

Channelling: The New Age euphemism for *spirit mediumship.*

Chi: In the mystical Chinese religion of *Taoism,* Chi is the invisible *spiritual energy* that is said to flow through all things and organisms as well as the universe. This spiritual *vital force* is said to be divided into two complementary opposites called *yin and yang,* and it forms the basic tenet of acupuncture-type therapies.

Christ (the): In the New Age world, this name must be distinguished from the Christ of the Gospels. The Christ of the New Age is an *avatar.* The Christ of the Gospels is God the Son, Lord, Saviour and Redeemer.

Christ-consciousness: An *intuitive* awareness of one's godhood status.

Christian Science: A cult founded in the late nineteenth century by Mary Baker Eddy. It stresses divine healing through the mind by manipulation of *spiritual* laws.

Clairvoyant: A person claiming the power to perceive things outside the range of normal sight. The term 'clairvoyance' is frequently used in association with *ESP*, telepathy, *psychics, paranormal* research, spiritism and so on.

Complementary Medicine: See *alternative medicine.*

Consciousness: Often used in the New Age world to describe self-awareness and preceded by the adjectives 'altered', 'expanded', or *Christ.*

Cosmic Christ: The impersonal divine force of the New Age that guides *spiritual evolution.*

Cosmic Consciousness: A state of awareness in which one perceives that *All is One, One is All.*

Cosmic Humanist: Whereas the secular humanist is thoroughly man-centred without any point of *spiritual* or *transcendent* reference, the cosmic humanist remains self-centred and has a point of spiritual or transcendent reference, but this is outside a biblical context.

Cosmopolitan Spirituality: A name I have coined to encompass all forms of nonbiblical *spiritual* or religious beliefs, practices, rituals and so on which are prevalent in the West today, regardless of their extent of influence.

Counterculture: The 1960s movement of young people whose values and lifestyles ran counter to the status quo. It was a seedbed for much that is called 'New Age' today.

Crystals: Colourful stones of various sizes, shapes and weights which are used by New Age seekers during *meditation* and healing therapies to enhance their access to the *universal life-energies* of the universe.

Deep Ecology: An attempt to develop a religious philosophy about ecological concerns in which the chief tenets are *biocentrism* and *Self-realisation* as articulated by Norwegian philosopher Arne Naess.

Dualism: As used in this book, the term applies to the dichotomy people often make between *secular/spiritual*, or body/spirit, or matter/ mind, or two equally powerful antagonistic forces of good and evil.

Eastern Religions: Used in this book chiefly to designate *Buddhism,* Confucianism, *Hinduism* and *Taoism.*

Energy: The New Age term for the animating 'life force' of the universe. May be called: animal magnetism, astral body, astrum, auras, bioplasma, *Chi* (Qi), ethers, *The Force,* The Innate, life energy, life force, mana, Odic Force, orgone, para-electricity, prana, *universal* *life-energy*, vital energy, *vital force*, voodoo, *yin and yang*.

Enlightenment: A noncommunicable mystical experience in which the recipient receives inner, intuitive, illumination about his or her divinity or Oneness with all things.

Entities: A New Age euphemism for *spirits*.

Entropy: The irreversible degradation of matter and energy.

Epistemology: A branch of philosophy that investigates the origin, nature and theory of knowledge, including how we come to know things. Several schools of thought that have made a contribution to this area are Empiricism, *Rationalism*, Idealism and Realism.

Esoteric: Whereas 'exoteric' is that which is not confined to an inner circle of disciples but is known to the larger public, esoteric is knowledge (most likely) that is confined to a select group of initiates. *Arcane.*

ESP: Extrasensory perception. The supposed ability to perceive or sense an object or event by means other than the physical senses. Made popular in the early twentieth century by the work of the *Society for Psychical Research* and *paranormal* research. All of the largest bodies of credible evidence and studies that have been conducted in the past one hundred years in this area still show no convincing proof of the existence of ESP. ESP has been shown to account for some instances of mediumistically transmitted information. *Clairvoyant.*

Existentialism: This is not easily defined because of the broad range of different emphases and characteristics placed upon it by philosophers. It is a kind of metaphysics in that it tackles the natural order; it is a kind of anthropology in that it explains human nature. It is frequently associated with philosophical or cultural rebellion against established ideas and institutions, such as *rationalism, materialism, naturalism.* Though diverse in how it is propounded, several common threads are: high regard for individual human existence; affirmation of freedom; strong emphasis on choice and its effect on the future; refusal to subordinate decisions to 'outside authority', such as existing social structures; stresses living in the 'here and now' with little or no regard for the past; history and the universe often seen as meaningless, irrelevant, absurd. Existentialism was a prevailing philosophical motivation for the 1960s *counterculture.*

The Force: Term popularised by George Lucas in his 'Star Wars' movies to describe 'an energy field generated by all living organisms. It surrounds us and penetrates us. The Force is where the Jedi gets his power,'—so says Obi-wan Kenobi to Luke Skywalker. But the Force is also where Darth Vader, or the Dark Side, gets his power. Thus the Force is but another attempt to invent monistic energies for any sorcerers, white or black, who wish to wield it. *Energy.*

Gaia (hypothesis): The personification of the

earth after the ancient Greek goddess 'Gaia'. In the hands of British atmospheric scientist James Lovelock and American microbiologist Lynn Margulis the planet earth is reinvented as the living goddess (creature) Gaia, who must be treated accordingly. The implications for ecology, politics and religion are considerable.

Gnosticism: A religious and philosophical system of the early Christian era whose central concept was that salvation comes through knowledge ('gnosis') rather than faith in Jesus Christ. It usually contained elements of Jewish, Christian, Greek and pagan thought. Christ is considered noncorporeal and matter is believed to be evil. Salvation results from transcending matter. Carl Jung did much to popularise gnosticism in the West, as did the discovery in the 1940s of the Nag Hammadi gnostic documents, which were found buried in a large earthenware jar that dates from the fourth century.

Going Within: See *centring, meditation, stilling.*

Greens: A pseudonym often used of people who are ecologically minded from a spiritual point of view.

Grounding: See *centring.*

Guided Imagery: A type of *meditation* in which the person closes his eyes and is mentally walked in his imagination through a scene usually created by another person. It is frequently used by students, instructed by teachers, as a means for visualising a 'helper' or 'wise person' who will act as a 'guide' for problem solving or motivation. Very easily becomes a mediumistic point of contact with *spirits*.

Guru: An Eastern religious teacher or holy man who has a following of disciples to whom he hands down his teaching. In the New Age world, often a *spiritual* teacher who shows the way to *enlightenment* or *spiritual evolution*.

Higher Self: Traceable back to Madame Blavatsky's theosophical teachings. Popularised by Shirley MacLaine as a *spirit guide* who can be *channelled* for great wisdom and infinite knowledge. Many New Agers do not see it as a separate *entity* but as an unresourced potential of their own personal unconscious and so worth getting in touch with.

Hinduism: A complex body of religious and cultural practices that forms the predominant religion of India. Central beliefs include *reincarnation, karma* and a Supreme Being who takes many forms and shapes.

Holism (holistic): From the Greek word 'holos', which means 'whole' in the sense of 'entire' or 'unified'. When informed by New Age wisdom, holism is an attempt to explain the integration of body, mind and spirit and develop and practise healing therapies in such a context. Also used ecologically. See *alternative medicine.*

Holistic Health Care: See *alternative medicine.*

Horoscope: A diagram, or map, of the stars and planets at the time of one's birth, and the interpretation thereof by an astrologer.

Humanism: As used in this book, a *secular* belief system whose central tenets are: man is totally autonomous from God; opposition to historic Christianity; rejection of the Bible. Man is his own authority and therefore answerable to no Higher Power than himself. This has led to the various kinds of moral and ethical *relativism* which has been thrust into education, science, politics, the arts and so on in the twentieth century.

Hypnotherapy: A complexity of various kinds of hypnosis in which the patient is placed in a trance state and coaxed to recall past experiences (traumas, repressions, hurts and so on) which the hypnotist then uses to create the conditions to bring the patient through to healing, sometimes called catharsis. It may be used in medical practice to treat a myriad of habits and diseases such as smoking, overeating, bulimia, improving memory and so on. In the New Age world, hypnotherapy is very dangerously allied to so-called *past-life recall therapy*.

I Ching: The Chinese practice of divination associated with *Taoism* and using sticks or coins and a book of sayings for telling the future.

Inner Healing: A complexity of various kinds of procedures, Christian and otherwise, for healing and transforming hidden hurts and wounds of the past and their deleterious influences upon present behaviour. The purpose is to produce increasing degrees of inner renewal in order that the person may live more wholly and fully in the future. Has been a highly controversial area.

Intuitive (the): Often used in the New Age world as a term to describe the act or faculty of sharp insight or knowing something without the use of rational processes.

Karma: The good and bad deeds, actions and works of one's present and supposed past lives and the total accumulation thereof. Every deed, good or bad, has an inevitable consequence, and the laws of karma are sometimes known as the laws of sowing and reaping. This provides an explanation for one's present condition, and it also offers a solution to suffering, for one can improve one's lot in this or a next life by doing good now. Ultimately, it is a doctrine of self-salvation through *reincarnation.*

Krishna: An *avatar*-manifestation of the Hindu god Vishnu.

Koan: Used chiefly in Zen Buddhism, koans are paradoxical riddles or questions to be used in *meditation* and which have no logical answer. Their purpose is to aid concentration and gain *intuitive* knowledge. Koans become meditation objects, day and night, and their lack of logical, rational solutions forces the meditator to experience altered modes of *consciousness.* Examples: show me your face before your mother and father met; or, what is the sound of one hand clapping?

Left Brain: It is still controversial, but theories now describe the left hemisphere of the brain as predominately involved in analytical, logical, rational thinking, especially verbal and mathematical functions. See *right brain*.

Life Force: See *energy*.

Macrobiotics: It may seem like a diet to outsiders but it is a spiritual discipline and way of life to initiates. The term was coined by George Ohsawa, a westernised Japanese, who had studied ancient Eastern religious philosophies and reinterpreted some of their central ideas, especially that of *yin and yang*, into macrobiotics.

Mandala: Usually a four-sided symbol, sometimes surrounded by a circle, used as a visual aid to restrict awareness during *meditation* and so focus attention and concentration on one object.

Mantra: In *Hinduism*, a vocal sound that is a secret formula believed to embody the divinity invoked by it; also thought to possess magical or supernatural powers. Used in *TM* and other meditative techniques as a word or sound repeated countlessly over and over and over again to focus attention, outwit the rational mind and enter meditative states. Becomes a ritualistic kind of prayer or incantation.

Materialism: A philosophical theory that physical matter in its movements and modifications is the only reality and that everything in the universe, including thought, feeling, mind and will, can be explained by physical laws.

Meditation: Chiefly used in this book to describe a deeply relaxed state and an emptying of the mind of rational thought in an effort to attain an *intuitive* kind of knowing and insight or even to contact *spirits*. There is a rapidly increasing number of New Age schools of meditation, each with their own overlapping or unique techniques, ranging from *TM* to breathing exercises to chanting a *mantra* to practising *visualisation*, and much more.

Medium: See *spirit medium*.

Mesmerism: The forerunner to hypnotic induction involving the phenomenon called animal magnetism, coined by Austrian physician Franz Mesmer (1734–1815).

Metaphysics: A branch of philosophy concerned with the systematic study of first principles and the nature of existence, including the study of being (ontology) and often the study of the structure of the universe (cosmology).

Monism: A system of *metaphysics* in which all reality, both the material and the *spiritual*, is conceived as a unified whole. There are various kinds of monistic systems. The popular buzz-phrase *All is One, One is All* sums up the New Age version. See footnote 2, chapter 7.

Monotheism: The doctrine of belief that there is only one God.

Mysticism: A *spiritual* discipline through which a practitioner hopes to attain contact or union with 'God' or 'Ultimate Reality' through deep or trance *meditation.* Christianity teaches that access to God is through the cross of Jesus Christ.

Naturalism: The theory that all phenomena can be explained in terms of natural causes and laws without attributing moral, *spiritual* and supernatural significance to them.

New Age Movement: A now imprecise term to describe the Aquarian Age.

Numerology: The study of the *occult* meaning of numbers and their supposed influence in human life and affairs.

Occult: Of or pertaining to demonic supernatural influences, *spirits* or phenomena and the practices by which one accesses such power.

Oneness: See *monism.*

Pantheism: The doctrine or belief that everything is God or a part of God. See *pantheistic monism.*

Pantheistic Monism: The word 'pantheism' comes from the Greek words 'pan' meaning 'all' and 'theos' meaning 'God'. The word 'monism' comes from the Greek word for 'single' or 'one'. The term 'pantheistic monism' is being used more frequently to describe what is perhaps the dominant metaphysical presupposition in the

New Age world. It can be summed up in the saying, *'All is One, One is All,* All is God'. This gives New Age wisdom both a God-concept and a theory of unity-in-diversity.

Paranormal: Various kinds of phenomena, usually known as *psychic,* which lie outside the range of normal sensory experience and of the scientifically explainable. *Psychic phenomena.*

Paradigm: A large framework of thought, or conceptual model, for understanding and explaining various aspects of reality, natural occurrences or phenomena. For example, there was Newton's 'paradigm' for describing the predictability of mechanical forces and how this would explain everything in terms of trajectories, gravity and force. As science evolved, the framework of Newtonian mechanics became increasingly unable to handle new discoveries and data, which placed stress and strain on this now 'old paradigm' so that a new framework of thought was necessary to contain and explain later discoveries and data. Enter Einstein's 'Special Theory of Relativity', which became a 'new paradigm' in the sciences to supersede Newton's physics. Paradigm shifts also occur in education, economics, health care, politics and so on.

Past-life Recall: This generally occurs within the domains of deep hypnosis or trance states in which the person 'remembers' incidents from his or her supposed past lives.

Past-life Recall Therapy: Identifying the traumas, hurts and bad experiences of one's supposed past lives in an effort to understand one's lot in this life and bring greater freedom and healing. Usually connected with the laws of *karma*.

Presupposition: An assumption about life that people do not think about and take for granted but which influences their actions in varying degrees. For example, a Christian prays because he assumes in advance that God is personal in nature and therefore able to hear his prayers. But he does not come to every time of prayer thinking, 'I'm going to pray because God is personal in nature and so will hear me.' This is simply taken for granted. A person's presuppositions, however, may not necessarily be true.

Psychic: From the Greek word 'psuche', meaning 'soul'. Used in this book chiefly to describe the wide range of *paranormal* phenomena, such as *ESP,* telepathy, *clairvoyance,* automatic writing, spoon bending, poltergeist activities and other 'supernormal' occurrences that lie outside the range of normal sensory or scientific explanation. Also used as a term to describe a person who is responsive to such 'forces'. It is not uncommon that psychic activities are breeding grounds for mediumistic activities with *spirits*.

Psychic Healing: The practice of healing (usually painless) by someone claiming to be able to manipulate 'universal healing energies'. Some attribute their healing powers to God. Most psychic surgeons, however, practise sleight-of-hand tricks on the bodies of their patients, which makes it seem as if the 'evil tissue' or 'negative energy' of a disease has been removed. There is much fraud and charlatanry in this area, as well as the potential danger of *spirit* contact through the trance state of the 'surgeon'.

Psychic Phenomena: See *psychic*.

Psychic Therapy: Usually done by a *spirit medium*, *channeller*, crystal healer or other persons claiming to have 'supernormal' powers. May easily lead to spirit contact.

Psycho-spiritual Technologies: A name for New Age transformative remedies, therapies, practices and processes that may not be *occult*-sounding but have Eastern religious, mystical or pagan *presuppositions*. These would include much that is called *alternative medicine* as well as disciplines like *A Course in Miracles*, *TM*, *visualisation* and others which incorporate the *cosmopolitan spirituality* of the New Age into their transformative 'technologies'.

Rama: Like *Krishna*, another beloved and adored divine manifestation in human form in *Hinduism*. *Avatar*.

Rationalism: From the Latin word 'rationalis', meaning 'belonging to reason'. As used in this book, it represents a complex *secular* belief system whose march through the West has been chiefly to combat the claims of religion, faith and spirituality by declaring that reason alone is the only valid source for knowledge, belief and action. God and the Bible have no place in informing human affairs and decisions.

Reductionism: Theories that reduce complex phenomena to separate simple parts, in order to try to explain the whole. When applied to psychology, for instance, reductionism may reduce the whole wealth of human behaviour to biological events and reflexes. Or, when informing the universe, it may reduce all of life to only that which is seen. Or, when applied to human beings, it may reduce a person to a collection of atoms and physical laws, or thoughts to a mere combination of sense impressions. Reductionist principles are frequently the presuppositions of the natural sciences and psychology, which is why they are futile for explaining the 'whole'.

Reincarnation: The doctrine or belief based on the laws of *karma* that people live many hundreds or thousands of lifetimes.

Relativism: Used in this book for the theory that there are no longer any moral absolutes; truth, therefore, becomes an ethical relative to the individual or group who holds it. This appears in the New Age world as the popular saying, 'You've got your truth, I've got mine.'

Right Brain: A still controversial theory that the brain's right hemisphere is predominantly involved with the creative, artistic and *intuitive* aspects. It is highly emphasised in the New Age world as that which needs great development and expression in Western people. *Left brain.*

Rolfing: Developed by biochemist Ida Rolf, this

particularly aggressive type of massage is
thought to help the body rebalance its energies
by softening muscles and so freeing the body
from poor postures. Someone has called it
massage with a vengeance.

Samsara: In *Hinduism* and *Buddhism*, the
eternal cycle of birth, suffering, death and
rebirth.

Secular: Pertaining to that which is worldly or
temporal rather than religious or *spiritual.*

Secular Humanism: See *humanism.*

Secularism: The view that the present well-
being of mankind excludes any religious or
spiritual considerations, especially in civil affairs
and public education.

Secularisation: The process of drawing away
from a religious or *spiritual* orientation as a chief
influence in a culture's activities and beliefs.

Self: In simplest terms, when the word appears
capitalised in New Age teaching, it is generally to
describe a God-concept. See *Self-realisation.*

Self-realisation: In *Hinduism* 'Atman' means
'Self' and is identified with *Brahma* (the
Supreme). The object of human life becomes to
discover one's unity with this Supreme Source.
When one becomes enlightened to this, it is Self-
realisation.

Shaman: In ancient times, a medicine man,
principally of northern Asia but also found in

Mexico and among American Indians, who worshipped *spirits* and practised healing through magic and power received from the spirits. A shaman claims the power to compel spirits by various rituals and incantations and to be able to protect clients from harmful influences of spirits. There is a revival of shamanism in the New Age world, especially among women.

Siva (Shiva): The Hindu god of destruction and reproduction; a member of the Hindu trinity along with *Brahma* and *Vishnu*.

Society for Psychical Research: Founded in 1882 by a number of scientists and philosophers to investigate *occult* phenomena. Lost some of its noteriety in the 1930s with the rise of so-called *paranormal* research activities and parapsychology.

Spirit(s): Used in this book to describe demonic supernatural beings with a power greater than that of humans, who can at times interfere in human affairs and who may be communicated with through *occult* means. Often labelled an *entity* or *spirit guide* in the New Age world and contacted through *spirit mediumship* or *channelling*.

Spirit Channelling: See *spirit mediumship*.

Spirit Guide: See *spirit*. In the New Age world, often thought to be a highly evolved deceased person who is between incarnations or who no longer has to reincarnate.

Spirit Medium(ship): A person thought to be able to contact the spirits of the dead and the process through which this is accomplished. Seances, ouija boards, tarot cards and *channelling* are popular means for this occultism. Channelling is a popular New Age practice in which a person enters a deep trance state and permits a *spirit* to completely take over the personality and so speak to a client about matters mundane or metaphysical. After a 'session' the spirit leaves the *channeller*, who returns to normal *consciousness* often without knowing what the spirit has said through him. Women who are channellers frequently speak in male voices when channelling a spirit.

Spiritual: The areas of life that relate to things which are not tangible or material but are concerned with the soul, God, religion or the sacred.

Spiritual Evolution: A way of describing the gradual process of New Age *spiritual* development both in this life and through *reincarnation*. This is thought to be accomplished by practising any of the numerous spiritual disciplines such as *meditation, yoga, asceticism,* doing good works and so on. Spiritual evolution asks the rhetorical question, 'Is a human being the best the "system" can produce?' Of course not, comes the answer. If we have pulled ourselves up this far from the biotic slime by our own bootstraps, maybe we can throw up a whole new 'order of being' someday. And the next stage towards that ultimate goal, it is generally agreed, is to pay off all of our bad *karma* so that we will not have to reincarnate any longer in our 'earth suits' and thus we can be highly evolved sheer *spirits*. After that, who knows? The potential is limitless because we are 'God'.

Spiritualism: Sometimes referred to as 'spiritism', and in this book includes spiritualist churches within its context. In its broadest meaning, includes communication with the dead or with *spirits* through a *medium* or *psychic* and a wide range of *occult* or *psychic phenomena*. Spiritualist churches are often confused with Christianity even though they stand opposed to cardinal Christian doctrine and belief.

Spiritualist: One who practises *spiritualism*.

Stilling: Often used in classrooms as a generic, non-religious label for Eastern religious forms of *meditation*.

Synchronicity: A term largely popularised by Carl Jung to describe 'meaningful coincidences' of events or actions that may otherwise seem unrelated to each other but now have perhaps a special or *spiritual* meaning.

Syncretism: The tendency to blend or reconcile differing beliefs, often religious or spiritual. In the New Age world, these attempts are usually made by trying to take cardinal Christian beliefs and make them compatible with *occult* or Eastern mystical or pagan beliefs. For example, using the name 'Jesus' to mean an *avatar*, or redefining 'forgiveness' as a change of 'perception', or saying that the *spirit guides* are angels or highly evolved human beings.

Systems Theory: A view of looking at the world as a whole system of interrelated smaller systems. It is a reaction against *reductionism* and the prevailing analytical way of examining things and the world by breaking them up into an unrelated multiplicity of objects. In systems thinking, which is often characterised by words like organic and holistic, the universe is seen as one indivisible dynamic whole whose 'parts' are interrelated. Within this whole are innumerable systems in their own right, e.g. an anthill, a beehive, the human family, and these form a complex web of interrelationships between them that make up the bigger system which comprises all the interrelationships. In a systems view things are not remaining static but are part of a continual dynamic process of evolution, as frequently depicted by the saying, 'The whole is greater than the sum of its parts.'*

Taoism: 'Tao' is an ancient Chinese word meaning 'the way' or 'the one', and it describes the ultimate essence, or universal principle or *energy*, by and through which all things have their existence. It manifests itself in all things in a process of antithetic but complementary 'rhythms', such as *yin and yang* or macrocosm and microcosm, and these correspond with and counterbalance each other. Taoism, which can be traced back to the teaching of Lao Tse in sixth-century BC China, is 'The Way' of recapturing and preserving the harmony of this supposed 'spiritual rhythm' that animates all things.

---

* This description has been distilled from Elliot Miller's book *A Crash Course on the New Age Movement*.

Tarot: A deck of twenty-two playing cards depicting vices, virtues and *spiritual* powers. These are used in *occult* forms of character analysis and fortune telling.

Teleology: In its broadest sense, the philosophical study of design or purpose in the universe, as opposed to the view that the universe can be understood by purely mechanical or natural causes or explanations.

TM: Transcendental meditation. It was introduced to the United States in 1959 by the Hindu monk Maharishi Mahesh Yogi and became widely popularised in the West when promoted by the Beatles in the late 1960s. When this Eastern mystical form of *meditation* was redefined in a thorough-going scientific language (complete with research graphs and documentation), it moved from the counter-cultural fringe to mainstream culture, hailed as it was as a great key to physical and mental relaxation, stress management, blood-pressure reduction, anxiety relief, job performance improvement and increased sexual enjoyment. There is much ritual initiation which includes the giving of a *mantra*.

Transcendent: Often used of Deity to describe that which is above and independent of the material universe.

Transformation: Used in the New Age world in very broad contexts to describe one's 'passage' from old traditional ways (paradigms) of thinking to an awareness or awakening to New Age ways of thinking and acting. Marilyn

Ferguson has written that transformation is a journey without a final destination, and she analyses it (Ha!) in four stages. First comes the entry point, in which something catastrophic shakes up one's old understanding. LSD, for example, did this for the hippies. Then comes exploration, in which the seeker searches and practises the *psycho-spiritual technologies* designed to free the tight hold one has on the old and so expand consciousness to an acceptance of New Age thinking. Then comes integration, in which New Age thinking and its practices are more thoroughly influencing the person's life. The fourth stage she calls conspiracy, in which the *paradigm* shift is so strong that the person seeks to communicate the ideas of the transformation to others and incorporate them into his work and family because the social implications of it have been seen and understood.

Transmigration: Used of 'souls' in *Eastern religions* to describe *reincarnation* from body to body as determined by one's *karma*. Past and future bodies may include animals as well, which is why cows and rats, for example, are treated specially in India and not killed or eaten.

Transpersonal: In the New Age world, a term describing levels of *consciousness* above and beyond the strictly personal. Often associated with New Age *spiritual* disciplines and practices and the *intuitive*, or when describing contact with *spirit guides*.

Transpersonal Psychology: A vast and bewildering constellation of psychological practices and therapies that incorporate spirituality into counselling. They would include their own blends of *syncretism* from influences such as Zen Buddhism, contemporary Sufism, *TM*, alchemy, hypnotism, *gnosticism, Taoism, mysticism,* the Cabalistic tradition, Carl Jung and much more. *Spirit* contact roams through transpersonal psychologies like a particularly bad Los Angeles smog.

Unity: Officially, the 'Unity School of Christianity'. Called by Dr Walter Martin 'the largest gnostic cult in Christendom'. Highly syncretistic and rejects the cardinal tenets of Christianity. Accepts *reincarnation*. It is easy to find many books promoting *astrology* and the *occult* in Unity church libraries.

Universal Consciousness: A New Age term for 'God consciousness' which is impersonal. See *energy*.

Universal Life-energy: See *energy*.

Vishnu: Whereas *Brahma* represents the Creator and *Siva* the Destroyer, Vishnu represents the third aspect of this Hindu triad of the Supreme as the Sustainer.

Visualisation: Often called 'creative visualisation' and not necessarily New Age in practice; but when it is, it is a kind of *spiritual* discipline using 'mental energies' to manipulate or create one's own goals, realise dreams, greatly improve or transform health, relationships and beauty. It is practised in the context of setting goals, developing *paranormal* senses, relaxation exercises, deep *meditation*, affirmations and other mystical techniques. It promises that as you control and shape your thoughts, dreams and desires, you can create your own reality. After entry-level stages, it usually involves one in contact with *spirit guides* and occultism.

Vital Force: Used loosely in the New Age world to describe *energy*, but it was chiefly popularised by the founder of homeopathy, Samuel Hahnemann, who wrote that 'the spiritual vital force [is] the dynamism that animates the material body'. According to Hahnemann, 'when a person falls ill, it is only this spiritual . . . vital force . . . that is primarily deranged', and so responsible for outer bodily symptoms, which are secondary.

Wicca: A new label for white *witchcraft*. Very popular among New Age pagans and feminists.

Witchcraft: The practice of sorcery or ritual magic, either black or white, to manipulate supernatural powers thought to exist in nature, animals and humans. Often associated with a revival of pagan religions and animism.

Worldview: James Sire has written that a worldview is a set of *presuppositions* one holds about the basic make-up of the world. That is about as simple and clear a definition as you are likely to find. Such assumptions about the basic make-up of life and the world include what one thinks about the nature of personal and societal concerns and dimensions, such as

education, politics, religion, the family and so
on. In this book I have used the term 'wisdom'
in its biblical sense in place of 'worldview'.

Yin and Yang: The two fundamental rhythms
or *spiritual* forces in *Taoism* that make up *Chi.*
They are said to be complementary opposites
forming a harmonious whole when balanced.
They are an essential part of *macrobiotics* and
most acupuncture theories, methodologies and
treatments and their derivatives, such as
acupressure and shiatsu. In the Western New
Age world, yin and yang have taken on a
wealth of opposite though complementary
characteristics. For example, yin: dark, cold,
feminine, below; yang: light, heat, masculine,
above. Yin and yang have no basis in material
reality.

Yoga: From a Sanskrit word meaning 'yoking'
or 'union', usually with 'God'. The aim of the
Indian Yogi is the self's liberation from matter
and union with the Supreme *Self.* This is
attained gradually through stages by means of
scrupulous practice of self-control, prescribed
bodily postures, strict regulation of breathing,
meditation and focusing of the gaze. Miraculous
powers are promised to the one who attains
absorption into the Supreme. In the West,
attempts have been made to demystify yoga by
marketing it as merely a physical discipline, for
training and expanding *consciousness*,
experiencing tranquillity, receiving *spiritual*
insight or doing exercise. Various aims of yoga
are represented by its different schools, such as
hatha, gnana, karma, bhakti, tantra and
kundalini. The hatha, kundalini and tantra

schools, probably in that order, are the most popular in the West.

Zeitgeist: The outlook or spiritual characteristics of a certain period of time. From the German 'zeit', meaning 'time' and 'geist', meaning 'spirit'.

Zen Koans: See *koans.*

Zen Macrobiotics: See *macrobiotics.*

Zygote: The organism that develops from a mature sperm and egg participating in fertilisation.

Recommended Reading

(including cassette tapes and useful organisations)

New Age and Related Topics
(listed alphabetically by author)

Abell, George O. and Singer, Barry (eds.), *Science and the Paranormal: Probing the Existence of the Supernatural* (New York, NY, Charles Scribner's Sons, 1981). From a secular viewpoint, many eminent scientists evaluate topics such as The Bermuda Triangle, Big Foot, UFOs, ESP, Uri Geller, TM, pyramids and more.

Albrecht, Mark, *Reincarnation: A Christian Appraisal* (Downers Grove, Ill.: InterVarsity Press, 1982). A short, clear and informative critique of this cardinal New Age belief. Topics: history of, past-life recall, arguments against, theological objections to.

Amano, J. Yutaka and Geisler, Norman L., *The Infiltration of the New Age* (Wheaton, Ill.: Tyndale House Publishers, 1989). Examines central New Age beliefs. Chapters on Self and inner healing. Five helpful appendices.

Ankerberg, John and Weldon, John, *Astrology: Do the Heavens Rule Our Destiny?* (Eugene, Oreg.: Harvest House Publishers, 1989). A wide variety of astrological principles and practices receive extensive Christian criticism.

———, *Can You Trust Your Doctor?: The Complete Guide to New Age Medicine and Its Threat to Your Family* (Brentwood, Tenn.: Wolgemuth & Hyatt, 1991). The most exhaustive Christian analysis of holistic health care and alternative medicine that I know of so far. Worth the investment.

Bishop, Steve and Droop, Christopher, *The Earth is the Lord's: A Message of Hope for the Environment* (Bristol, Eng.: The Regius Press Ltd., 1990). A very brief introductory work explaining the basis for Christian earth-steward-ship. But what do the authors mean by 'cosmic Christ'? Extensive bibliography is worth the price of the book.

Campolo, Tony, *How to Rescue the Earth Without Worshipping Nature* (Milton Keynes, Eng.: Nelson Word, 1992). Partially reviewed. Stretch your thinking with these fresh insights about Christian earth-stewardship.

Chandler, Russell, *Understanding the New Age* (Milton Keynes, Eng.: Nelson Word, 1989). Chock-a-block with information. Chandler's job as religious correspondent for the *Los Angeles Times* newspaper gave him access to many New Age and Christian leaders, whom he interviewed for the book.

Clark, David K. and Geisler, Norman L., *Apologetics in the New Age: A Christian Critique of Pantheism* (Grand Rapids, Mich.: Baker Book House, 1990). A scholarly defence of Christian belief against five kinds of pantheism and their New Age expressions.

Cole, Michael, et al., *What is the New Age?* (London, Eng.: Hodder & Stoughton, 1990). Multiple authorship gives this book breadth of insight into topics such as New Age origins, conspiracy theory, spiritual powers, the real new age and more.

Cooper, Tim, *Green Christianity* (London, Eng.: Spire, 1990). Though the book virtually ignores the occult potential of New Ageism, it provides a critique of New Age earth-stewardship ideologies and makes a convincing case for Christian earth-stewardship. Cooper is a prominent figure in Britain's growing Green movement.

Culver, Roger B. and Ianna, Philip A., *Astrology: True or False?: A Scientific Evaluation* (Buffalo, NY: Prometheus Books, 1988). May be the definitive scientific criticism of astrology from a secular viewpoint. Written by two professors of astronomy. Well-researched and thought through.

Drane, John, *What is the New Age Saying to the Church?* (London, Eng.: Marshall Pickering, 1991). This lecturer in religious studies at the University of Stirling, Scotland, interviewed leading New Agers for the book. Somewhat unsettling criticisms of Christian failure with New Age people.

Ellis, Roger, *The Occult and Young People* (Eastbourne, Eng.: Kingsway, 1989). Clear warnings about occult power and practices from astral projection to witchcraft, and help for those involved in them.

Geisler and Amano, *The Reincarnation Sensation* (Wheaton, Ill.: Tyndale House, 1987). This biblical evaluation includes examination of the psychology and injustice of reincarnation; also, a look at 'Christian' belief in it.

Gordon, Ian, *The Craft and the Cross* (Eastbourne, Eng.: Kingsway, 1989). Autobiography. Insights about the New Age are woven throughout this fascinating account of Gordon's rise in the Masons, which he thought was compatible with Christianity, until . . .

Groothuis, Douglas, *Unmasking the New Age* (Downers Grove, Ill.: InterVarsity, 1986). May be the best 'get acquainted with the New Age' book on the market. Topics include: 'All is One, One is All'; human potential in psychology; New Age science and politics; Christian response.

——, *Confronting the New Age* (Downers Grove, Ill.: InterVarsity, 1988). A good companion book to *Unmasking* . . . Topics include: New Age education, business and music; visualisation; three chapters on witnessing to New Age people.

——, *Revealing the New Age Jesus: Challenges to Orthodox Views of Christ* (Downers Grove, Ill.: InterVarsity, 1990). In-depth coverage of pagan, gnostic and New Age views of Jesus Christ. Other topics: the 'lost years' of Jesus; Jesus the Essene, the Spirit, the Cosmic Christ. Very helpful bibliography.

Hoyt, Karen, et al., *The New Age Rage* (Old Tappan, NJ; Revell, 1987). From eight Spiritual Counterfeits Project writers comes a careful exploration of the New Age, holistic health, quantum physics, transpersonal psychology, tantra, an appendix on Christian and New Age worldviews and other relevant ideas and practices.

Korem, Dan, *Powers: Testing the Psychic and the Supernatural* (Downers Grove, Ill.: InterVarsity, 1988). A psychic detective finds a missing body; a mind reader knows your thoughts; a psychic points and the pencil moves. This investigative journalist and magician exposes how psychics fool us. The section on 'cold readings' is worth the price of the book.

Lewis, C. S., *That Hideous Strength* (New York, NY: MacMillan, 1972). Take a break. Want a novel that actually does what everyone (almost) thinks Peretti's tales are doing? A chilling good yarn. Was Lewis playing the prophet?

Logan, Kevin, *Close Encounters with the New Age* (Eastbourne, Eng.: Kingsway, 1991). After spending time at Findhorn (Scotland) and Glastonbury (England), the author shares his observations about the esotericism of those places.

Maharaj, Rabindranath R., with Dave Hunt, *Death of a Guru* (London, Eng.: Hodder & Stoughton, 1978). Also published as *Escape into the Light*. Autobiography. A convincing Eastern mystical connection with the Western New Age is made in this young yogi's poignant search for meaning within Hinduism and his parallel struggle towards Jesus Christ.

Mangalwadi, Vishal, *In Search of Self: Beyond the New Age* (London, Eng.: Hodder and Stoughton, 1992). This L'Abri Fellowship associate writes with refreshing insight from his background and experience as an Indian Christian. Endorsed by Os Guinness.

Martin, Walter, *The New Age Cult* (Minneapolis, Minn.: Bethany, 1989). Unreviewed. Written by one of Christianity's foremost investigators of cults and the occult.

Matrissiana, Caryl, *Gods of the New Age* (Basingstoke, Eng.: Marshall Pickering, 1985). Autobiography. A fashionable Londoner enters the New Age and later becomes disillusioned and turns to Christ.

Michaelson, Johanna, *The Beautiful Side of Evil* (Eugene, Oreg.: Harvest House, 1982). Autobiography. The unmasking of psychic healing from someone who was a personal assistant to a psychic healer in Mexico, and her conversion to Christ.

Miller, Elliot, *A Crash Course on the New Age Movement* (Grand Rapids, Mich.: Baker Book House, 1989). Some autobiography. Chiefly a survey and critique of New Age ideology from the editor-in-chief of the 'Christian Research Journal'. Topics include: mysticism, general systems theory, New Age activism and channelling.

North, Gary, *Unholy Spirits: Occultism and New Age Humanism* (Fort Worth, Tex.: Dominion Press, 1986). Also published as *None Dare Call It Witchcraft*. An intelligent look at things, from the crisis of Western rationalism, to Carlos Castaneda, to Edgar Cayce, to UFOs, to the end of the world(?).

Osborn, Lawrence, *Angels of Light?: The Challenge of the New Age* (London, Eng.: Daybreak, 1992). Unreviewed. Foreword by Christian thinker Lesslie Newbigin, who commends the book as 'necessary reading'.

Pement, Eric (ed.), *Contend for the Faith: Collected Papers of the Rockford Conference on Discernment and Evangelism* (Chicago, Ill.: Evangelical Ministries to New Religions, 1992). More than 20 contributors on a wide variety of subjects—discernment, worldview, apologetics, Islam, Buddhism, Mormonism, Jehovah's Witnesses, astrology, channelling, exit-counselling and much more—make this unique volume appropriate for your reference section. Limited print run.

Perry, Michael, *Gods Within: A Critical Guide to the New Age* (London, Eng.: SPCK, 1992). Makes some good points at times, but the book clouds the borders between paranormal phenomena and Christian spiritual gifts, does not take a firm stand against visiting spirit mediums and includes occultist Rudolph Steiner in a list of Christian 'oracles'. Not recommended for young Christians or those already confused by the New Age. Does not seem to me to live up to its subtitle.

Pfeifer, Samuel, MD, *Healing at Any Price?: The Hidden Dangers of Alternative Medicine* (Milton Keynes, Eng.: Nelson Word, 1988). A good Christian appraisal of the twilight zone of holism and alternative medicine. Topics include: reflexology, acupuncture, homeopathy, iridology, herbal medicine and more.

Reisser, Paul C. MD, Reisser, Teri K. and Weldon, John, *New Age Medicine: A Christian Perspective on Holistic Health* (Downers Grove, Ill.: InterVarsity, 1987). A good introductory assessment of popular holistic practices. The chapters on energy and Chinese medicine are particularly helpful.

Rhodes, Ron, *The Counterfeit Christ of the New Age Movement* (Grand Rapids, Mich.: Baker Book House, 1990). This associate editor with the 'Christian Research Journal' surveys New Age teaching about Jesus Christ. Discusses David Spangler, Elizabeth Clare Prophet, Matthew Fox and others.

Seaton, Chris, *Whose Earth?* (Westchester, Ill.: Crossway Books, 1992). Unreviewed. Foreword by Mike Morris, International Secretary of the Evangelical Alliance, who commends the book for 'informed insights with radical proposals for action'.

Sire, James, *Scripture Twisting* (Downers Grove, Ill.: InterVarsity, 1980). Reveals many ways in which the Bible can be taken out of context. New Age relevance.

Smith, LaGard F., *Out on a Broken Limb*

(Eugene, Oreg.: Harvest House, 1986). A Christian response to Shirley MacLaine's New Age bestseller *Out on a Limb*. Shows the flaws of MacLaine's New Age beliefs and her misuse of Scripture.

——, *Crystal Lies: Choices and the New Age* (Ann Arbor, Mich.: Vine Books, Servant Publications, 1989). A plethora of Bible verses helps move the book along and helps readers make wise choices about their beliefs.

Taylor, Mike, *Ley Lines and the Christian* (Market Harborough, Eng.: Diasozo Trust, 1992). Booklet. The soundest explanation of the subject that I know of. May challenge some Christians to give up beliefs not founded on the Bible.

Evangelisation, Outreach and Counselling Resources

Brooke, Tal, *Riders of the Cosmic Circuit* (Batavia, Ill.: Lion Publishing, 1986). Autobiography. This former Western disciple of Sai Baba writes to New Age seekers about his life, his assessment of leading gurus and his conversion to Jesus Christ.

Buell, Jon A. and Hyder, Quentin O., *Jesus: God, Ghost or Guru?* (Grand Rapids, Mich.: Zondervan/Probe, 1978). This Christian Free University Curriculum book is an apologetic for an orthodox view of Jesus Christ, with a response by F. F. Bruce. Will help New Agers to see other choices.

Enroth, Ronald (ed.), *Evangelising the Cults* (Ann Arbor, Mich.: Servant, 1990). Ten Christian contributors write chapters on Mormonism, Scientology, occult groups, Eastern religions, the New Age and more, in the context of how to share Jesus with such people.

Green, Michael, *You Must Be Joking: Popular Excuses for Avoiding Jesus Christ* (London, Eng.: Hodder & Stoughton, 1976). Great material to use in conversations with New Agers who lean on typical objections to Christianity.

Halverson, Dean, *Crystal Clear: A Small Group Discussion Guide for Understanding and Reaching New Agers* (Colorado Springs, Colo.: Navpress, 1990). Just what the subtitle says. The nine sessions in this compact work will help you explore the salient characteristics of the New Age belief system and how to approach New Agers with understanding and sensitivity. Leader's Guide runs parallel to the sessions.

Koch, Kurt, *Christian Counselling and Occultism* (Grand Rapids, Mich.: Kregal Publications, 1972). Ought to be read slowly and carefully by any Christian involved in ministry to people who are thought to be influenced by occult phenomena. Hundreds of pastoral case studies cited. Principles for discernment given.

Lewis, C. S., *Mere Christianity* (New York, NY: MacMillan, 1952). This lucid defence of the Christian faith can be given to New Agers to speak to them about the reality of God, Jesus, morals, forgiveness and other cardinal Christian beliefs.

Martin, Walter Dr, *Kingdom of the Cults* (Minneapolis, Minn.: Bethany, 1985, rev. edit.). Still the definitive work for nearly two dozen major cults. Also carries chapters on dealing with the language barrier and the psychological structure of cultism. Ought to be on the shelf for any Christian who needs a handy and dependable reference. Chapters on New-Age-related topics include: theosophy, spiritism, scientology and Eastern religions.

McDowell, Josh, *Evidence that Demands a Verdict* (San Bernardino, Calif.: Campus Crusade for Christ, 1972). A good book for doing a series of Bible studies on the fact and meaning of the Resurrection.

Petersen, Jim, *Evangelism as a Lifestyle* (Colorado Springs, Colo.: Navpress, 1980). How to reach people in your world who have little or no understanding of Christianity. Identifies problems with traditional evangelism and offers solutions for communicating the gospel to a secularised world.

——, *Evangelism for Our Generation* (Colorado Springs, Colo.: Navpress, 1985). Very helpful material on worldview and understanding our times, and how these affect our evangelism. An appendix with a step-by-step evangelistic study of John's Gospel.

——, *Church Without Walls* (Colorado Springs, Colo.: Navpress, 1992). Unreviewed. Foreword by Dr Gene A. Getz, who writes that this 'veteran missionary . . . has earned the right to speak out' about why traditional church structures have outlived their functions and impede the gospel in today's world, and how forgotten New Testament ideas would help us correct this.

Richardson, Don, *Peace Child: An Unforgettable Story of Primitive Jungle Treachery in the Twentieth Century* (Ventura, Calif.: Regal Books, 1976). Autobiography. Shows how Don and Carol Richardson overcame unbelieveable odds to communicate the gospel to a Stone Age Sawi tribe. A real faith builder for Christians who feel terribly up against it with New Age people.

Strohmer, Charles, *What Your Horoscope Doesn't Tell You* (American edition—Wheaton, Ill.: Tyndale House, 1988; Milton Keynes, Eng.: Nelson Word, 1991). I put myself on the other side of the typewriter while I was writing the book and asked, 'What would have made sense to me from a Christian point of view when I was into the New Age, to help me see its dangers and get out of it?' Out of that came a weighty exposé of astrology, written for non-Christian spiritual seekers. It is a book you can put into their hands that will challenge them at their level and also offer the gospel. It has been very influential towards this end.

Christianity and the Modern World

The following books will assist readers who are interested in knowing more about the importance of worldview as it relates primarily to the cultural shift that is occurring in the West today, and how we as Christians should understand it and respond.

Guinness, Os, *The Dust of Death* (Downers Grove, Ill.: InterVarsity, 1973). A critique of the counterculture as it journeyed out of a rationalistic and technological wasteland into the Promised Land of radical politics, Eastern religion, psychedelic drugs and the occult.

Newbigin, Lesslie, *Foolishness to the Greeks: The Gospel and Western Culture* (London, Eng.: SPCK, 1990). A healthy dose of understanding for the problems we face in communicating with a modern Western world. The author is especially concerned with the problems represented by modern science, social structures and political practices. Deeply thoughtful.

Niebuhr, H. Richard, *Christ and Culture* (New York, NY: Harper & Row, 1975). Unreviewed. Analysis of the problematic relations of Christianity with culture. Sections include: Christ against culture, the Christ of culture, Christ above culture, Christ as transformer of culture.

Peck, John, *Wisdom in the Marketplace* (London, Eng.: Greenbelt, 1989). Penetrating and ground-breaking. This Christian philosopher and theologian helps us faithfully meet the radical questions that beset the modern world with the 'wisdom of God'. The book is about more than building up ideas and making them work. It aims to assist the personal development of a biblical viewpoint that will become instinctive and govern actions in a spontaneous, godly manner.

Schaeffer, Francis, *The God Who is There* (Downers Grove, Ill.: InterVarsity, 1968). Surveys the intellectual and cultural climate of the second half of the twentieth century, shows the relationship of the New Theology to that climate, explains how historic Christianity differs.

——, *He is There and He is Not Silent* (Wheaton, Ill.: Tyndale House, 1972). 'This book,' Schaeffer wrote, 'deals with the philosophic necessity of God's being there and not being silent, in the areas of metaphysics, morals and epistemology.'

——, *Escape From Reason* (Downers Grove, Ill.: InterVarsity, 1968). A penetrating analysis of trends in modern thought. Starting with Aquinas and coming up through the Renaissance, the Reformation and early modern science, the book shows what has led to modern man's despair and his blind existential leap into whatever he thinks will bring the answer to life's meaninglessness. (These three books by Schaeffer make a unified base for much of the author's thought and work.)

Sire, James, *The Universe Next Door* (Downers Grove, Ill.: InterVarsity, 1976). Different worldview perspectives, including Eastern panetheistic monism and the New Consciousness.

——, *Discipleship of the Mind* (Downers Grove, Ill.: InterVarsity, 1990). Unreviewed. Topics include: introduction to worldview analysis, the nature of human nature, knowing and doing, the meaning of human history. Includes an appendix to Christian students and an amazing bibliography.

Walsh, Brian J. and Middleton, J. Richard, *The Transforming Vision: Shaping a Christian Worldview* (Downers Grove, Ill.: InterVarsity, 1984). Unreviewed. Sections include: what are worldviews?; biblical worldview; modern worldview; Christian cultural response.

Webber, Robert E., *The Church in the World* (Grand Rapids, Mich.: Zondervan, 1986). Unreviewed. A historical and theological survey of the Church–World issue, from New Testament times to modern day. Explores how Christians can have a redemptive influence on the world and guide decisions of government. Assesses Christian activists as diverse as Jerry Falwell, Tim LaHaye, Ron Sider, Richard Neuhaus and Gustavo Gutiérrez.

Cassette Tapes

Charles Strohmer has two popular cassette tape courses on the New Age. These are not composed of assorted messages collected from various conferences, but were designed and taught as whole courses, in an effort to provide continuity of thought throughout. These have an international flavour to them, and they bring more than twenty years of experience as an 'insider turned outsider' to the subject. Each course uses biblical wisdom to evaluate the theories, beliefs, practices and therapies of the New Age. They answer the questions that most people are asking and bring perspectives we may have missed. They also help to equip the listener with effective communication skills. As *Wise as a Serpent, Harmless as a Dove* has been chiefly about effective communication, both the courses below are designed for gaining a much more thorough understanding of New Age wisdom in particular, and a biblical response to it. Either course makes an ideal tool for use alongside *Wise as a Serpent, Harmless as a Dove.* Churches, Sunday school classes and home Bible study groups also use the courses to run studies on the New Age and stimulate small-group discussions and activities.

1. New Age Spirituality and Christian Belief
This popular in-depth course is one of a kind. It contains more than fifteen hours of teaching on ten cassette tapes. It includes classes on:

- principalities and powers
- man as god
- rebirth theory
- spiritual evolution
- mystical experience
- New Age occultism (3 classes)
- New Age wisdom in culture (2 classes)
- New Age wisdom in health care (2 classes)
- communicating with New Agers (2 classes)
- psychic powers and the paranormal
- Carl Jung and New Age psychology
- Charles Strohmer's testimony

2. A Crash Course on the New Age
This is not a shortened version of the above

course.   It stands on its own, consisting of six classes, five hours of teaching.   The classes include:

- common misunderstanding about the New Age
- what we are up against
- New Age occultism
- holistic health care
- New Age wisdom in education and business
- effective communication

To order in the United States:

For 'New Age Spirituality and Christian Belief', send $39.95, or for 'A Crash Course on the New Age', send $12.95 to:
Charles Strohmer, Tapes, PO Box 4325, Sevierville, TN, 37864.   Make cheque payable to C. Strohmer.

To order in Great Britain or elsewhere in Europe:

For 'New Age Spirituality and Christian Belief', send £24.95, or for 'A Crash Course on the New Age', send £8.95 to:
Manna Christian Centre, 147–149 Streatham High Road, London, SW16 6EG.   Make cheque payable to Manna.

If you wish to write directly to Charles Strohmer from outside the United States and order your tapes that way, please send only an *International Money Order* in US dollars only.   (Each course comes in an attractive album and cover.)

Useful Organisations

Great Britain

Beacon Foundation, 3 Grosvenor Avenue, Rhyl, Clywd, LL18 4HA, Wales.
Helps both professionals and churches monitor the occult problem in Britain. Will assist in rehabilitation of victims of occult abuse.

Christian Information Outreach, 92 The Street, Boughton, Faversham, Kent, ME13 9AP, England.
Offers films, tapes, books, research, etc. Newsletter.

Deo Gloria Trust, Selsdon House, 212–220 Addington Road, South Croydon, Surrey, CR2 8LD, England.
Books, leaflets, research, etc.

United States

Christian Research Institute, PO Box 500, San Juan Capistrano, CA, 92693.
Publishes a popular quarterly journal and a bi-monthly newsletter. Offers books, tapes and many timely helps.

Evangelical Ministries to New Religions, PO Box 10279, Denver, CO, 80210.
Research, conferences.

Jesus People USA (JPUSA), Eric Pement or John Trott, 4707 N. Malden, Chicago, IL, 60640.
Publishes *Cornerstone* magazine and offers

counselling, lectures and timely research, as well as an extensive 'Directory' of both evangelical and nonevangelical agencies, cult, occult and New Age research organisations (hundreds of listings, international).

Spiritual Counterfeits Project, PO Box 4308, Berkeley, CA, 94704.
Publishes noteworthy journal and newsletter. Offers a wealth of research at your fingertips through their 'Access Line', phone (415) 540-5767, 10.00 a.m. to 2.00 a.m. West Coast Time only. Lectures and conferences.

About the Author

Charles Strohmer is an author, editor, seminar speaker and ordained Christian minister. Before becoming a Christian in July 1976, he spent many years as a professional astrologer. He also practised meditation and visualisation with 'spirit guides'. After his conversion, he studied Christian spirituality under the late Dr Francis Schaeffer's L'Abri ministry and took extensive courses in Christian philosophy and worldview under English theologian and philosopher the Revd John Peck. An American, he lived in Great Britain where his wife was a missionary for several years. He now resides in the Smoky Mountains of Tennessee.

Wise as a Serpent, Harmless as a Dove is his third book. His second, *Explaining the Grace of God*, is being distributed as a teaching booklet in CIS and Third World nations. His first book, *What Your Horoscope Doesn't Tell You*, is having wide success in numerous translations. He has been a guest on radio and television, including the '700 Club' and the BBC, and his articles have been published in several magazines, including the *Spiritual Counterfeits Project Journal*. His work also takes him across the denominations on both sides of the Atlantic, speaking in churches, colleges and mission organisations.

He is associated with the Trinity House Arts Group in Livonia, Michigan, is listed in the fourth edition of *Who's Who in Religion*, and is currently at work on his autobiography.

WHAT YOUR HOROSCOPE DOESN'T TELL YOU

Charles Strohmer

In a world controlled more and more by technology, astrology offers people a system to help them figure out how to live peacefully in an unpredictable world.

Astrology has been the leading practice of the so-called New Age movement for more than 25 years. But is astrology's 'wisdom' true wisdom? Is it science or religion? Real or counterfeit? Is astrology in harmony with the will of God?

Charles R. Strohmer answers these questions from his experience as a former astrologist. He explains where astrology came from and how it 'works'. He shatters the myth that astrology is a benign 'game' that people play, and he reveals what is behind it—what your horoscope *doesn't* tell you.

'An astonishing book'
    Keith Ewing, *Evangelical Alliance*

'Astrology often "works". Something more than mere coincidence is involved. No Christian book to my knowledge has addressed this crucial factor in astrology's longstanding popularity—until now. In eminently readable language, *What Your Horoscope Doesn't Tell You* lucidly sets forth the case.'
    Elliot Miller, *Christian Research Journal*

'Astrology has been debunked more than the tooth fairy. Strohmer goes beyond debunking. His book is a first word of exceptional importance.'
    Brooks Alexander, *Spiritual Counterfeits Project*

'Read this. And give it to that friend who leans on advice from the stars.'
    William H. Smallman, *The Baptist Bulletin*

Catalogue Number YB 9235   £3.25

UNDERSTANDING THE NEW AGE

Russell Chandler

Crystals . . . Pyramids . . . Channelling . . . Gurus . . .
Holistic . . . Healing . . . Reincarnation . . . The Earth
Goddess . . . Astrology Charts . . . 'The Force' . . . All
features of the New Age Movement.

'The New Age has touched you,' says Russell Chandler.
'You've heard its ideas, listened to its music, viewed its
artwork, watched its superstars, read its literature and
bought its products. You may even have participated in its
therapies, shared in its rituals and embraced its
philosophies—all without knowing them as New Age.'

Before writing his book, Chandler interviewed more
than thirty proponents and critics of the movement. He
quotes extensively from New Age writers and thinkers like
Shirley Maclaine, Marilyn Ferguson and M. Scott Peck, as
well as from their critics, and his reporting is balanced and
fair.

In this five-part book Chandler examines:

- the prevalence and premises of the New Age
  Movement
- who's who in the New Age
- its influence on many aspects of our culture
- how to discern and evaluate it
- the Judaeo-Christian alternative

His compelling conclusions will challenge all who read this
book.

Catalogue Number YB 9300   £3.95

HOW TO RESCUE THE EARTH WITHOUT WORSHIPPING NATURE

Tony Campolo

*Is ignoring the destruction of nature a sin?
If the world is to 'pass away' some day, should
Christians care about the environment?
Is concern for the earth just a distraction from
the issues in which the church should really be
involved?*

Strange questions? Not for a Christian who believes that rescuing the earth is commanded by Scripture. Reckless disregard for the environment, whether out of ignorance or greed, is sinful, says best-selling author Tony Campolo.

Yet Christians, who *should* lead the crusade to save our planet, are often put off by ecological approaches that seem anti-Christian or extreme.

How to Rescue the Earth Without Worshipping Nature draws on biblical and other Christian writings to develop a system of 'creation care' that offers down-to-earth suggestions for churches and individuals who want to be responsible stewards of God's world.

*If the kingdom of God is to come on earth as it is
in heaven, then there is much work to be done.
The urgency of the situation requires that we
begin to act now!*

Catalogue Number YB 9571   £4.25

HEALING AT ANY PRICE

Samuel Pfeifer M.D.

' . . . destined to become one of the most informative books on the subject of alternative medicine that has yet been written.'

From the foreword by Selwyn Hughes

Many people, feeling increasingly alienated from modern technological medicine, have turned to alternative medicine remedies. But what are their underlying philosophies? Following extensive research, Dr Pfeifer discussed various branches of New Age medicine, including acupuncture, homoeopathy, iridology and radiesthesia. He looks at the beliefs of those who pioneered their use, and concludes that some have their roots in Eastern philosophy and occult practices. Dr Pfeifer estimates the success of each of these methods, and suggests possible reasons for their effectiveness.

Catalogue Number YB 9153 £2.95